Don't Say Anything to Anybody

Don't Say Anything to Anybody

A German World War II Girlhood

Brigitte Z. Yearman with Anika Hanisch

Third Path
Bozeman, Montana

Published in the United States by Third Path Press,
an imprint of Third Path, LLC, Bozeman, Montana.

Author's Note: This book is true to my recollection of events. To protect privacy, I have changed the names of some people. Wherever possible I have confirmed the dates of specific attacks and post-war events. I am not entirely clear on the exact timing of certain refugee movements at the end of and after the war, but I do know with certainty that my journey in 1946 took place during cold months, and it took us five weeks. You will notice that when German words are included, I use the eszett (ß)—the symbol for the German double-s (ss)—as it would have appeared during the war and post-war years.

Cover design by James Bennett Design
Cover images and interior photos courtesy the Zobel Yearman Family

Library of Congress Cataloging-in-Publication Data
Don't Say Anything to Anybody: A German World War II Girlhood / Brigitte Yearman
and Anika Hanisch
p. cm.

ISBN-13: 9780692891216
ISBN-10: 0692891218

1. Yearman, Brigitte. 2. World War II—Personal narratives. 3. Refugee experience.
4. Childhood trauma—survival.
I. Hanisch, Anika—Coauthor II. Title
Library of Congress Control Number: 2017907577
Third Path Press, Bozeman, MT

To my four daughters,
who inspired me to write my life experience,
and also to my grandchildren
and future generations to come.

Acknowledgements

We first thank Mary Wagner, who introduced us to each other and made this co-authorship possible. You are an amazing woman, and we are deeply grateful for your constant community-building efforts. Numerous friends and colleagues read multiple drafts and were deeply involved in revision and editing. Our heartfelt thanks to all of you, especially to Alanna Brown for encouraging Brigitte at the earliest stages of writing and for providing comprehensive line editing later on; to Nicole Cohn for her clear-headed troubleshooting and invaluable developmental editing, especially in the opening chapters; to Mary Carroll Moore, writing instructor at the Loft Literary Center in Minneapolis, for her genius advice on story structure; to Troy B. Kechely for his wealth of military knowledge and benefactor support; to Janet Chaikin for exceptional final copy editing; and to James Bennett for his brilliant cover design.

Many others contributed insight as beta readers during the revision process: Janel Carino, Gail Gettler, Susanne Pannwitz Mueller, Rabbi Ed Stafman, Sally Tange, Ben Tone, and Richard Wolff. This book would also not have been possible without generous benefactor support from Marlo Arthun, Jack and Tawnie Lehman, Laurel Lint, Ellen

Macfarland, Patti Marshall, Vicky Merchant, Elisabeth Morell, Ingrid Nemzek, Thomas J. Scanlin, Richard and Betty Schledorn, Lynn Speakman, Mary Ann Staab, Kathy Tone (in memory of Ben Tone), and Spencer and Kerry Williams.

From Brigitte: Thank you to my daughters for being the ones who originally asked me to write down my memories: Angelika, Evelyn, Christina, and Mary Ann. Thank you to my sister, Elke Breitlauch, and my brother, Rainer Zobel. And of course, thank you to my partner in life, Frank Schledorn.

From Anika: Deepest thanks for the endless encouragement, inspiration, and tech help from: Mark and Ingrid, Chris and Val, Urs and Joe, Andy and Carrie, Lauren, and all my nieces and nephews. Thank you to Eileen Hosking, Sara Lee, and Amy Pass for your heartening friendship and editorial insight. Most of all, thanks to John Hosking for ongoing feedback and loving support.

Every book has a team behind it. Ours is numerous and represents over half a dozen countries. You have carried us along in love and encouragement. Thank you all.

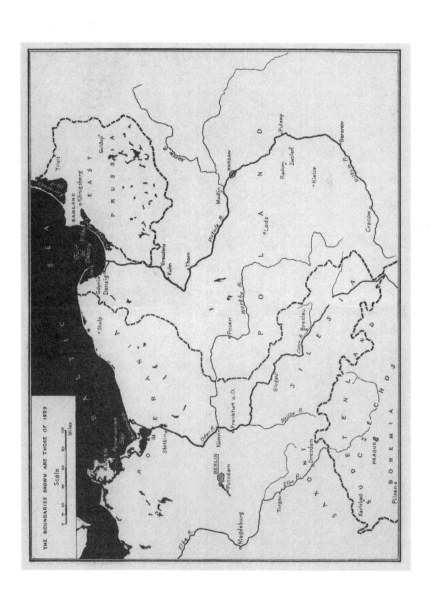

Part 1

Wartime
1939 – 1945

Brigitte and her paternal grandfather, before the war, c. 1938

One

Kiel, Germany

The day the war began, I broke my doll's face. My dear sweet doll, with her porcelain face, brown eyes, and curly hair, like mine. Just minutes before I dropped her, I sat in the stairwell outside our apartment door rocking her in my arms like a baby. Mother and the neighbor woman stood on the landing above me. They spoke in the hushed serious whispers that parents use when they do not want a child to hear precisely what they are saying. Though they want the child to hear a few scraps to sense the gravity of their words.

Father came home from work. He rushed past me, and he and mother went into our apartment. The neighbor woman stepped outside to shake a rug. For a moment, I was alone. I stroked my doll's hair and held her out in front of me. As I held her like that, about to give her a hug, Mother dashed out onto the landing, shouting to the neighbor woman.

"We are at war! We have invaded Poland."

Mother's fear hit me like a punch—my chest, my arms, my knees. My hands. The fear snapped my hands open and my doll fell. She hit the edge of the stairs, her face shattering into a million pieces. Behind me, Mother cried, "It is the end. What will become of us?"

I cried. But Mother never did console me about the broken doll. No hugs or kind words. She was not that kind of mother to begin with, and the war made her even less so. For my part, I was the kind of child who ran straight down the street when told to stay close to home. I ran even faster when Mother called for me to come back.

Mother was young—eighteen when she married, twenty when I was born. We were poor, and she made her own clothes, sewing skirts and blouses and even coats that copied wealthy styles and earned compliments from her girlfriends. She pinned her curly brown hair up away from her face and was quick to smile when my father was around. I did love to look at her, my pretty Mother. But her sweet smile often turned to a scowl when speaking with me.

The day after the war began, Mother knelt down and spoke firmly to me, "Brigitte, you broke your doll. I am not getting you a new one." She told her friends that she had a doll carriage for sale.

The following week, a woman came to our door with her little daughter, a girl about my age. I looked on as Mother shoved the carriage toward the woman. Mother took the coins in payment, gave a quick nod. That was that. The other mother carried the carriage down the stairs and out the front entrance to the sidewalk. I watched from the kitchen, then scurried out onto the landing and down the stairs. I peeked out the entryway door. They were already down the street; I could hear the little girl pushing the carriage.

Soon Kiel was burning. Germany invaded Poland in 1939, and within two years British planes began bombing us. My parents must have known that might happen. The very reason we moved to the Baltic harbor town made it a risky place to live. We moved from Glogau to the coast when I was three because Father needed work. There were good jobs in Kiel, a German submarine base. Father was an electrical engineer, so he found work installing and testing the electrical systems in submarines, the *Unterseeboots*. The work paid well. But the existence of such work made our city a target. Our government wanted to build more ships; the British wanted to destroy them.

Once the air raids began, there were many nights when I lay in my bed and, through my curtains, saw lights flickering in the sky—our forces looking for British planes. Sometimes I heard incredible explosions in the distance, like a single crack of thunder. Our military had big guns that could shoot the British planes and keep us safe. I was, surprisingly, not frightened by the flickering searchlights and anti-aircraft guns at night. They were simply a part of my world.

By day, there was the noise of construction as the city built bomb shelters. We lived in a neighborhood on the hills above town. From the row-house steps, we could see down to the harbor. After an air raid one evening, I sat with the neighbor boys watching tall flames devour the buildings down by the water. Uncomprehending, we watched the glow in smiling wonder.

For a small child, the world is a delight; it is supposed to be a delight. You have no language for horrors, no words. I rarely dwelt long on any sadness, always looking for the next playful curiosity. *My doll is gone, but it is sunny out today. I will climb the apple tree in our backyard.* Even as the sirens rang and flames leapt high, there was curiosity: *What are they building in town? What are bunkers? Why do we need more bomb shelters?* Early on, there were moments when the war seemed like a fantastic adventure. At first. Soon enough, there would be only fear.

Kiel was not a place where children should be. Throughout Germany, the government had come to similar conclusions about other potential airstrike targets. The order went out: All children between ages six and ten in the vicinity of major military targets were to be transported from their homes into the countryside. They called it *Kinderlandverschickung*—children's countryside relocation. On an autumn day in 1941, Father sat down with me to explain.

It was evening, but he was dressed like he was about to head to an occasion. It was his way. Father often dressed down for his electrician work and then, when he came home, cleaned up and donned a fresh shirt and tie. Like Mother, he liked to look good. He was a laborer now, but his family had money in the past. Father's eyes were stern and dark, his thin lips usually turned down at the corners, a man with hard things on his mind. But whenever he looked at me, those eyes grew warm, the frown softened. I called him *Vati*—Daddy—and I knew he adored me.

"It is too dangerous for you to stay here," Vati said. "You're going on a train to a pretty little village. Won't that be nice?"

"Are you coming with me?"

"No, but your Mother and I will visit," he said, and stroked my hair. "You will be fine. You are a good, brave girl."

If I really wanted something, Vati was the one who would give it to me. But the way he said no this time felt conclusive, binding. There was no way to coerce him to accompany me. I looked at my feet. Mother, too, had nothing to say.

Regardless, I was excited about the train ride the day I left. I had ridden the train before with my parents; it always took us someplace interesting, such as Glogau or Breslau to visit family. At the station, hundreds of children were gathered, along with their parents saying goodbye to them. We children were all taking a train into the country. Who knew where we'd go or what we'd get to see. I stood on the platform waiting, dressed in my best: my dark blue peacoat, my best dress and white beret, and a nametag pinned to my lapel. It was a special day. Vati and Mother hugged me and helped me load into the train car with my suitcase.

The adventure turned strange as we pulled out of the station. Shouldn't a train ride be a good time? Shouldn't you get to kneel on your seat to get a better view? Shouldn't we play games and have something good to eat? On this train, the only allowed activity was to sit still. We were not to leave our seats without permission and a justifiable bodily necessity. Every train car had one adult escort, and ours was a strict and sour woman who paced the aisle. She prowled like that, back and forth, looking for the slightest infraction. *Sit up straight. Get down. Be quiet. Quit squirming.*

Barely an hour in, the other children began to cry. The sour woman kept pacing, and we all cried as quietly as possible. The next time she walked past me, I mustered up a scrap of courage.

"I want to go home," I said. Other children whispered, "*Ich auch.*" Me too.

But the escort shushed us all. "Stop it. You won't get to go home for a very long time."

This prospect made us cry more, which made our escort even more cross. She was right though. My father had been under the impression that my trip was temporary, just until Kiel was safe again. A few weeks, maybe two months at most. But the prowling lady in my train car was right. I wouldn't go back to Kiel for a very long time, and it would never be home again. Not really.

The journey lasted all day, long into the evening. Eventually I fell asleep. I woke when we came to a stop and the doors of the train car squeaked open. We had finally arrived in Koslin, some three hundred miles to the east. One by one, we lined up in the aisle, and our chaperone guided us out of the train and assembled us in the station. Several grown-ups with pencils and lists scrutinized our group. One looked like a schoolmaster. He rushed about reading the medallion nametag pinned to each child's coat. He sorted us, each word punctuated by a bony finger pointing this way and that, "You, there. You, here." Older children, here. Younger children, there. Boys. Girls. Soon we were neatly arranged by gender and age.

Men and women from nearby villages gathered on the other side of the station. These strangers were from farms and small shops.

Most had children of their own to care for, but each one was about to become a foster parent to one of us. One by one, other children paired up with a new parent. I shivered. Soon the man who looked like a schoolmaster came to me. A village woman followed him, and they discussed me.

"She is too small!" said the woman. "My son is gone, fighting in the war; I need one that can actually work."

It was no small thing, taking in a foster. Each of the foster families would receive a small compensation and extra rations for our care, but it was clear many of the families wanted us to act as free labor as well. The schoolmaster man tried in vain to persuade the woman otherwise. The two moved on to look at the remaining older children, ones who would be fit for farm work.

Not only was I one of the youngest children in the group, I was the shortest too. I knew I was small; my height sometimes made it difficult when playing games back home. *Now this, too?* Did my height mean no one would want me? Soon everyone had been assigned a family, except me. As troubling as it was to consider living with strangers, this new prospect was surely worse.

There were no children left in the train station except me. The head official with the clipboard and a few grown-ups stood at the other end of the hall. They spoke—doubtless disparaging words about me. I sat down on my old raggedy suitcase and cried, my face buried in the sleeve of my peacoat. I was still crying when the official cleared his throat. I hadn't heard the adults approach me. Another man was with him. This new face looked down at me and smiled.

"I have just the right place for you," he said. He signed some papers, and the official walked away from us. "My sister will love you," the smiling man said. "Come here."

I did not care that I had never met him before; I jumped up and took his hand. The smiling man picked up my suitcase with his other hand, and I held tight to him as we walked to another train. Whoever he was, he was the only adult who looked at me with kindness in his eyes since my father had hugged me goodbye that morning. He wore a dark pinstriped suit coat and pants like my father, but his face was more round and gentle. The smiling man told me his name was Otto, and from then on he was Onkel Otto to me. He worked for social services in Koslin, so it was his livelihood to help children who were in trouble. When he and his sister heard of the *Kinderlandverschickung*, of course they planned to take in at least one. And of course Onkel Otto volunteered to take the one that no one else wanted.

Onkel Otto lived in Seidel, a tiny farming village about five miles south of Koslin. During our short train ride, I snoozed next to my new friend. But I was wide awake once the train arrived at Seidel. Otto held my suitcase with one hand and me with his other hand. He explained where we were going and that I would stay at his sister's house, not at his. I wondered about that; I didn't want to stay with anyone but him.

"My sister will be so happy to meet you," he said. "Her name is Anna Arndt."

Her home was a short walk from the train station. There she was, standing at the end of her driveway. Just as warm and sweet as her brother, she held her arms open to me. I cringed. Tante Anna was lovely, but Onkel Otto was my savior. Clinging to his hand, I looked away. There was no letting go.

"This is my sister. You're going to live with her," he said, trying to coax me to look at her. He told Anna my name and age.

An old couple came around from the back of the house—Otto and Anna's parents. They lived with Anna. All three of these new faces came close, ready to take me in and fuss over the poor little girl from the city: Anna with her curly brown hair and concerned eyes, her father in his smart gray coat and pencil mustache, and her mother in her starched black dress and black scarf around her hair. Completely exhausted from my trip, I found them strange and frightening.

"I live right there," Otto said, and pointed to another house across the street. "You can visit me anytime."

This appeased me just enough to loosen my grip on Otto's hand. My new Tante Anna wasn't bothered by my lack of appreciation. "Come, Brigitte," she said. "I'm sure you're tired." She took my suitcase, coaxed my hand into hers, and guided me into her home.

Countless children in the *Kinderlandverschickung* were used as free labor at their assigned farms. Not so for me. I was the only child from this program who was placed in Seidel, and I was small, so all the villagers were excessively concerned about me. Anna and her parents and Otto and all their neighbors looked at me with sad faces, patted my head, and prescribed the German cure-all for the low-spirited: an abundance of potatoes, meat, and cream. But, really, I was hardly dispirited. I did not pine for my parents or lament over my burning hometown. I didn't cry at night or stare out the window waiting for someone. At six years old, I thought only of what was immediately at hand: my new Tante and Onkel and foster grandparents lavishing me with food and attention. In my mind they were my new family, and I was sure they would always be with me.

Aunt Anna and Brigitte, when she first arrived in Seidel

Two

Seidel, Germany

There were clear perks for being Anna's poor little city girl. The Muttis and Omas—mothers and grandmothers—of the village decided my primary objective during my stay in Seidel was to eat. Constantly running from house to house and exploring fields and barns, I did not gain much weight, but I did grow taller and precocious. Within weeks, I was unafraid of pretty much everyone. With all those new friends, I did not miss my parents at all initially. I knew Anna and my mother wrote to each other regularly. I listened to Anna read excerpts from Mother's letters, and I did like to hear the news from home. But my young girl's mind was on other things.

My primary diversion in Seidel was the food. My first morning at Anna's, I woke to the smell of warm barley coffee—the malt drink everyone made instead of real coffee. I lay in Tante Anna's bed listening to the rustling in the kitchen. Anna shared her double-twin with me, as her husband, Richard, was gone, drafted to fight in the war. I got out of bed and found Anna and her parents in the kitchen. Anna poured the malt coffee while Oma and Opa set out black rye bread, butter, and marmalade.

I sat with them at the table. I watched my new Opa cut the crust off his slice of rye bread. He said it hurt his teeth. Oma told me how she and Anna baked the beautiful black bread every two weeks in the outdoor kitchen next to the barn. This was where they smoked sausage too. I watched Opa spread marmalade on the soft center portion of his bread. I eyed the crust.

"Are you going to eat that?"

"No."

"May I?"

"Of course, Brigittchen." Little Brigitte. I liked the sound of that.

I took the crust and spread butter all along the length of it. This became our daily ritual. It's hard to say which food I would come to love the most—the buttered black-bread crust in the morning or our buttermilk soup every evening.

After breakfast, Oma sat on a stool by the green tile oven peeling potatoes for the midday meal. In German families, this has always been the main meal of the day, and when we ate the potatoes that Oma had peeled in the morning, along with some chicken or pork. In the evening we had a light meal, either buttermilk soup or home fries, and it was the former that I loved the most. Buttermilk soup began with a few strips of bacon in the bottom of a pot, then buttermilk, then boiled potatoes—so rich and warm and salty sweet. Wherever my farmyard expeditions took me, the smell of buttermilk soup drew me home. When Oma baked apples in the green tile oven, that smell called to me too. These were simple farm foods, but I had never had them before and regarded them as delicacies.

After breakfast each day, I explored another field, stream, or pond, venturing farther and farther away from Anna's house. Every day I walked farther up the road and knocked on another door, acquainting myself with each family. There were other children to meet and, most notably, more foods to eat. Women touched my shoulders and arms and commented on my size. It became the village project to put weight on Anna's city girl. Everywhere I went, people asked me, "*Magst du eine Stulle?*" Would you like a sandwich? The word *sandwich* did not do it justice. The *Stulle* was a giant roll sliced in half and slathered with a thick layer of homemade butter and molasses. I never refused such an offer. After a few weeks of making such friends, I rarely made it home for the midday meal anymore, which Anna served promptly at half past noon. I feasted with a different family every day and came home in the evening. My favorite lunch destination was Armin's house. My Tante had a cousin down the road, and that cousin had a son named Armin, who was about my age. I spent plenty of time at his house. His mother's potato pancakes and malt coffee were the best in Seidel. Everyone knew that.

Here in Seidel, I had both shelter and love for a few years: a farm village, a single street lined with homes and a school, a post office, a fire station, and a small mercantile. I walked almost everywhere on my own—with the exception of the Schnapps factory across from the school; I was clearly not allowed on that side of the street. Behind every house, there was a garden. Beyond every garden, fields and forests. Everyone knew the color and markings of each other's milk cows, which roamed freely in shared pastures. Every cow knew its barn and returned home in the evening. Children roamed freely too. Seidel had no fences, for none were needed.

For a little while, I was a city child seeing cows and pigs and geese for the first time. For a little while, I did not wonder where my parents were. For a little while, there was no war. But it was in Aunt Anna's house that Seidel would discover the war was no longer a far-off thing. It was in her sitting room that her closest family and friends would speak their opinions. They spoke freely in Anna's house, but hid their opinions as soon as they left. For there were informants everywhere. Still, for a little while, there was none of that, and I was simply Anna's city girl—walking into the barn, looking at a giant milk cow and seeing the evening light in her soft brown eye.

As Anna's foster child, I was not used as farm labor, but was assigned a few small chores. I looked forward to my occasional assignment to pick up war ration goods at the general store on the other end of town. The shop owner, who was Anna's brother-in-law, always gave me a free piece of candy. One obstacle stood between me and the rock candy—the children who lived near the mercantile, up the hill at the east end of the village. They did not think kindly of the children who lived on the west end. Who knows how this rift began, but there was much name-calling.

The shop owner's daughter, my surrogate cousin, often came to my rescue. Heidi was a few years older than I, and she could make any little bully shrink back. Günther was one of the bullies, and as soon as he and his friends began taunting me, Heidi would appear at the shop door with her hands on her hips.

"Leave her alone!" she shouted, and the mean boys scattered. That gauntlet complete, I walked into the store, approached the counter, and presented my *Lebensmittlekarte*, a wartime ration card. Heidi filled my order and stamped my card. At the end of the transaction, Heidi's father looked around as if he had a secret to share. Then he bent down and gave me a piece of rock candy. This was a treasure. I did not eat it right away, but tucked it in my dress pocket for later.

Heidi and her father loaded my mesh grocery bag with flour and sugar, and then took the ceramic bowl I had brought from Anna's kitchen and filled it with sauerkraut. It had a loose-fitting lid, so I needed to carry the load carefully to keep it from spilling. An even greater challenge was resisting the urge to nibble on the way home. I adored sauerkraut—yet another farm food delicacy—and always stopped a few times during my return walk to taste test. I plucked a few scraps out with my fingers and savored the kraut. They were small bites. No one would notice. Except, by the time I got home and looked down, all my little bites had resulted in a bowl that was more than half empty.

Anna would open the door and look down at me, shaking her head. "Again?" she asked. "Is there any left for us? What will I do with you?"

Just as consistently, my Oma, Anna's mother, would be standing behind her, saying, "Do not lay a hand on that girl." My Oma's black dress, black shawl, and starched white collar seemed so stern, and yet she was the one who tempered any frustration Anna expressed toward me.

Eventually Anna resigned herself to the sauerkraut problem. She would sit on the stoop next to me, peek into the mostly empty bowl, and we would eat the last little bit together. After several weeks of Anna joining me in this fashion, Oma approached us and said, "I suppose anytime I see the two of you sitting on the sidewalk, I can assume there will be no sauerkraut for the rest of us." Her words were sharp, but there was laughter in her eyes. That was the sternest discipline I received from Oma or her daughter—a verbal warning now and again, a warning steeped in doting love.

Initially, growing up in Hitler's Germany affected me minimally. Most notably, the war meant that Anna's husband, Richard, was gone most of the time. Like my father, he was a soldier. When Richard came home on leave, his visits were an interruption to my perfectly happy life. I had to sleep upstairs in Oma and Opa's bed, and I didn't care for that at all. And Anna and Oma cooked all the finest food when Richard was around, but I didn't care for the menu change either. We ate much more meat than usual. On one such visit, I grew bold and confronted the man.

"When are you leaving?" I asked.

"In two days," Richard said. "Why, Brigittchen?"

"Because we don't get any buttermilk soup when you're here."

Apart from Richard's visits, I could blame the new German government for only one other irritation. In this new Germany, girls were to cease school by the time they were in their mid-teens. After that, they were to serve in domestic internships, in which they cleaned and cooked in another household in order to learn to be good wives and mothers. It was part of the *Hitlerjugend* program—Hitler's Youth. No one really knew why a young woman needed to serve in someone else's home to learn these things, but the government said this was best. That is how one of my foster cousins, Gerda, came to be the one who bathed me once a week.

Gerda lived across the street. Her father, Walter, was Onkel Otto's brother, and the two families shared a duplex. Gerda had a younger sister, Lilly, who was about my age. I liked Lilly so much that seeing her teenage sister come over on bath day was a grand disappointment. I waited for the perfect moment to let Gerda know what I thought of the arrangement. In the kitchen, Gerda had me strip down and step into a big basin that held the gray water from laundry day; this was my bath. Gerda commenced to scrub me all over, and right then I began to scream till Aunt Anna came running.

"What are you doing to her?" Anna demanded. She scowled at Gerda—just as I'd hoped.

Flustered, Gerda insisted she'd done nothing to provoke me. But as soon as Anna left the room, I resumed my screams. Anna was forever suspicious that Gerda was truly unkind to me in some fashion. The poor girl. Her only offense was that she was not Lilly.

Anna's house was grand, but, like all homes in Seidel, it had an outhouse. I'd never used a chamber pot before, but I learned about them quickly once the weather turned cold. When the snows arrived in earnest, the drifts were easily four-feet high. Opa carved a path to the outhouse, but the chamber pots became a necessity. No one wanted to walk along that cold, snowy hallway after dark or before dawn.

So I was baffled one December evening when Opa took me by the hand and said we ought to go to the privy before bedtime. That hadn't been a part of our routine for weeks. Aunt Anna and Oma smiled, as if they had shared a secret with each other and possibly with Opa too. It was truly strange, but I obliged. We bundled up in the mudroom with boots, coats, hats, and mitts—such a fuss to use the bathroom—and headed out into the frigid farmyard, a good thirty-meter walk to the outhouse on the other side of our barn. After we took our turns in the privy, Opa dallied, insisting that we check on the animals. The cows and pigs and geese and chickens were all fine and cozy, bothered only by our waking them. Finally we returned to the warm house, shed our layers in the mudroom, and thawed our way through the kitchen and into the living room.

While we were gone, Aunt Anna and Oma had transformed a corner by the couch. The blue spruce, they insisted, was not their do-ing, but the work of *Weihnachtsmann*. I'd never seen a Christmas tree up close before. Its boughs sparkled with silver tinsel and several lit candles. A set of carved farmyard figures stood on the floor under the tree. Anna and Oma and Opa waited for me to approach, but I stayed a few paces back, staring at the tinsel in the candlelight.

Opa coaxed me over. "Der Weihnachtsmann delivered a present from your Vati," he said, picking up one of the carved figurines. "He made these for you."

"It's Christmas, Brigitte," Anna said. "The presents are for you." Anna had no children of her own. In the past, she went across the street to celebrate Christmas Eve with Walter and Otto. That night it was Christmas in Anna's house.

Outside that house, the wind blew and the drifts grew. Beyond our farmyard, other families in other homes celebrated as well. Some worried about their husbands and sons in the military; some were remarkably unconcerned, still sure that the war would end any day. Beyond Seidel, Germany continued to devour her neighbors. Across the Atlantic, an isolationist United States had just experienced the attack at Pearl Harbor, and Germany, in solidarity with Japan, had declared war against America. All these things had happened a couple weeks before, but if Anna and her family knew of these events, if they had speculated at all about the implications, they never let on to me. I knew only of the sparkling tree and this curious Weihnachtsmann who brought me carved animals from my Vati.

The next day was a Thursday, but Anna walked to church as if it were Sunday. Oma and Opa never attended services, but Anna usually did. No one told me why; it was just their way. I also knew I was not allowed to go to church. No one told me why that was either. If I looked longingly at Anna on a church morning, she gave me a stern glance that silenced my request before I had a chance to open my mouth. Christmas morning was no different. Whatever magic der Weihnachtsmann wielded, he could not alter the unspoken rules about churchgoing in the Arndt household. I stayed home and watched Oma sit on the bench by the green tile oven peeling potatoes. It was like any other day—except for the new toys and the goose roasting in the oven.

Throughout the winter, I continued in my role as grocery-getter. I was also commissioned with straightening the family's shoes in our mudroom every Saturday. Beyond that, I was free to explore the winter woods and warm barns on my own, or keep myself occupied playing with the carved animals from Vati. When spring came, I was commissioned with a new daily chore. I was to herd our flock of domestic geese in the pasture across the road. Opa taught me the finer points of this task. Our barn was home to four milk cows and several pigs, and the geese and chickens were kept in pens attached to that barn. Once the grass greened up, Opa let the cows out to graze every morning. In the evening, he called to them and they followed him home. The geese were more of a challenge.

Opa showed me how to gather the flock in the farmyard and usher them to the field on the other side of the street. Once in the field, sure enough, one goose wandered away from the flock. Opa ran behind the stray, waving his arms, scaring the bird back into the flock. I copied his technique. Within minutes, I could successfully herd the creatures—birds who were almost as tall as me. I only needed to watch out for the gander, who did not like anyone who interfered with his flock. He turned the tables on me, sneaking up from behind and biting my legs and rear end.

Sometimes my foster cousin Lilly helped herd the geese. When Lilly joined me, we could take the geese farther into the field. She also made a small improvement to the chore. Before heading out to round up the flock, we'd pack a bag with snacks and a blanket to spread out in the field. While the geese nibbled bugs and grass, we sat on the blanket eating our own treats. Whenever a goose strayed too far, we leapt up and chased the bird back to the flock. Then we hurried back to our blanket to lie on our backs and gaze at the sky and trees.

Despite Lilly's frequent assistance, the gander continued to give me trouble, frequently nipping at my legs and rear. Nasty bird. One day when I was in the farmyard alone, the gander charged at me as usual. But instead of running away and essentially offering him a target, I held my ground. He needed to learn a lesson for once. When he was inches from biting me, I shouted, "Not this time!" I snatched him by the neck, squeezed with both of my hands, and swung him around till I was dizzy.

The nasty gander didn't make a sound as I swung him about, but his flock made a commotion, honking and shrieking their concern. Tante Anna must have looked out the kitchen window right then. She rushed out the back door shouting. Anna grabbed the gander out of my hands and let him go free—miraculously, still alive. She took me by the shoulders.

"What were you thinking?" she said. "You could have killed him!"

"He's mean to me!" I insisted. I showed her the peck marks and bruises on the back of my legs. Anna sighed. And the gander, though he often hissed at me from afar, never pecked at me again.

Our resident tom turkey elicited similar spite from me. The tom never managed to bite me, but he was guilty by association. The two enormous birds strutted about with a similar arrogance, and the turkey occasionally charged at me, threatening to attack. So, despite Anna's reaction to the gander incident, I schemed to deal harshly with the turkey as well. I had learned this much: it needed to look like an accident. I devised a perfect scenario.

All the farms had a giant cistern that collected rainwater to water the garden and the animals. I was intimately familiar with ours, as I'd fallen into it once. I remembered the fear, the feeling of Opa's hands around my waist as he pulled me out, and the embarrassment afterwards. It was the hard way to learn that a cistern's lid should always be left tightly in place any time it wasn't raining. Still, sometimes we forgot to replace the lid. I decided the ugly turkey could have his "accident" at the cistern.

Alone in the farmyard, I pulled the lid off the cistern and herded the turkey over. It was a wooden barrel sunk into the ground a little. The top edge was just a couple feet above ground. It was feasible that the giant bird might hop up onto the side of the barrel, peer into the water, and maybe, just maybe, slip inside. I shooed the frightened bird across the yard, cornered him between the cistern and the wall of the barn. Then I grabbed him by the neck and hefted him into the water. He flapped about and uttered a few garbled gobbles. I heard him clawing at the wooden sides and feared he might climb out. So I dragged the cistern lid back over the top. That would do. He needed to stay in there a while, long enough to get a really good fright.

I slipped back into the house, oblivious to the error in my foolproof plan. This time it wasn't Anna, but my sweet Opa, who confronted me. Later that evening, he came inside looking for me and asked me to take a seat on the bench in the kitchen.

"Brigitte, how did the turkey get into the cistern?"

"I don't know, I said. "Maybe he fell in."

Opa, who thought the world of me, would have believed me if it weren't for my scheme's fatal flaw. "Really?" he said. "And the turkey pulled the lid over himself? What a strong bird."

I felt my face flush. I was caught.

"The bird is dead," he said.

I felt awful. I never meant to kill the mean bird, only scare him. My stunned silence must have been enough punishment in Opa's book. I wasn't even spanked for that incident, or for any other. Though I surely deserved it.

That first year, I should have started first grade with the other six-year olds, but Aunt Anna held me back, presumably out of concern that I adjust well. *Kinderlandverschickung* was supposed to be a temporary arrangement, and she thought that I might as well wait till I got back to Kiel to start school, since Germany was supposed to win the war any day now. Starting my education in one town and resuming it in another might not be worth the fuss. Also, Anna was in her early thirties, married but childless; it's possible she simply liked having me around.

Not that I spent much time indoors. I spent a full year in that village as a rather feral child. My foster cousin Armin had started school, but as the weather warmed, he joined me in the afternoon after classes were done. We roamed the meadows and sat in the shallow stream to cool off as the weather grew warmer.

In June, I learned something astounding. One sunny morning, Tante Anna took me aside after breakfast and made a strange announcement to me. "Do you know what day it is?" she asked. "It is your birthday today."

"My what?" I asked. I didn't know what the word meant. Anna held a lovely crocheted something folded in her hands.

"A birthday—everyone has one," she said, unfurling the cloth. It was a pink crocheted dress. "Why don't you try this on. Your mother made it and sent it to you. There's a blue one as well."

My mother made me two dresses? I had seen her crochet before, but never something for me. She never did such things. I took off my threadbare checked dress, and Anna helped me into the pink crocheted sundress. It fit perfectly. My eyes wide, I marveled at the fine stitches.

"You really don't know what a birthday is, do you?" Anna said. "It's the day you were born. You're seven today."

I had never heard of birthdays until that moment. Unable to afford gifts or sweets, I'm sure my parents never called attention to my earliest birthdays. "I have a birthday," I said, and Anna laughed. "It's my birthday," I repeated, then tore out the door, down the street, knocking on doors and announcing my news: "It's my birthday!" I gleaned smiles, congratulations, and several gifts from our neighbors' gardens. An hour or so later, I hurried home with an armload of flowers.

Burdened down and struggling to see around the blooms in front of my face, I slipped. I stumbled not onto dry ground, but straight into the drainage sludge along the side of the road. This was no pretty little creek, but the rivulet of farmyard waste channeled to the fields outside the village. I kept my arms up, saving the flowers, but my new dress was a disaster. I arrived at Anna's door in tears. I held the precious flowers out in front of me, but there was no hiding the manure-covered dress. From Anna's perspective, there was no guessing the full extent of the trouble I'd just caused.

"God in heaven, did you steal all of those?" she asked, pointing at the bouquet.

"No, no. These are my birthday presents," I said, and sniffled. "Everybody gave them to me."

That matter cleared up, she turned her attention to the dress. But how could Anna punish me? It was my birthday. Besides, I heard Oma rustling in the kitchen. With Oma nearby, Anna wouldn't rebuke me too harshly. The dress went directly into the basin in the wash kitchen, and then I got a good scrub too. Anna's silence and rough hands were loud enough. She decreed that for the rest of the day, I was to sit on the bench next to the big green tile oven. I did just that, and cried.

So go the crises of childhood. And in Seidel, for a couple of years I really did get to be a child: messy, selfish, curious, and the cause of all sorts of trouble. I recovered from the birthday fiasco. So did the dress—Anna's scrubbing restored it entirely.

Three

Shortly after my birthday, my mother sent a letter informing me that she was coming to visit. She planned to take the train to visit her own mother, and said she could pick me up en route. She also informed us that my Vati would not be with her; he had been drafted and was fighting against Russia on the Crimean Peninsula. This news was thoroughly disappointing, but I didn't understand that my father's life might be in danger. I only looked forward to another train ride—this one would be fun, not like that train from Kiel to Koslin.

Mother collected me and a little bag of overnight things, and we rode together to my real Oma's place. I knew my biological Oma was a widow and quite poor, nothing like Anna and her parents at the big farmhouse in Seidel. Mother married my Vati when she was eighteen, and though her family had been destitute for generations, his family had some money. Unfortunately, Hitler's regime seized my paternal grandfather's hotel in Glogau a few years before the war began. There were rumors that he had made too much money working for Belgium and England, and such trade relations were unacceptable to the new regime.

Though Vati's parents lost their wealth, they still lived in Glogau. Sometimes we visited them for an hour or two. I did not relish these encounters. Vati's mother was a scary woman, who had a habit of suddenly shouting at her husband in the middle of a family meal.

Grandfather just sat and took the verbal tirades. I heard from an aunt that back when the family still owned their hotel, this Oma of mine carried a monstrous ring of keys that clattered against her heavy skirt wherever she went. Whenever the hotel staff heard the rattle of those keys from down the hall or up a stairway, they all scattered. Thankfully, we never spent the night with my Vati's parents. When my mother visited Glogau, she of course stayed with her own Mutti.

My maternal Oma had a miniscule second-floor, two-room apartment. It held a kitchen and a small room divided by curtains to suggest a bedroom and living room. Oma was sweet and kind to me, but she was painfully sad all the time, and there was very little to do at her place. Glogau was Mother's hometown, and a day into our visit, it became clear that we were there so Mother could party with all her old friends. I did not attend those parties; I wasn't sure why she'd taken me to Glogau at all.

One morning, Mother dressed up to meet a friend at a café. On her way out she said, "Brigitte, I'll be back this afternoon to take you to the ice cream parlor."

Mother was so bright and happy, and the promise of ice cream made me happy too. I didn't mind staying back with Oma, even if she napped most of the time. I'd find something to do. Sometimes Oma sent me out to play in the square by the church or pick up cold cuts at the deli, where the shop owner always gave me the ham ends as a snack. After Mother left, those diversions lost their lustre. I was too excited about the ice cream to play or run errands. I feared Mother would come home and might head back out again without me if I wasn't there.

I walked down the stairs to the apartment building entrance and took my post, standing there waiting for Mother to return. The shadows under the trees outside grew small in the midday sun. Slowly, the tree shadows grew longer again. Sometimes Mother was late for things. It was okay.

She'd be back soon; she promised. I stayed at my post. Eventually, Oma called down to me. She asked if I wanted something to eat. Of course I didn't; I was waiting for ice cream. My legs got tired, and I sat down on the stoop. Hours passed. That evening I heard Oma at the top of the stairs again.

"Come up child," she said.

"I'm waiting to get ice cream."

"Come up here."

I looked at her and stood, then took a few sleepy steps up the stairs.

"Your mother is not coming back till late," Oma said. "I know my daughter."

We were in bed when Mother finally got back, but I was still awake. She didn't say anything to me that night or the next morning. Never apologized. I was quiet on the train ride back to Seidel, and when I got off at the station, I ran the short path back to Anna's house. Mother stayed the night at Anna's before heading back to Kiel, but I didn't talk to her much. I missed Father—my world would end if anything ever happened to him. But what could I say about Mother? She promised she would visit every couple of months from then on, but part of me wished she wouldn't visit me anymore at all.

Four

Summer passed quickly, and soon the wheat and barley fields turned gold. All the farmers helped each other with harvesting the grain. We didn't have a mechanical thresher—the threshing would be done by hand. But the farmers shared two horse-drawn wheat cutters. I watched as they made their way up and down each field. The rest of the village followed, gathering and tying bundles of wheat. When we had a half-dozen of these bundles, we stacked them in a pyramid, leaning against each other. The women served lunch at tables set up in the field. That was my favorite part—the giant picnic.

The harvest was decent that year. Anna also ran a trucking business on the side—two canvas-topped trucks that delivered produce and other goods in the region. That business made good profits as well. One day Anna announced she would take the train to Koslin to make a significant purchase.

"I'm buying a bicycle," she said. Only a few people in the village had such a luxury, and Anna did not like to be outdone.

"A bicycle?" I said. "Can I go with you?"

"No, you need to stay here and help Opa."

Anna left when it was still dark the next morning. I cried, but made the best of my day by helping Opa around the farmyard. A far greater disappointment awaited me that evening when the train pulled into the station. I stood outside and watched for Anna, eager to see the shiny new bicycle and hoping she'd let me ride it. There was Anna getting off the train, but no bicycle. She held an unwieldy package in her arms instead.

Anna said nothing as she entered our house. She had a serious look in her eyes, and I got the impression I shouldn't say a thing about the bicycle. Some happening in town, some news perhaps, had made her change her mind about her purchase. She set the strange package on the kitchen table and opened the box. The gleaming brown plastic device stood a little over a foot tall, a rectangular-shaped box with rounded edges. A rough mesh cloth covered a round portal on the front right, and there were three knobs near the base. It was called a *Volksempfänger*, a radio. Anna set it up on a shelf in the living room.

Oma walked in and said, "What do you need that for?"

Opa joined us. Anna's parents stared at the device and at their daughter. They were not impressed. But the rest of Seidel was. By the next evening, everyone on our end of the village knew about the radio. Anna's family and closest friends gathered to listen to the 6 p.m. report. This was the only purpose of the Volksempfänger; it broadcasted the German government's nightly propaganda and war news. The radio was intentionally designed to be incapable of receiving other stations. Though some people modified their radios with stronger antennas, such adjustments were illegal. Anna and her family knew that.

Impressed or not, Oma and Opa joined everyone to listen to that first report. Walter and his wife came over. Otto and his strange wife, Wanda, came too. They lived just across the street, but I hadn't seen much of my beloved Onkel, as his wife usually hid in the back bedroom anytime I came over. I'd taken the hint and quit visiting his house. So it was nice to see Onkel Otto. Five other couples who lived nearby joined us too. It would have felt like a party, except there were no other children and no one was smiling. Everyone squeezed onto the couch and the kitchen chairs, all huddled near the radio. I sat in the corner on the floor, watching. At 6 p.m., Anna turned one of the knobs and the radio crackled to life. I listened, but couldn't understand the twenty-syllable words, the complicated bulletins and stern, rough voices clattering out of the radio's speaker. I could have left to play outside. But despite the unintelligible reports, I was curious about their effect on my family. The adults listened with tight lips and furrowed brows, and when the report ended, they spoke hushed and worried words. Something big was happening.

For the next two-and-a-half years, this was our ritual every evening. Oma and Opa came to appreciate the radio, even if they disagreed with the propaganda. Everyone in this close group of friends and family asked Opa for his opinions. Opa, I learned, was not German. He was an American citizen—of German descent, but born and raised on a farm in Minnesota. He had visited Germany in the late 1880s to connect with extended family. On that trip he met Oma and decided he wouldn't be returning to America. He still held his citizenship though.

I didn't understand the radio reports at all. I sat in the corner and used the radio time to relish a piece of rock candy from the general store. I paid attention when Opa spoke. One thing was vividly clear to me: he was thankful America had joined the war. He hoped U.S. forces would take our region someday—the U.S. and not Russia. My surrogate family hoped Germany would lose, and their closest friends agreed.

Seidel was so small. That village's greatest tensions had always been over neighborly gossip or the weather's effects on the grain harvest. Suddenly we had far greater concerns. The nightly reports convinced everyone that the war might take a very long time, and within weeks of Anna's radio purchase, there was a swift and personal ramification in my world. Anna came to me after one of the reports and tilted my chin up to look at her.

"Brigitte, this is no holiday," she said. "You need to go to school."

She had rethought her decision to keep me out of school and have me wait till I returned to Kiel to begin first grade. Even though the government had billed the *Kinderlandverschickung* as a temporary arrangement—weeks or months only—I'd lived with Anna for almost a year. It was clear the war was taking longer than anyone thought it would, and it might be a very long time before I would move back to Kiel.

Five

Initially, school was another big adventure for me. I liked the chance to see my village friends each day, though we knew we needed to keep quiet once we were in the classroom. There were four rows of desks, with each row representing a different grade. The teacher, Herr Schmidt, gave me a seat in the middle of the first row; I was in first grade, but needed to catch up due to my personal four-month vacation. I had already missed the first school term, which began in the spring for us. Herr Schmidt was not about to coddle me either. He set several papers on the desk at the front of my row, and the first student obediently took one sheet and passed the stack behind her. As we each took our assignment paper, the teacher approached me and slapped an additional sheet on my desk.

"Write this," he said. "Copy each letter. Now."

I looked at the paper, the lines and swirls of the letters. Theoretically, I knew what the characters were, but I had never tried writing before, never been taught a single letter. I watched how the other children looked at their papers and copied the characters onto their slates. Mimicking them, I dove in, scratching out a semblance of the letter *A* with my chalk.

We didn't have a Nazi flag in our classroom, though if the teacher had his way, we would have. At the beginning of each day, Herr Schmidt checked his clock then stood at the head of the classroom. We knew we had to stand then as well. We greeted him, as he required us to, with the right-arm salute and a loud "Heil Hitler." Then our lessons began.

Everyone in my world spoke about Hitler and always with heavy, quiet words—except Herr Schmidt, who liked to shout when he talked about him. It frightened me when he ranted like that. It was hard to tell which was worse—the frightened whispers at home or the arrogant shouts at school. Herr Schmidt barked at us to be proud of being German youth and to always say the Deutsche greeting. If we didn't say it, we were disrespectful, maybe even an enemy of the new Germany. By the end of my first week, I understood I had to go to school, but I wasn't too fond of the teacher.

He didn't like me either. Unfortunately, I gave him good reason for that dislike early on. Opa had crafted wooden clogs for me, and Tante Anna told me I needed to wear these wooden shoes to school instead of my leather ones. Everyone in the family had a pair of clogs, and I was happy to wear them around the farmyard. But no one else at school wore wooden shoes, and I already stood out because I was shorter than the other children and behind in my studies. So one morning, after Anna had double-checked that I left home wearing my wooden shoes, I walked out the door heading in the direction of the school building, but as soon as I was near the school yard, I crossed a narrow bridge to a road that led to the hay fields. The hay had been cut and stacked, and the great mountains of cut grass called to me. They needed climbing.

When I reached the first haystack, I slipped out of my clumsy clogs, pulled off my stockings, and began to climb. I walked barefoot often enough that my feet tolerated the hay and field stubble. It was easier to climb without the wooden shoes anyway. At the top of the stack, I sat down on the edge and launched myself down the hay, sliding to the bottom. This was endlessly fantastic, and I set about climbing and sliding over and over.

I didn't know that Herr Schmidt had planned an outing that day. As stern as he was, he did allow the whole class—about twenty-five students in four grades—to take an occasional walk in the countryside. The fresh air was good for young German children; it would help them grow up sturdy and strong and proud of their nation. What were the chances that my class would walk to the same field where I was playing? Perhaps there was actually a very good chance; it was the field closest to the school, after all. I was so intent on my climbing and sliding, my world reduced to the crunching straw below and the crisp sky above, that I did not even hear the footsteps. Finishing my two hundredth slide down the haystack, I landed at the bottom and saw Herr Schmidt's shoes. I received a substantial verbal rebuke and, of course, had to return to school with the class. At the end of the day, my teacher walked me home and personally informed Anna of my wrongdoing.

That day set Herr Schmidt and me on rather poor footing with each other. Aunt Anna was not pleased either. There would be no more playing hooky. Neatly caught, I knew I must attend school from then on—timely and prepared, with my lessons complete. My benevolent Tante, who wasn't all that fond of Herr Schmidt herself, allowed me one compromise. As long as I attended school every day, I could wear my leather shoes.

Herr Schmidt wanted us to say the *Heil* to him not only in school, but also when we passed by him in the village. One day, I was walking through the church courtyard and saw an adult approaching. I realized it was Herr Schmidt, but I was too scared to say the Deutsche greeting. I froze. He kept walking toward me. Then he walked past me, and I thought I'd been spared. No—his footsteps stopped, then doubled back. He returned, stood in front of me, and slapped me on the face.

"Brigitte! You don't say 'Heil Hitler' to me anymore?"

"Heil Hitler," I said, shaking.

"Walk past me ten times and say 'Heil Hitler' every time," he said. "Now!"

I obeyed. I shouted those words at him over and over as he counted off one through ten.

I still didn't know who Hitler was—other than that his name made my teacher act like a monster. Herr Schmidt's demands confused me. When Anna or Opa requested that I do or not do something, it usually made sense. *Don't shove the tom turkey into the water cistern—we want to keep raising turkeys so we have good meat in the winter. Take your weekly bath—you don't want to smell. Don't eat all the sauerkraut—Oma wants to enjoy some too. Wear your wooden shoes more often—we don't want your leather shoes to wear out.* These things made sense. This latest altercation with my schoolteacher made no sense at all.

Six

One afternoon in late fall, I was playing in the farmyard after school when I heard crying coming from the kitchen. I ran inside. Anna was sobbing, trying to tell Oma and Opa something.

"They've taken him!" she said, when she finally got the words out. "They've taken Otto!"

Who's taken Otto? Where have they taken him? No one spoke directly to me; I caught the story in fits and starts as Anna cried and Oma and Opa drew the details out of their daughter. Otto, my dear Onkel who saved me at the train station in Koslin, had been taken by the Secret Service. To the best of Anna's knowledge, he was to be interrogated regarding his opinions about the Führer. What would the SS care about what rural villagers thought? Otto worked in Koslin with social services, overseeing the care of foster children. That was why he'd been so compassionate with me when he first saw me. It might also explain why he was reported. He was not just another farmer. He had some influence in regional policies.

"Who reported him?" Anna cried. "Why my brother? He's done nothing!"

For several days, we had no idea where Otto was. But he was returned. For the crime of harboring and propagating ideas that could harm German security, Otto had been sentenced to serve a week in a regional labor camp. The experience did little to brighten Otto's opinion of Hitler, but it was effective in making him very, very quiet. It made all of us turn quiet. It was an effective punishment as far as the SS was concerned.

After Otto returned, he sat with our evening radio report group, his closest family and friends. There was still a measure of trust in that group; Anna's family was convinced that whoever reported Otto was in Koslin, perhaps a colleague in the city. Still, the discussions after the evening news were more hushed, more careful. That winter, everyone became more guarded about their opinions. Yet life continued. We lived with the big things that we must not talk about. We lived with the silence. We ate the crops from our good harvest, and Anna and Richard's trucks continued to ship grain and potatoes. We young children went to school, teen boys completed their advanced studies, and teen girls worked in their domestic internships.

At school, I learned math and reading and why we must always speak well of Hitler and be proud of the new Germany. At home, when I told Anna about everything that Herr Schmidt said, she and her parents grew upset. Then Anna's face would change and she seemed more worried than angry, and she always ended these conversations with the same exhortation. She bent down, took me by the shoulders and said, "Don't say anything to anybody about this."

I stared at her, concerned that I might accidentally talk about the Anything, purely because I didn't know what the Anything was. The fear in Anna's eyes told me this was a bad time to ask silly questions, so I kept my mouth shut. I knew this much: everyone was afraid of saying something that could get you sent to a work camp.

She offered one clarification. "Remember when it was your birthday, how you went to everyone's house? How you talked to everybody about anything that came to your mind?"

"Yes."

"You must not do that anymore. You must not talk to anyone."

"I won't, Tante Anna," I said. "I promise."

Seven

I knew I must not talk about the big Anything. Given that I did not know which conversational Somethings might tumble into an illicit conversation about the big Anything, I made it my practice to say Nothing at all. A pleasant nod and *Guten Tag* were fine. *Wie gehts?* was also acceptable. But if I was likewise asked how I was faring, I answered "*Gut, danke*" and hurried on my way. This was how Anna dealt with any neighbors who were not members of our evening radio group, and I modeled her with precision. Apart from that, life continued as it had before Otto's detention in the labor camp. This is what happens under a dictatorship. The regime settles around you like a deep snow—it mutes every sound and limits your sense of mobility. But in your home, in daily life with relatives and safest friends, you attempt to embody a semblance of normal life.

The rest of my days in Seidel are a tight string of summers and Christmases punctuated by occasional news from my parents in Kiel. I remember the Christmas when two dolls disappeared from my room in early December, then reappeared under the tree wearing newly knitted white and green caps and dresses. I remember the summer that Anna finally bought a bicycle and I learned to ride it, and the summer that Anna boarded the train for Koslin and came home with a brown and white puppy named Bengel. I remember that the sheepdog mutt was no help with the geese; he followed Lilly and me out to the meadow and conked out in the shade while we herded the flock. I remember new farm laborers arriving in Seidel—Polish prisoners of war. We did not have any assigned to our farm, but I remember how the neighbors dealt kindly with these men and, over time, earned their trust. No one knew then that such choices might help spare their own lives in years to come.

I remember picking blueberries in the summer and mushrooms in the spring and fall. I remember climbing onto the barn roof with a neighbor girl so we could reach the branches of the pear tree and sit on the roof eating its sun-warmed fruit. I remember the Christmas when I spied through the keyhole into Oma and Opa's room, discovering that this was where my Tante prepared the tree and presents. Seidel was my home. I rarely thought of my parents except when we received a letter, or when Mother picked me up for our visits to Glogau, or when I made two or three brief visits back to Kiel.

Those memories linked together in my mind like a string of beads, and in the middle, there was a shiny pendant. The initial news came in early autumn of 1942. My mother wrote to let us know that she was pregnant. I was going to have a new little brother or sister. Months later, we heard that Mother went home to Glogau to have the baby; she felt safer going into labor in a town that wasn't an airstrike target. The baby was born the last day of the year, a healthy little girl named Elke. By March, Mother and my baby sister were back in Kiel. The city was getting bombed a lot, but the neighborhood bunker was close to her apartment, so everything was fine. She arranged for me to come home for a week that spring to meet my new sister. Father had been granted a brief family leave as well. He would meet me in Seidel and accompany me on the train. I had no idea which news was more exciting: a baby sister or a chance to see Vati again.

Eight

Kiel

My father was not a big talker, but he gave me a warm hug when we met, and I was content to curl up next to him on the train for the whole five-hour ride back home. It was evening when the train slowly swayed into the city. Kiel had changed; so many bombed-out buildings, especially down by the harbor. I had seen destroyed buildings like that back when I lived in Kiel, but there were a lot more now. Plenty of people still lived there. My mother was there. It was still home. A bigger city meant plenty of work and food. Besides, I barely remembered a time when Kiel was not being bombed. We all knew to run when the sirens went off. I remembered what that was like; there would be nights and some afternoons when the whole neighborhood packed into the bunker for hours. We'd see all our friends, and I would talk with the other children. It wasn't so bad.

Those who stayed in Kiel learned to live lightly; you never knew when you might exit a bunker after an air raid night and discover your home was flattened. You had to be ready to move. It turned out, Mother knew that experience firsthand. As Vati and I left the train and boarded a bus, he explained how the apartment building where we lived before had been bombed out. Mother found a new apartment a little farther away from the city center. She hoped it would be safer there.

We spent that evening cooing over baby Elke. I was the proud seven-year-old big sister. Vati and I sat on the couch together, and he handed Elke to me, showing me how to support her head and hold her tight so she wouldn't cry. Father and Mother did not expect me to help with caring for Elke, so I was free to enjoy her when she was happy and hand her off if she grew fussy. When the latter inevitably happened, I excused myself to go outside and explore the new neighborhood. No one was concerned about this, despite all the broken glass and a hundred ways to get hurt in the shells of bombed-out buildings. I had become quite independent during my time in Seidel, and my parents seemed happy to have a break from me too.

Regardless, I quickly found other children my age playing and exploring the ruins. "Look at this," I heard a young boy's voice call from the crumbled half of my parents' apartment building. A few of his pals scurried over to him, and I joined them. The first boy had found a piece of colored glass from a broken lamp. "This one's really nice, isn't it?" The shard caught the light from the sunset; how it sparkled! I joined the children scavenging for especially pretty glass shards.

Every day that week, I was free to hold Elke for a little while, then shoot off to explore the ruins outside. I only needed to dash home when the sirens went off. This happened almost every day and most nights. I remembered the routine from when I used to live in Kiel. There were three sirens. The first meant grab your bag—the bag you always had packed and ready to go—and hurry to the bunker. The second siren meant that if you weren't already at the bunker, you'd better hoof it; the planes were very close. By the third siren, if you weren't already in the bunker, you were a fool, because the bombs were already falling.

I knew this. No one had to remind me. Whether we were preparing a meal, taking a walk, sitting on the couch after dinner, or sleeping, we lived ready to cease any task or wake from any dream as soon as the first siren sounded. It was muscle memory: the moment you grabbed your bag, your brisk walk down the street, and your settling in and chitchatting with friends. Both the British and the Americans were bombing us now. I did not marvel at this or wonder why there was a war or if it would ever stop. I did not think to ask my father why so many countries were bombing Germany. For me, it was the way of things; I had little memory of a time without war. As far as I knew, every child in the world grew up in a land where the big cities got bombed regularly. During bunker visits, we sat within the concrete cocoon and listened to the planes overhead. Sometimes there were no explosions; we were in the bunker only as a precaution. Sometimes there were explosions, and we felt the inner concrete wall shudder faintly. Eventually the skies grew silent and the doors opened. We headed home and sighed with relief to see our home still standing.

Near the end of my visit to Kiel, we made an evening jaunt to the bunker. All four of us arrived, safe and snug. Father crossed the room to speak with a neighbor. He had not seen many of his acquaintances in months, so everywhere he went, people wanted to speak with him and get a little news from the Crimean front. This was nothing unusual, the easygoing socializing juxtaposed with the muted thunder outside. Mother sat on the floor next to me holding Elke, bouncing her lightly. My sister began to fuss.

Mother gasped. "I forgot the bottles!" she said, urgently but hushed. She didn't want anyone else to hear of her oversight. She placed Elke in my arms and raced out of the bunker. This did not frighten me. The bombing was always worse down at the harbor; it was rarely all that bad in our neighborhood.

Vati walked up to me, brow furrowed, and asked where Mother was. I replied with genuine calm. "She ran home to get Elke's bottles," I said. "She'll be right back."

I thought only that Mother was silly for forgetting the bottles and felt a little put out that I had to hold my crying, squirming sister. If there was any fear in Father's face at that moment, I did not catch it. Perhaps he debated in his mind, weighed the risk of racing after her, of possibly leaving his girls entirely orphaned. Perhaps he thought such things, but he did not even wince under their weight. He nodded and sat down next to me.

Elke began yowling in earnest and I handed her off to Father. He held her tight to his chest. Right then, an explosion shook the wall behind our backs and resounded through the bunker with impossible force. That bunker was constructed of two sheltering concrete walls, a building within a building. On entering, one passed through two doors with several feet between them. The exterior wall was meant to absorb the worst of an explosion. If it gave way, there was still a whole other structure with foot-thick walls inside. For us to feel an explosion like that, the bomb must have actually hit the exterior wall.

I looked at Father, for the first time really frightened by the sound of bombing. He looked not at me, but at the door. I followed his gaze. There was Mother, very much alive, but all the blood drained from her face. She walked up to us shaking, clutching one of the two forgotten bottles.

"The other bottle broke," she said. Mother sat down next to Vati and stared straight ahead. Then she began to cry and told us what happened. She did not hide this story from me. She did not hide her shaking hands.

As she ran to the house, there were no explosions. It was only a few blocks away—not far, but it was a marathon for her, and she hoped against hope for the silence to continue. The only sound was of the British planes, their engines—retreating or approaching, it was hard to tell. Mother opened the door to our apartment, and there were the bottles on the small table by the door. She grabbed them and slammed the door shut behind her.

She heard a plane. Approaching. Yes, the engine noise grew louder. She ran as fast as she could, one bottle in each hand. At the bunker, she opened the exterior door and heard a sound like a strong wind above her. The moment she latched the exterior door behind her, about to open the inner door, the bomb hit. The impact threw her against the interior wall, and one of the bottles flew out of her hand. Somehow, the other bottle was still in her hand when she stood up from the floor.

She was alive. She had no broken bones, no wounds. She stood of her own accord, stood and opened the second door into the bunker, passed through, and closed the door securely behind her.

"If I'd left a second later, if the door hadn't shut—" Mother's words were cut short by another explosion. She did not cry anymore, and neither did we. We sat still and quiet. Feeding Elke her milk just a little at a time, Mother was able to stretch the one bottle through the whole night.

In the morning, the skies were silent. The bunker doors were opened, and we saw where the bomb had hit. Everyone had to step carefully around the crater; its edge was right at the bunker door. By the end of the next day, the hole was filled. Just in time for another raid.

While bulldozers and dump trucks repaired the crater, I began to cry that I didn't want to stay in the city anymore. I wanted to go home to Seidel. Vati distracted me with a happy surprise. He would accompany me back to Seidel the next day, and he still had three more days left of his leave after that. He would spend those days with me at Anna's place.

I was hardly sad when I hugged Mother goodbye. The next three days were a marvel. I had my favorite adult with me in my favorite place. It was spring and the fields were greening up. We walked in the meadows and through town, and I introduced Vati to my friends and foster cousins. I showed him the stream that ran past Walter and Otto's house. We walked through the tall grass, and I was so excited about the stream and telling Vati about the pond that I didn't watch my step and fell into the water. It wasn't deep, but my dress got soaked. Vati laughed and picked me up out of the stream. Later I returned the favor. When we were back at the farm, the old gander rushed at my father, hissing and snapping. I stepped between them. The gander, remembering who I was, immediately waddled away in retreat. Vati was impressed with my persuasive ability with the creature.

I could not understand why Father had to go back to the war. He obviously didn't want to go. He never said anything about his life in Crimea, never spoke of what he had to do there. But the day he left, he knelt down to give me a hug and his brown eyes were so sad. None of the adults in my life had ever looked at me with such transparent grief. Hours after he left, as I lay down to sleep that night, I realized I might never see him again. The sadness and fear I'd seen in his eyes were not unfounded. It was surely the last time we were happy together.

Nine

Seidel

The summer that I turned eight, Anna's husband, Richard, came home for a brief leave. When he spoke with Anna, he had the same fear and sadness and grief in his eyes that I'd seen in my father's face.

"If anything happens, we'll all meet in Melsungen," Richard told Anna. They were standing in the hall. He held her hands.

"Melsungen. Your brother's house," she said, confirming his words.

Melsungen was west and inland, over three hundred miles away. It must have seemed far enough away that no foreign army would pass through. And so small it would not attract air raids. When they spoke like that, I could tell they were talking about the big Anything. I listened in, but never asked any questions about the matter. Another harvest season, Christmas, and birthday would pass before we learned the extent of the German retreat from the eastern line. It was that retreat which would eventually bring the Russian army straight through Seidel.

Throughout my second year of school, Herr Schmidt continued to insist that our Fatherland would carry on, ultimately victorious under our fine Führer's command. Germany would win. Any day now. Yet at home, everyone waited and hoped for a successful assassination attempt. I don't know how Anna heard about the countless unsuccessful ones, but I remember her speaking of them at the supper table. "He almost got it again," she'd say, and Opa and Oma would shake their heads in disappointment.

Ten

By spring of 1944, the evening radio reports were honest enough about battle locations along the eastern line. We knew Germany was in retreat. The Russian front advanced. Germany, at her arrogant height, was within a stone's throw of Moscow. Now Russia took back its land and began pushing Germany out of Poland too. We began to see more and more wounded soldiers on our trains.

Seidel was remote, but our rail line connected the eastern front with the cities on the Baltic coast. Wounded troops often came through our town on their way to safer regions in the west. Many who had been drafted from our region came home permanently, discharged due to injuries. When the train stopped in Seidel, anyone with provisions to spare headed to the station to give food to the soldiers. In return, the young men shared news from the last battle they had fought in. I accompanied Anna on some of these trips, watching these strangers, wondering at the bandages, the splints, the unmoving bodies lying on cots. Blood soaked through the bandages, bright red against white cloth, or darkened the gray uniforms. I was never bold enough to ask the questions I had for those wounded young men. Seeing them made me think of Vati and his sad, scared eyes.

In April, Anna received a telegram from my mother. "Your father has been wounded," she said. Anna touched my shoulder. "He's alive, but wounded. He is being shipped home."

My father was a wounded soldier, like the ones on the trains. The telegram said nothing of the exact nature of his injuries. Did he break his leg? Lose a hand? Did he have stitches? Were there bandages around his head? Did he lie on a cot, unable to stand up? Anna asked me if I wanted to go home to Kiel. I said no. No, I didn't want to go back to a city that was getting bombed. I didn't want to stay in Seidel either, where something big and bad was coming. I wanted to find my Vati and get out of here. I wanted to get out of all the places that weren't safe anymore.

Having seen so many injured soldiers pass through our train station, I was convinced that every one of them was shipped home on our rail line. After all, Vati had picked me up on our train when we visited Kiel together. In my mind, Seidel was the only rural stop between Crimea and Koslin, and I was sure I could find my father on one of the trains passing through.

When I sat in school, I could not pay attention to my lessons. I thought only of Vati and how I needed to return to him, to find him, to make sure whatever wound he had mended quickly. Whatever our lesson work, whether it was math or grammar or more rants about how our Fatherland would soon win the war, when I heard a train whistle, I stood up and ran out the back door of the school. To hell with Herr Schmidt. There was a shortcut that led straight to the train tracks. When the train stopped, I ran from car to car calling, "Vati! Vati! Are you in there?" I never found him, but refused to listen to the explanations Tante Anna gave me. What did she know? What did anyone know?

As for my teacher? As foul as Herr Schmidt was, he did nothing when I returned to class. Not even a look. He carried on with his lesson as if nothing had happened. It was the only thing that man ever did that even resembled kindness.

Eleven

There was no hiding Normandy, no hiding America's full involvement in European battles, and no hiding the Allies' new victories. I remember Anna's family and closest friends sitting in a circle around the radio, remember their faces lighting up with hope and fear at once. Hope that the Americans would rescue us, certainty that the Allies could destroy Hitler; fear that Russia would get to our region first. We knew that we could, to an extent, trust the Americans and the British, but we were terrified of Russia. We had heard that the Russian forces were especially ruthless toward civilian populations.

The war had turned. Everyone knew. Even Herr Schmidt. In the winter of 1944, the big Anything grew to encompass rumors that we ought to be ready to leave Seidel. Just as Anna's family planned to meet in Melsungen, other families made similar plans, arranging to meet each other in some inland city where they had a cousin, a brother-in-law, a close friend.

Twelve

At the dawn of 1945, both the radio reports and injured soldiers confirmed that the Russian front was only a hundred miles or so to our east. In February, school was cancelled indefinitely. By day, I helped Opa take care of the animals, not knowing whether we might have to leave them behind for good. We ate and kept house, all the while wondering whether we would see the house again once we left. Today? Tonight? Two days from now? How would we know anyway? It was the same feeling I had in Kiel knowing the air-raid siren might go off at any time. Except in Kiel, you knew there would be a siren and there was a bunker where you could hide. In Seidel, something was coming, something very bad, but no bunker. There was only this general idea of heading west, running ahead of an unstoppable wave. Almost every day, we'd hear the sound of approaching planes and see them flying overhead in formation, in threes. Always headed west, coming from the Russian front.

My parents wrote us saying they wanted to come and pick me up, bring me back to Kiel. Tante Anna read me that letter and I said, "No, I don't want to go back there." Anna agreed and wrote back. It was hardly safer for me in Kiel, and not entirely wise for them to travel east at this time. She told them we would head west soon. We would find them. Somehow.

Everyone waited for the right moment to leave. We ate, cared for the animals, slept fitfully, and listened to the radio. We listened as the reports named towns now under Russian control. Soon the list contained villages that Anna and her family had heard of, only miles to our east. Each evening we listened about the battle line coming closer. One evening, Oma was feeding the chickens when the radio report started. Opa called to her and she came running. She was so flustered, she stumbled on the steps and fell and broke her nose. We had no access to a doctor, so Anna did her best to care for her mother's injury.

Just days after that, when Oma's face was still badly swollen and red, a wave of retreating German soldiers passed through Seidel—not just the injured ones on the train, but healthy men fleeing on foot. So this was how we would learn when it was time to leave. Instead of sirens, there would be young men from our country. Every night, another group of haggard men came through our streets. Anna fed them, for we had plenty stored in the pantry from two good harvest seasons. All the villagers let the soldiers sleep in their homes. In the morning, the men boarded the train to Koslin; they were all headed west. One of the soldiers who came through looked so much like Vati, I clung to him. The sweet man humored me when Anna explained the situation. I wept when he shipped out, and he waved to me from the train until they were out of sight.

Germany had not yet surrendered, but one evening, the soldiers who sat with us at our table did not mince words.

"We have lost," one man said. He was not as young as the others with him and spoke with authority. "Be ready to leave. The Russians will not be merciful to you."

The next morning, the soldiers made formation in our street before heading out. One young man leaned out of line and whispered to Anna, "If you're smart, you'll get out of here now."

"Get inside," Anna said to me. "We need to start packing."

I tried not to think of my father or how I would ever find him again. There was work to do. Anna and her family loaded our belongings into one of her shipping trucks. Thank goodness for that little side business. The whole family would be able to ride in the back of the flatbed truck.

On March 27, 1945, we woke wondering if today was the day. Our bags were packed. The truck was ready. Yet we kept the tile oven hot in the kitchen. We still needed to eat. How long would we be without a warm meal? That morning, while everyone busied themselves with packing, I longed for a little sweetness. My mouth watering, I set an apple in the tile oven. It was a new apple, just harvested. Oma often made me baked apples. It was easy; I could do it myself. Set the apple in the top oven. Then when the smell of warm apple wafted out, it was ready.

I opened the oven door to check on the apple. Who knows why I did what I did next. I knew how to take something hot out of the oven; it was a familiar task. Perhaps the constant fear that lived in our house had infiltrated and boggled the part of my mind that normally engaged common sense. Whatever the case, I was thinking only of the apple's sweet taste, and I grabbed it with my bare hands. Oh it seared! In less than a second it was out of my hands—and on the ceiling. That's how much I jumped at the pain.

No one was in the kitchen to see this foolishness, and I intended to keep my embarrassing mistake a secret. As I doused my hands with cold water from the wash bucket, I heard the apple plop onto the floor behind me. My hands soothed, I gathered my dignity and the apple—both bruised but surprisingly intact. A portion of the apple had broken off and the rest was a bit dusty, but I rinsed it off and gulped it fast. Who knew when I might get a warm apple again in the future? I noticed a spattering of apple guts on the ceiling; I could not reach to clean it and hoped no one would notice.

But nothing got past Tante Anna. I was standing just outside the kitchen door when she walked in from the farmyard. As she perused the kitchen, looking for any more items she might like to pack in the truck, her eyes wandered up one cupboard and then to the ceiling nearby.

"What is that?" she said to the ceiling, then turned to me. "Brigitte, do you know anything about that?"

"No," I said. "That's strange." I approached and looked at the odd splatter on the ceiling, feigning surprise and curiosity.

Had Tante Anna looked at me, she would have known I was lying. But she was captivated by the ceiling, turning her head, shifting her weight, squinting. "Oh God," she said, suddenly solemn. "Oh God, it's a sign."

She called her parents in and pointed to the strange thing on the ceiling. All three marveled. The odd markings looked exactly like the stars on the Russian flag. Everyone agreed. We must leave the next morning. I stood in the doorway perfectly still, way too frightened to laugh.

That evening, the sign was confirmed. Seidel's mayor declared that all those who wished to leave should do so immediately. We would get what sleep we could and leave before dawn. Before we went to bed, Anna and Opa prepared a cache of canned meat and coins and other valuables. In hopes that we would return someday, they buried the stash in the nearest farm field.

Part 2

Refugee
1945 – 1946

Thirteen

Anna drove, with Oma seated next to her in the front of the truck. Opa and I sat in the back of the truck perched atop our tarped belongings, in the hope of hiding anything worth stealing. All those days of saying Nothing to our neighbors, all those days of quiet distrust—that was nothing compared to what we now feared. Between the advancing Russians and the poverty in Germany's bombed-out cities, we knew that our food alone was attractive loot. Anna and her parents weren't entirely sure where we were going, whether we needed to head to Melsungen for refuge right away or if we could leave home temporarily and come back after the Russian front had passed through. Rumor had it that they let residents return to their homes after a region was stable.

It was cold and damp the morning we left. Our tarped belongings below us and a canvas tent above, we huddled in the back of the truck as Anna drove. We traveled rural roads, hoping to avoid military convoys on the major highways and heading southwest, away from the advancing Russian front. Everywhere we went, every road held a stream of refugees fleeing on foot. We'd heard Koslin was under siege, so we pushed further west, hoping Stettin would be stable. For two days, we traveled over bumpy roads and spent our nights in barns—nestling into the hay at night was a warm and cozy relief compared to our cold travel by day. We did our best to avoid the battle zones in major towns. But ultimately we would need to enter a city to find fuel for the truck and to determine whether we needed to head much farther west or wait out the Russian advance and see if we could go back home.

When we reached the outskirts of Stettin, one hundred miles from Seidel, there were hordes of others like us heading into the city, refugees from farther east. But there seemed to be just as many residents trying to escape. The streets were crowded with people on foot and in vehicles, everyone trying to go somewhere—who knew where. Apparently, we had the bad luck of arriving in Stettin on the same day the Russian Army was moving in. Anna stopped the truck. We were considering the possibility of turning back when several German soldiers approached us. This seemed a good turn until they spoke.

"Leave your vehicle now!" one barked at Anna and Oma. Others pulled Opa and me out from the back. We stared at them, stunned.

An officer grabbed Anna's arm to yank her out of the driver's seat, but he hesitated. She looked directly at him.

"This is my truck," she said.

"It belongs to the Führer now," the officer said. "The Russians are shooting us on sight, even if we surrender."

The four of us lined up outside the truck—a child, a lovely woman, and her elderly parents. The officer softened for only a moment. "Realize you are doing us a great service," he said. "Take whatever food and clothing you can carry. We need the rest."

We were permitted then to quickly gather a few items. Anna and Opa and I threw food and clothing into three potato sacks. Mostly food. We'd each carry one bag, though Oma was hurting, so she couldn't carry anything. There was little time to consider the situation, to think or feel anything as we watched members of our own military steal our truck, our clothing, and our food. Now on foot in an unfamiliar city under siege, we had to find a way out. Other foot travelers informed Opa that trains were still running. The station was not far. We joined a group of other refugees walking along the tracks. We found more chaos at the train station. Yes, there were trains. But everyone was trying to get in them. There were no tickets to buy; everyone tried to cram into a train as soon as they heard where it was headed. Everyone in that jostling fearful crowd was either a resident of Stettin or a refugee from outlying areas trying to get somewhere else. Anna and Opa tended to Oma, helping her through the crowd. I held onto my potato sack and kept up.

Somehow Anna found a train with open seats. It probably had room on it because it was headed north, not west, but this would have to do. We wanted only to get away from the direct path of the Russian siege coming from the east, and Anna managed to find us a compartment on a train to Swinemunde on the coast. We settled into our seats, and Oma began to cry. She must have been in great pain, her nose still bruised from her fall a week before, and now this awful day with no known end to our journey. She leaned on Opa.

When the train arrived in Swinemunde, we found out it was the end of the line. The train would go no further. Oma couldn't go any further anyway; she desperately needed to rest. We had to find shelter fast.

Swinemunde was already Russian occupied, and we quickly learned that this was slightly better than arriving in a city still under siege. Having taken control of a town, the Russians set up a command post, a *Kommandantur*, and usually permitted civilians to move back in—if they chose to. Many former residents chose not to move back into their bombed-out homes, chose to stay on with relatives farther west, farther inland. Every wave of refugees left empty houses in its wake, and there was no shortage of people like us searching for shelter. As soon as we disembarked from the train, we began our hunt for a fairly intact roof. We found it amid rubble.

The house had one solid room left, enough space for two mattresses that we salvaged. Eventually we found a small table and chairs that fit in that room as well. A hallway and bathroom were also intact—remarkably, the faucet worked. For Anna and her parents, this was their first time living in a home with running water. Too bad the kitchen and front sitting room were dust and rubble. The basement below our living quarters was also sturdy; we would set up a kitchen and pantry there. But that first evening, all that mattered was protection from the rain and a soft surface where Oma could lie down. We had the mattresses and the food in our packs. That was enough.

The next day, the urgency of our situation set in. We needed food. What we had in our packs might last us three days at most. We felt moderately safe in our sturdy room, with its one locking door, but we'd have to leave to find provisions. Oma was in no shape to travel. Anna, normally so quick to take charge of such tasks, said that she had better stay back with Oma. Opa agreed with Anna. "I don't want you out there ever, if possible," he said. With a hostile military policing the streets, my beautiful Tante had the strongest reason to fear heading out of doors.

That left food gathering to Opa and me. He took my hand and we walked into the gray day, heading up one street and down the next. We weren't sure what we might find, or really what we ought to be looking for. Without any plan, we made our way to the harbor, simply because all roads led there. What we found there was even more valuable than food. At the harbor, I recognized a boy my age: it was Günther from Seidel, the boy who lived near Heidi's house. Technically, he was one of the boys who had bullied me; Heidi had to scare him off many times. But there he was, standing on the pier.

I loosened my hand from Opa's and walked up to Günther. We stared at each other.

"Brigitte?"

I nodded. "Is your family staying in Swinemunde too?"

"Yes. My mother and grandmother found a house up that lane there. Yesterday."

"We did too. Over that way, not far."

That was that. Günther did not tell me to go back where I came from or laugh at me. He was, no doubt, as relieved as I was to see a familiar face in the midst of so much strangeness. He joined Opa and me in our food gathering, which included an abandoned basket of fish, still quite fresh. We divvied up our finds and headed to our respective shelters. What fortune to find that food; what fortune to find a friend amidst the rubble.

Fourteen

Swinemunde

We lived in our little room for several weeks, waiting for word about our home region. Anna found a wood stove in the basement, below our room. The stove had a flue; it was usable right where it stood. Two tiny windows in the basement allowed just enough light for Anna to cook down there. Each day she managed to cook for four people in that makeshift kitchen. Every day I ventured out to scavenge our groceries. In general, the Russian soldiers had the decency to leave children alone. So in every family, children around my age—about eight to eleven years old—were the safest candidates for food gathering. I was nine, the perfect age. Any younger and the child might get hurt rummaging in the rubble; any older and they might draw the harassment of the Russians. In the same way that I had been sent to the mercantile in Seidel to fetch sauerkraut and flour, so I was now sent out into the town to scavenge each day.

Günther and I worked together, and we always found just enough to feed our families for a day or two. There were plenty of bombed-out houses. We could freely search the ones that were not occupied by squatters. Within a few days, we developed a decent system of working together to find the best houses: clearly destroyed, but not so flattened that the food stores would be inedible. It was easier to scavenge if the roof was gone, as this let light in. But if the roof was

64

gone, that meant the walls might be crumbled too. We evaluated each property as we walked up and down each street.

Those were surprisingly contented days, at least for me. Give a nine-year-old a little chore, especially one that involves exploring a dangerous place—then give her a friend to accompany her—and that's all that's needed. She will feel bold instead of worried, as if she'd simply opened the door to the neighbor's barn—the barn she was told she must not enter.

One day, Günther and I found the abandoned German *Kaserne*, a cluster of army offices. One of the buildings was entirely bombed out on one side. We entered the structure easily, found rickety burnt-out stairs leading down to the basement, and felt our way down the steps. A little light came through a dusty window high up on the cellar wall. We let our eyes adjust, then discovered what we could have only hoped for. It was a true cellar, not just military office storage. There was food.

On one shelf we found a single miniature wooden barrel that held about a gallon of honey. Then we found a whole standard barrelful of partially peeled potatoes. Whoever had been peeling them left in a hurry—that was for sure. The barrel was full of water, the potatoes submerged. It was hard to tell whether this had slowed or caused the film of brown decay coating each potato. But there they were, a whole barrel of potatoes. Back in Seidel, such a find would hardly be worthy of the pig trough, but here in bombed-out Swinemunde, we'd discovered gold. Günther found an old sack and we set about extracting the potatoes and setting them in the bag. Then we filled our coat pockets too.

We returned to our homes to divvy the loot between both families. Günther carried the potato sack and I carried the honey. There was no way to get around the rot. Anna boiled them long and hard, and the honey covered up the moldy taste. Potatoes and honey—not a combination we'd eaten before, but it was decent. We ate well that night.

The next day, Günther and I found a couple sacks of dried peas. We delivered these to our families, then we headed back out to rummage more. We found an abandoned house by the waterfront that seemed promising, but someone else had beaten us to the food pantry. We kept exploring the structure and found an elaborate dollhouse in one of the bedrooms. What a find! Together we hauled the thing up the lane to my house. We sat with the dollhouse on the walk in front of my place. Even though my pal was a boy, he could still appreciate that this was quite the costly plaything. Besides, we weren't actually playing with any dolls. There weren't any. When Günther saw a June beetle crawling on the ground, I suggested we catch it and place it in the dollhouse, which had miniature doors and shutters that actually latched. We could trap the bug in the house.

Upon catching one beetle, we noticed all the others. We gathered several dozen of the little black bugs to people the dollhouse. I wasn't sure Tante Anna would be keen on the beetles, but we could hide the dollhouse in the bathtub. It wouldn't bother anyone there. So we did just that. Anna was downstairs in the cellar kitchen cooking the peas we'd brought earlier. Oma and Opa were resting. Opa called to me when he heard us giggling and shuffling down the hall.

"Yes, Opa, it's just me," I shouted back to him. Apparently that was all the assurance he needed; no one came out to check on us. We brought the dollhouse into the bathroom and settled it into the tub, quite undetected. The miniature door was shut tight, all the windows latched. We could hear the inhabitants rustling about, climbing the walls, scratching along the ceiling, falling to the floor. June bugs were such lumbering, stupid creatures. We laughed again, then left the bathroom, shutting the door behind us. We could play with the beetles again after supper. Or tomorrow. Or whenever we remembered them.

Günther said hello to Opa, then dashed off to his own home. Anna announced our food was almost ready. We ate our pea soup—it was great luck to find the big sack of peas; dry goods like that could last for months. I missed buttermilk soup, but I never complained about these humble meals. Food tasted better when you worked hard to find it yourself. Thinking of such things, I fully forgot about the beetles. And the dollhouse. And the possibility that the little bug people might want a better life for themselves.

Instead, Anna found them. After supper, she gathered our dishes and walked to the bathroom to wash them in the sink there. I still didn't think of the beetles, even as Anna walked down the hall. I jumped about a foot when I heard her scream. Both Oma and Opa froze, then Opa dashed from his chair to the door. He was about to race down the hall to save his daughter, when we heard Anna shout again, "Brigitte, what is this!?"

The beetles had mutinied. They may have been stupid and lumbering, but their repeated fumblings in the dollhouse eventually popped opened a window. They were everywhere in the bathroom. When Anna opened the bathroom door with her one available finger, the whole swarm flew out at her. Several landed in her hair and on her face; she almost dropped the dishes. How long had Günther and I collected beetles that afternoon? How many had we shoved into our ornate bug box? It could've been hundreds.

Oma, always my defender, had no energy for such things that evening. But I saw just the slightest smile on her face when Anna returned. My Tante shook her head and said, "What am I going to do with you, child?" For one blessed moment, everything was as it should be.

It was spring, and the longer we stayed in Swinemunde, the warmer and more pleasant the weather became. Simultaneously, the longer we stayed, the more we exhausted our food supply. It was still cold at night too, and we had burned up all the scrap wood in the crumbling walls around us. We still needed heat and a cooking fire too. We needed wood badly enough that Opa headed out every day to scavenge. This became increasingly risky, as the Russian soldiers had begun actively intimidating any adults they saw. It wasn't a patrol to keep order in the city so much as a very disorderly pastime. Drunk and shooting into the sky, the soldiers came into our neighborhood every day.

Still, I knew Günther and I retained a measure of safety. I'd had only one close call with a soldier so far. Günther and I had just parted company to bring home our day's paltry finds. I was alone on my street when a Russian soldier driving a horse and buggy came racing round the corner, headed directly for me. He held the reins in his left hand and shot a gun erratically at the buildings along the street. Then he saw me. He yelled a few angry words—at me or at his horse, I couldn't tell. I froze for a split second, then jumped to the side, barely escaping the horse hooves, as the buggy wheels hurtled past me. I caught my breath, then ran the rest of the way home.

Such harassment was rarely directed at us kids, but quite common for teens and adults. The streets became increasingly empty, the silence broken only by celebratory gunfire and drunken laughter. Everyone stayed inside whatever shelter they had. Only grade-school-aged children walked about, and we were skittish. Just as Günther and I foraged together, other children roamed the streets in twos and threes doing the same. They might walk in the opposite direction from us on the other side of the street. They might duck down another lane. We might see another child at a distance poking around in the same square block of rubble. Some became familiar in a way, but we rarely spoke. Never played. We all knew we must be light on our feet. We all knew that, with this particular enemy, we were safer when we scattered to individual hiding places. Every child watched for the brown Soviet uniform, listened for the heavy steps of soldiers' boots. We all learned how to disappear.

With that being the state of things, it was a great risk for Opa to head out into the streets to gather firewood each day, and only a matter of time before he ran into trouble with the Russians. We needed the heat. Oma was doing poorly. It had been weeks, but her broken nose had not healed. Günther and I had enough time to hunt for provisions or to gather wood, but not both. So Opa took on the task. He found a burned-out house down the street; its timbers and frame planks were shattered and strewn about on what used to be the main floor of the house. It was perfect. Opa even managed to find the owner of the house and formally request permission to scavenge the wood.

Opa worked alone at that site, while Günther and I hunted for food. One day, we planned to return to the firewood house to help carry the wood. But just as we arrived, so did two remarkably sober Russian lieutenants on patrol. Günther and I hid in the entryway of a house across the street and watched as they accused Opa of damaging property—this was a curious accusation, considering the property was already irreparably damaged. It didn't matter. These accusations and arrests had become more and more common. There was no other way for us refugees to feed and warm ourselves, but the Russians had begun arresting any adult found gathering firewood or looting food. It seemed like they wanted to starve us out over the coming months.

I gasped as the soldiers seized my Opa. They were taking him to their *Kommandantur* in the old police station. Horrified, Günther and I ran home to tell Tante Anna what had happened. She did not even flinch. She had no intention of going to the *Kommandantur* to plead for her father's release. It wasn't that she was afraid of walking outside or afraid of the soldiers. She simply was not worried for Opa's safety.

"Remember, my father is American," she said to us. "I don't think the Russians will do anything to him when he proves he is still an American citizen."

I wasn't so sure. I wanted to believe Anna was correct. But she hadn't seen the soldiers who arrested Opa, hadn't seen how rough they were with him.

"I've got to make sure he's okay!" I said, and bolted out the door, dragging Günther with me. My friend dug in his heels when we got to the street.

"Not me," he said, shaking. "No way."

My best buddy thought I was crazy. He ran to his own home, and I headed straight for the *Kommandantur*. There it was, in the middle of downtown, an old red brick building that had survived the siege. A few of the city offices around the town square were remarkably unharmed. One of the buildings across the square had stone archways framing the front entrance. I ran behind one of the columns and spied on the *Kommandantur* building from my hiding place. The square, like the rest of the town, was empty. I hadn't really thought of what I'd do once I arrived there. I peeked out from behind the column right as a Russian soldier stepped out. He was familiar. It was one of the men who had arrested my Opa. The soldier saw me and shouted something, then bounded toward me. I'd had plenty of practice running through that town and knew all the side streets. Outpacing that soldier wasn't too hard. But how my heart pounded in my ears when I finally stopped to catch my breath. I was sure the soldier was bent on arresting me. I took a circuitous route home, just in case he was on my trail.

By the time I got home, Opa was already there. Anna was right. He really did manage to talk himself out of that situation. I told him about the soldier who ran after me, and Opa laughed. He drew me close to where he sat at the table next to Oma. "I'm sure you left that man in the dust," he said. "But he probably meant to tell you that I'd been released. Of course, who knows how he intended to communicate that. Their German is terrible."

"How did you tell him you were an American, then?"

Opa patted his breast pocket. "An American birth certificate communicates clearly in any language. There was also one officer who spoke a little English." Whatever Russia and America thought of each other before the war, they were allied in their efforts against us. Russian officers wouldn't take any chances mistreating any American. For the rest of our days in Swinemunde, the soldiers left Opa alone.

We knew the war had ended. The news about Germany's surrender in May was hardly a significant event. It only gave a political seal on what everyone already knew: Germany lost, and our borders were being redrawn. As refugees, we had little energy to concern ourselves with the politics. We only wanted to know where we should live, where we'd get food. Even with our relative safety in Swinemunde, our situation became dire. We ate less and less each day as Günther and I exhausted our looting venues. Until we had the option to return home, we weren't sure what else we could do. Every refugee wrestled with this uncertainty. For my foster family, the situation was compounded by Oma's continued poor health. Leaving Swinemunde on foot was out of the question. Oma wouldn't survive another journey during which we might not find warm shelter each night.

Our best hope was if the ferries began running again. There were rumors that this might happen soon. The main delay was that there were German mines in all the coastal waters. These needed to be cleared—at least enough to ensure a safe passageway for the ferryboats. Once civilian ferries began running along the coast again, we could get back to the coast just north of Koslin. From there, hopefully we could hitchhike to Koslin, and maybe a train still ran from there to Seidel. Each day we chewed our food slowly and waited for word.

Fifteen

The streets of Swinemunde always seemed like a ghost town to me—so quiet except for other children my age scavenging and the occasional Russian soldier in a celebratory mood. We children had learned to move like mice, just a flash of movement now and then. The day the ferries started running again, we learned how many neighbors we actually had.

Günther's mother came to our door right at dawn. "There are two boats in the harbor!" she said, out of breath. "We must head down quickly to get tickets; there won't be enough for everyone." Who knew when ferries would come through again. Their presence in the harbor today certainly didn't guarantee predictable transport any time soon. For the moment, not only did we have a chance to board a boat heading toward our home region, but the Russians had also announced we were free to return to the villages back east. Seidel was occupied land, but the region was stable. We could go home.

Anna and I packed our three canvas sacks while Opa raced down to the harbor. We helped Oma walk down the cobblestone street to meet Opa by the docks. There we hit our first snag. Tante, Oma, and I stood back a few paces from the clamoring crowd. We saw Opa reach the ticket counter and pay for a purchase. We could tell from the unhappy shouts after his transaction that the tickets were now sold out. It was hard to read Opa's look when he approached us. His lips were tight, more a grimace than a smile. He wasn't waving four tickets in the air as I'd hoped.

"I have tickets," he said. "They sold me the last three."

My surrogate aunt and grandparents, all three of them, looked at me. For the first time, I realized I was not truly a member of their family. Something strange crossed my aunt's face, a heaviness I had not seen before. Perhaps for the first time she saw me as purely a burden. By all rights, I was. Even though I was adept at food scavenging and carrying firewood, I was also an extra mouth, another creature to be warmed and sheltered and cared for if ill. I should be with my own mother in Kiel, but who knew what was left of Kiel? Who knew whether my parents still lived in Kiel? There was no mail service, no way to communicate with my family. Honestly, that whole time in Swinemunde, I'd been so focused on the tasks of survival, I had not thought much of my parents. No one had time for missing those we'd left behind.

I looked at the three tickets in Opa's hand. I thought of my parents then.

Whatever Anna's feelings in that moment, there was no spoken debate that day, and there was no question in Opa's mind. "Someone must have mercy," he said. So the four of us headed into the harbor crowd, trusting that we would all board a boat together.

As anxious as we felt as we edged through the buzzing crowd, it was impossible not to feel the charge of celebration in the air. There had to be hundreds of people standing on the pier and along the roadway. Swinemunde was a loud place now, full of life. Everywhere, ticket holders discussed departure times, and countless others speculated about when the ferries would come again. Many families were split, some members leaving, some forced to stay back. These groups discussed the logistics of reuniting: *If my Uncle still has his delivery truck... If there is fuel... If the trains run again...* What kind of plans can you make when so much is out of your control? But everyone tried.

I lugged two of our rucksacks over one shoulder and held onto Anna's arm with my free hand. There had to be somebody with an extra ticket, someone who bought an extra in the hope of selling it for a fine profit. As a last resort, we'd plead our case to the ferry operators. Truly, who in our group could be safely left behind? Which one could survive alone in Swinemunde? They must understand. We jostled our way through the crowd onto the pier.

Then I saw Günther. I shouted to him through the crowd, and he made his way over to us, along with his mother and grandmother. Günther's mother smiled at us. "You got tickets, then?" she said.

Opa told her our plight. Günther's mother looked at her own family group, then at us. "I have four tickets," she confessed. "We only need three. I got the extra hoping to make a little cash, but here we are." There was no question about what needed to be done. We laughed and hugged our friends and swapped the two stacks of tickets. Three were for the first ferry, leaving about 8 a.m., four for the second boat. Ours would leave just minutes after Günther's. His family would wait for us on the dock at Groß Möllen. From there, we'd all find a way home to Seidel, another fourteen miles southeast from the coast.

What relief! In a moment, we became full members of the joyous crowd—the ones who had tickets, enough for the whole family. When the boats arrived, Günther's family and mine shook hands and patted shoulders and then headed to our separate boarding lines. "See you at home!" I shouted to Günther. He waved at me, then he was swallowed into the crowd on his boat.

Whatever the tension I'd seen in Anna's eyes, whatever the questions that fluttered through all our minds that morning, it all mattered very little right then. Even Oma—who struggled to stay standing, whose entire body ached most days, whose nose was still raw and weepy from her fall—smiled as we stood on the gangway. We were going home.

Günther's boat departed just as ours finished boarding. In the middle of the boat, a covered captain's deck rose up above the main deck. An awning stretched out covering the passenger space. There were no benches; the whole crowd huddled on the floor. Opa and Anna found space where we could all lean against the exterior wall of the captain's deck. As the ship's engine came to life, we headed out to open water. Anna sat close to her mother, letting her rest in her arms.

We were near the front of the boat. Several people sat on the floor between me and the railing, but I could see the water if I stretched to look over their shoulders. I could watch the buildings and trees on the shore growing smaller. I could see Günther's boat way ahead of us. They tracked a course a little farther out to sea. After about half an hour, we caught up to the other boat, traveling less than a hundred yards behind them.

That was when we heard the explosion. Everyone on our boat stood in unison and rushed to the railing, squeezing against each other to look ahead. Every conversation on the boat stopped mid-sentence. The crowd turned dead silent. I shoved my way to the front of the crowd and saw the debris still flying through the air. Ahead of us, the water was empty where there had been a boat before.

My eyes could not make sense of what they saw. Only my ears understood that my friend's boat had hit an underwater mine. My eyes did not understand, but I did see it all: debris crashed into the water. A woman next to me doubled over in shock, covering her head with her hands, but she didn't make a sound. I did not make a sound myself. I stared. I looked at the water, at the dissonant waves where Günther's boat had been. I stared into the water.

Our ferry did not stop. It couldn't. We were supposedly within safe passage; deviating would have hardly improved our own odds. Within seconds, our boat passed through the debris. Shattered boards. Clothing. Blood. Bodies. Parts of bodies. A carcass of a cow. I understood that animals died. I knew that. Then I realized, with clarity, that the people on that ferry had died too, just like the shattered cow floating in the water. I felt Opa's hands on my arms, pulling me away from the railing. There was no hiding anything. There were no gentle lies. No one said anything. Opa tugged me back to where he and Anna and Oma were sitting; he drew me back down to the floor. I was surely no safer from a mine sitting there with them. But my eyes were safe from the dead things in the water. I hid my face in Opa's coat and wept.

I was nine years old. I had seen our truck stolen. I had walked through strange towns unsure of shelter and food. I had seen enemy soldiers run around shooting their guns, and I had even outrun them. But I did not understand war until the day I lost my friend. It rendered me mute for several hours. I heard my aunt crying. I heard Opa and Oma and Anna speak frightened, desperate words, heard their decision to get off the ferry sooner than planned. I heard Anna say, "If we stay on this boat any longer, we'll be next!" Her words were sharp, but I heard them as if listening in through a closed door. Like hearing voices from under water. When I finally looked up, I saw the other people around us, faces frozen, staring, some red with tears, others pale and vacant. Some held each other; others could not move. Anna was still weeping.

I hid my face and cried again till I had no tears left, till my throat felt dry. Günther was my good friend. We'd found food together day after day, played with June beetles together, went everywhere with each other. He had teased me back in Seidel, but in Swinemunde that had changed, and somehow our friendship was especially close because of that change. When we boarded the boats that morning, we knew we'd be home that evening, and once we were home, we'd stay pals forever. Günther was gone. My friend was gone. He boarded the boat I should have been on, and now he was gone forever. After the tears subsided, I felt nothing at all.

We got off the ferry at Kolberg. Everyone else did too. Home was still thirty miles to the east. We couldn't walk the whole way—how would Oma survive? We hoped someone with a truck or wagon might have compassion on us. While Oma and I sat on crates near the end of the pier, Anna and Opa spoke with two fishermen. I overheard Opa telling them our story, how we lost our friends, how we couldn't risk another mile on the ferry.

The fishermen inquired about our destination. "We can get you to Groß Möllen safely," one of them said.

The other added, "We know the waters well; we work out there every day."

The fishermen were brothers. They loaded us onto their boat, and we sat out in the open in the middle of the main deck. While we were still docked, one of the men said, "You must be hungry." We did not deny this. The fishermen must have lived on the boat. One of them disappeared below decks and reappeared carrying two big pots. He set them on a crate, and we huddled around it as he removed the lids. We peeked inside: potatoes, ham, and, of course, steamed fish. Fresh potatoes. A few forks and knives were propped against the food inside the pots. Opa took a knife and sliced off a piece of ham and ate it. We all followed suit. Anna cut small pieces for her mother and fed her. All the food was cold, but it was so good. For weeks we'd been hungry. How awful it was to taste such good things. How difficult to feel gratitude, to taste delight on that day. God, we were hungry.

"Eat," the brothers said over and over. "Eat all that you need, all that you want."

So we did.

The fishing boat motored a slow and cautious route up the coast as we ate. It was late evening when the fishermen dropped us off at Groß Möllen. We had no luck finding any help at that harbor, so we walked through the small village, found a barn near the main road, and huddled together in the hay for the night. At dawn, we headed out to the road and flagged down a truck that was leaving the village.

Once again, Opa pled our case and was met with compassion. The driver was headed to Köslin, just ten miles from home. We could pile in the back of the truck bed, on top of his shipping crates. A canvas tarp was cinched tight over a frame covering the cargo bed. At least we'd be protected from the wind. We climbed aboard and huddled, with Oma in the middle to keep her warm and relatively stable during the jouncy ride. We coped well enough till we arrived at a checkpoint just outside the city.

Russian forces monitored all roads into major cities. Supposedly they were looking for any remaining German soldiers. But more often than not, they also searched for any goods worth stealing. We heard the soldiers speak gruffly with our driver. Then their boots approached the back of the truck. Between the four of us, the only items in our possession that might be considered valuable were Oma's fine, tall leather boots. As the soldiers came closer, Oma curled her legs under her and Opa discretely pulled the hem of her coat down over the boots. Initially, the soldiers rifled through the driver's crates—fish and potatoes that he intended to sell in Köslin. They took what they wished, then gestured at us.

We held completely still. Opa did not flaunt his American citizenship; the men were armed and had no superiors nearby. If they did not understand him, they might only perceive us as a threat. One of the soldiers opened our canvas rucksacks and examined the shabby contents in disgust. Another leaned over the side of the truck and reached toward Oma's coat to search her pockets. In that process, the coat shifted and revealed her leather boots. The soldier withdrew his grimy hands and called his buddies over, pointing out the find. One of the other soldiers stood at the foot of the truck bed grinning. He said something that was apparently funny. Based on the crass laughter, the quip had to be about the boots being a waste on someone who didn't have too many more steps to take. He held up his pointer finger and beckoned Oma to come closer. They wanted the boots.

They were four rogue soldiers, all armed. With Anna and Opa's help, Oma obeyed. Her hands shaking, Anna unlaced the boots, and Opa helped his wife pull her feet out of them. He tugged her threadbare stockings back up over her legs. Anna handed the boots to those mean-spirited hands, and Oma curled her legs back under her. She huddled closer to her husband.

The laughing soldiers, thus satisfied, let the truck pass. Opa held Oma close, but no one said a thing. No one cried. Everyone knew that Russian soldiers robbed civilians. We were lucky they were satisfied with only the boots.

Oma, who was barely strong enough to stand, now could not walk outdoors at all. We discussed our only option. Our driver could drop us off at the *Hauptbahnhof*, the central station, in Köslin. He'd heard our train line had been badly damaged, so the train to Seidel was not running. But Anna and Oma could at least wait indoors at the station. Opa and I would walk the ten miles along the train tracks, the most direct way home, and hopefully retrieve one of the handcarts in our farmyard. We'd return to Köslin and take Oma home in one humble chariot.

It was almost midday when Opa and I arrived in Seidel. We left the railroad tracks and headed down our village's single street. Just past the empty school building, there was Tante Anna's house. But it was no longer her house. Russian trucks were parked in front of it and in the farmyard. As the nicest building in the village, it had been immediately commandeered as officers' quarters. We stared at the home we could no longer enter. There was nothing we could do about it. Opa went across the street to Otto's house and knocked on the door. A few residents had chosen to stay in their homes as the battle line came through. We knew Otto had stayed because Wanda had been so ill that they couldn't flee. We could only hope they were still there. Relief washed over Opa's face when Otto answered the door.

"You are alive!" we said to each other over and over.

"And where are —," Otto asked. "Where are—" He could not complete the sentence.

"They are safe," Opa assured him. The two men slapped each other's shoulders, and Otto patted my head. I held my Onkel's hand as Opa explained the situation to him, how the truck was taken, how we stayed these past months in Swinemunde, how Oma was in Köslin and could not walk any further. "We need our handcart," he said, then looked at our occupied house. "Though I doubt I can get to anything from our barn."

"Use ours, of course," Otto said. He explained how he'd saved some of our animals from the Russians. He knew they'd occupy Anna's big house, so Otto raided potatoes and apples from our pantry, retrieved a few valuables from the hutch, and also rescued two cows, a sow and the hog, and several chickens—all before the Russians could claim them. Many of Anna's possessions were still safe.

I wanted to know who else remained in the village, if any of my friends were still there, but Opa felt the day growing short. We needed to get back to Köslin fast. As it was, it would be almost dark by the time we returned with Oma and Anna. We grabbed Otto's handcart and headed back up the train tracks, trotting at a brisk pace with the cart rattling along behind us. We took turns pulling it. Thank God for the meal we'd had on the fisherman's boat. My Opa and I needed to walk a total of thirty-three miles that day, and the generous meal from the day before fueled every exhausted step. Opa was surely sustained by a more pressing desire: to see his wife safe and warm once again.

With Oma curled up in the handcart, we had to take the main road instead of the train tracks. This route was a couple miles longer, but not so bone-jarring for our beloved passenger. By the time we turned east off the highway and onto the lane toward Seidel, it was almost sunset—but still plenty of light to see our way well. That was unfortunate. Anna and Opa were pulling the cart, and I was trailing several paces behind them, so there was no one to cover my eyes when we saw the bodies. They were German soldiers, six of them hanging in their dull gray uniforms. Most were boys a few years older than me. They were hung from ratty nooses in the woods along our lane.

"Look away," Opa called back to me. "Look away!"

The wind stirred a couple of the corpses. I couldn't look away. It is possible to feel so weary, even the most fearsome things no longer cause much of a ripple in your heart or in your belly. I stared at the swinging bodies. Anna left Opa to pull the cart and came back to me. She took me by the hand as we continued down our lane, away from the trees.

Sixteen

Seidel, Germany (Wyszewo, Poland)

Shaken, we stood on Otto's front stoop. I thought I saw a dark shadow duck around the corner of the house. I froze in fear. Then the shadow burst out from behind the house, racing toward us. It was Bengel, Anna's sheepdog. Otto had saved that sweet silly dog as well. There he was, jumping at our legs. I knelt and ran my fingers through his fur and let him lick my face. I filled my eyes and nose with dog. He was alive, and he still belonged to us. Seeing Bengel made me think of Lilly, how we used to tend the geese in the field, and how the dog did nothing to help us. And we'd sit on the blanket in the meadow and lie on our backs looking at the sky and the trees. Maybe we could do that again someday soon. There was only one problem. Lilly no longer lived in Seidel.

Onkel Otto answered the door and greeted us once more and embraced his mother and sister. He helped us all settle into Walter's side of the duplex, since Walter and his family no longer lived there. Initially, they had refused to leave when the rest of the village evacuated. Walter's son, Horst, had served in the army and returned to them during the retreat. The boy had acquired rifles and an anti-tank gun and thought he had all he needed to defend his village against the Russians. He would at least keep the invading force away from his family's house. When the family heard the Russian trucks turn off of the main highway, Walter, his wife, and their three daughters hid inside, but Horst ran out to stand guard at the stream bank along the edge of their property. He stood on the little footbridge, an anti-tank gun over his shoulder.

"There were trucks, and there were soldiers on foot too," Otto said. "They gave him no time to surrender. They saw Horst holding a *panzerfaust* and shot him down like a dog." After the region stabilized, Walter and his family left. They could not live so near the men who'd killed their boy, could not live so close to the memory.

Only months before, the adults would not have spoken so freely in front of me. Opa had not yet told Otto what I'd seen on the ferry, but Otto surely knew what I'd seen during the walk down our lane. There was nothing to hide from me anymore. I knew Horst. He was gone, just like Günther was gone. Horst had been aiming a gun when he died, but he was only sixteen. And my pal Günther hadn't done anything but board the wrong ferry. None of it made sense. I did not cry. But I asked if Lilly was safe.

"As far as I know," Otto said. "Walter left with Else and the girls. I do not know where they are. We still hope to meet in Melsungen. But Wanda's cough is much worse now; that's why I am still here. She needs to improve before we make the trip."

For the remainder of our days in Seidel, I slept in Lilly's old bed, but Lilly was not there and it all felt wrong. Walter's place wasn't my home; it was Lilly's home. And if Günther was dead and Horst was dead, who could say that Lilly was safe. No one could know anything at all.

There were others who had stayed in Seidel, hiding during the takeover, and some who had returned, like us. We all tried to re-build our lives, but the village would never be the same. Most of the livestock had wandered off, died, or been taken as food by the Russians. Other houses and buildings, in addition to ours, had been commandeered. Seidel was a fine base from which the Russians could monitor the activity of other farming villages in our region and keep their forces well fed.

Seidel was occupied. Still, it was, on the whole, stable. Walking down our single street was dangerous only if you were a young German man or an eye-catching woman. Opa was comfortable walking about outdoors. Among the items Otto had salvaged from our old house was Opa's old American flag. We hung it out our kitchen window, and Opa introduced himself to the officers across the street our first morning in Seidel. The Russians were courteous with him from then on. I gasped when Opa walked past a Russian military truck and reached through an open window to pick up a rifle perched on the back seat. He turned the gun over in his hands, nodded a few times, then set it back in the truck. The soldiers nearby glanced at him but didn't even move to stop him. They carried on their conversation, entirely comfortable with Opa inspecting their firearms. Despite that respect toward our patriarch, Anna didn't like to take any chances. She stayed indoors most of the time, and often sent me out instead to care for outdoor chores. She was also fine with me heading out into the village to explore on my own. Almost like old times.

One night, Opa and I checked on the cache of canned meat and valuables that he and Anna had buried in the north farm field. Everything was still there. The meat could stay in the hole; it would keep cool there, and it wasn't entirely unwise to keep a stash of food outside the house. But we gathered the tablecloth and the coin collection and brought these valuables back to the house. The tablecloth went into Walter's old hutch, and the coins went into a nightstand by the bed where Oma and Opa slept.

I overheard what had happened to Heidi. My sweet cousin with her blond ringlets, the girl who used to scare the bullies away from me, was gone. Anna and her girlfriends talked about what happened to her. The women sipped barley coffee at the kitchen table while I sat on the couch playing with a doll that Otto had saved from Anna's house. The women had discussed the coming winter and tallied the supplies they had on hand to get their families through the cold months. They discussed the closure of our general store. Then the conversation shifted toward the former store owners themselves.

"Do you know why your cousin and his family left?" one of the women asked Anna.

"No. Other than it's no pleasure to live with the Russians here."

"You need to know why. Heidi is gone," the woman said. The other girlfriends looked at their hands and everyone grew solemn. "Thirty Russians stepped on her."

The voices were hushed, but no one made any great effort to hide their words from me. I set my doll down and sat very still, shocked at the image of my beautiful friend crushed under the boots of thirty soldiers. It would be some years before I learned that those words implied something far worse than being trampled to death. Heidi was twelve years old—the girl who had always come to my rescue when there were bullies in the lane. She was gone.

Anna's girlfriends often gathered at our kitchen table. Listening in, I learned much more about what happened in Seidel while we were gone. Several families lost sons or daughters during the invasion and takeover. But some were spared. The families that had taken on Polish prisoners as farm laborers reaped the kindness they'd shown to these men. The Polish laborers left their quarters and approached the invading forces, shouting to them in Polish and halting Russian. Somehow they managed to communicate with the Russian soldiers, managed to defend the families that had fed them well. Their advocacy prevented many more deaths in our community.

One day, as I helped wash breakfast dishes, Anna spoke with me in a serious tone. "You need to know something important," she said. "Sometimes the Russians go into people's houses and demand food. Or they try to make a pretty woman come and cook for them or wash their clothes." Anna must have seen the flash of fear in my eyes. She tempered her words. "We can scare them off easily. You can help me."

My heart raced. How could I possibly help with such a thing? Those men trampled my friend to death, and Heidi had been taller and stronger than me.

"All you have to do is this: cough really hard if the Russians ever come to our door," Anna said. "Or if we are walking down the lane together and we see some soldiers, you hold my hand and cough like you have a terrible chest cold."

"I can do that," I said. "But why?"

"They're terrified of catching tuberculosis."

"What's that?"

"Lung disease. Many people are sick with it. We were lucky we had a warm shelter in Swinemunde. Others had to stay in barns and ruins with barely a roof; many of them are sick now. So what will you do if we see a Russian soldier?"

"Hold your hand and cough really hard." I coughed in demonstration, the way I would if I wanted to prove I was too sick to go to school.

"Just like that," Anna said. "And then they won't bother you or me."

I felt a surge of pride that I might be able to protect my family just by faking a bad cold. I could do that. Sure enough, Russian soldiers began to stop by our house several times a week. They demanded that Anna come cook and wash for them, but I put on a good show, hanging on Anna's dress and coughing and crying and carrying on. The soldiers eventually got tired of my fussing and walked on.

There was one soldier, though, whose presence did not require me to feign TB infection. His name was Ivan and he was what Anna and Opa called a White Russian. His ancestors were German and he spoke German as a boy, and so he hated having to fight for Russia. He felt sympathetic toward all of us and occasionally joined Anna and her parents for malt coffee. He also drank exorbitant quantities of vodka—even more than the other soldiers. So we often saw Ivan riding his bicycle down our lane and singing at the top of his lungs, always a bit wobbly. We called him Ivan the Happy. He would eventually have mercy on us on a day when all other compassion ran dry.

Seventeen

Autumn came and brought the first chilly precursors of a mean winter. Every day, Anna cooked and cared for her mother. Oma was feeling a little better lately, but she still never left the house. Opa, Onkel Otto, and I cared for the cows and pigs and chickens, and we all subsisted on our combined larders. The countryside had been torn apart right before planting time, so no one had planted any fields. There was no grain to harvest. We ate last year's potatoes and our stash of canned meat. And the cows kept giving milk, thanks to Otto continuing to milk them while we were gone.

Around that time, we learned that all of eastern Pomerania, the province in which Seidel was situated, had been transferred to Poland. We were German, but we now technically lived in Poland. In the fall of 1945, Polish families began to move into Seidel, and the Russian soldiers oversaw the assignment of vacant German homes to these incoming families. Our village had many such empty homes; soon more Poles than Germans lived in Seidel. We learned that the Russian forces would eventually leave and hand all governance of our region over to the new Polish residents. For now, they shared administration and had devised several unwieldy requirements of the German residents.

We had to supply two-thirds of each day's milking to the Polish dairy that had been established in Seidel. The remainder we could keep for our own milk and butter. I was not strong enough, or brave enough, to milk a cow. Instead it fell to me to carry the milk pails up the hill to the dairy. I was ten and one of the youngest people delivering milk each day. Over time, I managed to charm the men, chatting with gestures and limited German. One day, one of the Polish men showed me how to lean up and over the collection vat to pour my pails myself. From then on, the men merely waved hello to me when I arrived. I handled my own buckets, pouring our milk in without their oversight.

One day we woke to an early freeze. It had rained the day before and the street was full of slick, frozen puddles. It was awfully cold for October. I slipped on my way to the dairy and dumped half the milk out of my two pails. Horrified, I walked back home to confess to Anna. She was upset, but said she always shorted the delivery pails, so we could still refill the buckets and have enough left for us to drink that day.

Anna refreshed the pails and I set out once more. I was so careful with my steps. I passed by the puddle of spilled milk. Just steps away from the walkway up to the dairy, I slipped once more. God in heaven, this was serious. We'd have to refill the pails with all our remaining milk, and it would still look like the pails were half full. As I scrambled to my feet and turned back for home, I shook from both the cold and fear. Anna knew what had happened as soon as I walked in the door.

"We will have nothing!" she said. "And they will come after us! Do you understand what you've done?"

"I'm sorry," I said. I stared at the floorboards.

"I have no idea what we will do!"

A thought came to me. Hopefully Anna would hear me out. "We could water the milk down."

"They will know. They will see it!"

"They might not. They always let me pour my pails myself," I said.

"What?"

"They never look at our milk," I said. "They trust me."

Anna took a breath. She considered this. It was our best option. Our only option. Together, we poured the skimpiest amount of milk into each delivery pail, then topped them all off with water. It was almost translucent. As I inched back up the hill to the dairy, I hoped beyond hope that they wouldn't look in my buckets. From several paces away, it might pass as milk. Up close, it was blazingly obvious that our delivery was mostly water. As always, I smiled at the workers at the dairy. As always, they were joking with each other and hardly paid me any attention. Our milk looked more like dishwater, but I poured it right in, and got away with our deception without a hitch.

My accident angered Anna, but I was fast restored to her good graces. We began thinning our milk delivery every day—though certainly never as severely as that first time—and we had much more milk, butter, and cream at home. Our cows kept our bellies full heading into the cold months.

The early ice storms were not all bad. The handful of other German children who still lived in Seidel decided to make an ice-sliding hill. There had been no school in session since we moved back, and no chance of school resuming anytime soon, so we grade-school kids were constantly inventing new pastimes. Late one evening, we poured buckets of water on the hill, down to the frozen creek bed. By morning it was frozen and perfectly slick. We took turns sliding down on our rear ends. After an hour or so of this delight, I climbed the side of the icy hill once more and was surprised to see a man waiting for me at the top. It was Herr Schmidt. I panicked. I didn't even know he still lived in Seidel.

My fear-filled training kicked in, and I immediately stood stock straight, raised my right arm, and belted out the Heil.

He slapped me on the face and said, "Don't you know the Russians are here now?"

Then he turned around and left. I ran home and told Anna what had happened. She was furious with Herr Schmidt, but she was equally afraid to confront him. Opa agreed. It was too risky. Herr Schmidt was not above retaliating by inventing some offense he could report to the Russian *Kommandantur*.

It was never easy, but we did coexist with the Russians and the Polish settlers for several weeks. But then we learned that we now faced a tough choice: learn Polish and become Polish citizens, or leave. At first, the hostility was evident only among the adults in the village; settlers scowled at Opa or Anna when I walked with them outside. But the children seemed friendly. A few watched my friends and me playing a ball game. But when the parents of the Polish children saw their kids watching us, they broke up our games, and their children got a good scolding for standing too close to us. Then even the children began to treat us with hostility.

They would chase us down the street and encircle a German kid and demand that he take off all his clothes. Then they would take the boy's clothes and make him run back home in his underwear in the freezing cold. It never happened to me, but I saw it happen to a few of my pals. At that point, I decided to stay inside most of the time, just like Tante Anna and Oma. Looking out the window in coming days, I noticed most of my friends had made the same choice. Only Polish children played outside now.

At night, mobs of Polish men raided German homes. One night the mob came to our house. I woke to pounding on our door and angry shouts. I heard Anna and Opa's frantic whispers. There was no way we'd open our locked door, but the mob sounded like it was capable of kicking it in. Someone began pounding on our sitting room window, and it sounded as if they might break the glass. Just then, we heard a louder voice stand out above the Polish mob. It was Ivan. Doubtless he was well armed. The hoodlums quickly dispersed. At least we had good old Ivan looking out for us.

As the Polish people took more control of village life, we became prisoners in our own homes. Anna and Opa decided it was time to leave—this time permanently. Knowing that eastern Pomerania was now Polish, Anna's husband might never come looking for us here. It was time to head to Melsungen, 450 miles southwest and safely within German territory. Oma felt stronger lately; she could tolerate the journey. The only question was when to leave.

We got our answer late one night in mid-December. We were heading to bed when we heard a knock at our door. It wasn't a loud, angry knock, but we were still scared.

"Yes?" Opa called through the door.

"It is me, Ivan," our friend replied.

We let him in and he spoke quickly. "The Poles are planning to expel all of you in the morning," he said. "They don't want to give you any time to pack. They want to raid your houses afterward."

We needed to ready ourselves. We thanked Ivan, and he raced off to warn all the other German families. We spent the night packing, each of us choosing our most valued possessions to place in a drawstring canvas sack. We would each wear all the clothes we possibly could: double layers of socks and underwear and knitted wool stockings, which itched like mad, and extra shirts and sweaters. It was a long way to Melsungen, and the less we schlepped in the canvas bags, the better. At least it was winter; our layered clothing would not be entirely uncomfortable.

Anna surveyed me, completing a checklist in her mind. She clipped a shimmering amber necklace around my neck and tucked it under my countless layers. "This will be safer on you than on me," she said. Then she had me don Opa's work pants and suspenders over my entire ensemble. I was wearing an undershirt, a blouse, and three sweaters, and I tucked them all into the pants. Anna wrapped a fox fur around my midsection. Over all this, I would wear Opa's work coat. That coat would normally wrap around me twice, but given all my other layers, it fit just fine. A sturdy belt—also Opa's—cinched it all together. I was a walking suitcase.

Anna and Opa searched the house for the most meaningful valuables and food items that would carry well. As they rushed from room to room, I noticed the gold coin collection sitting on the couch. Someone had removed it from Opa's nightstand, but hadn't packed it yet. I tucked the coin purses into the deep pockets of Opa's work pants. If we were on the move again, that meant I would need to find food for my family once more. The coins could come in handy. The coins reminded me of the red velvet tablecloth in Walter's hutch. Both items had once been in the cache in the north field. I checked the hutch. The tablecloth was still there. Since it had been a part of the cache, I figured it must be valuable. I placed it in the bottom of my bag, layering ragged clothing on top of it. I still had room for any foodstuff Anna might want me to carry. I was about twenty pounds heavier, but I was ready to go.

It was past midnight when there was an unfriendly pounding at our door. They must have seen one of our lamps still lit and wondered what we were up to so late at night. They shined their own flashlights into our windows. I was terrified and bolted out the back door. The clatter in the back farmyard only drew their attention. I heard them rush around the side of the house, and I dashed past Otto's barn into the nearest hiding spot: the outhouse. I had never been as scared of the Russians as I was of the Polish mob that night.

There was a small heart-shaped opening in the privy door. I had never really noticed it before. In the pitch black, that little heart was all I could see. My own heart pounded in my ears, surely louder than the men's boots crunching across the frozen dirt and snow in the farmyard. I wished I didn't have to breathe, just for a few minutes. I held my breath as several men walked past the outhouse door. Their footsteps headed past the outhouse, around the barn, into the barn, back into the farmyard. Again they walked past my hideout as they headed back toward our house. They said gruff words to each other. How did they miss the privy door? How did they not hear me? The yard turned quiet. I exhaled, but had no idea what to do next. I waited a long time before I returned to the house, and everyone was very relieved to see me.

"Don't leave the house anymore," Anna said. "Stay here with us till we all must go."

We got a few fitful hours of sleep. I did anyway. I'm not sure my foster family got any sleep at all. Right at dawn, men arrived with a giant hay wagon and loaded us onto it. They'd already gathered several of our neighboring families. We all scrambled into the wagon and squeezed in next to our friends. That was when I saw Onkel Otto standing on the footbridge in front of his house.

"Onkel!" I shouted. No one told me he had to stay back again.

"Where are they taking you?" he called to us.

"We'll see you in Melsungen," Anna said. "Come when you are able to."

"Why isn't he with us?" I cried.

"Wanda is still too sick," Anna said. "It's hardly kind of them, but they are letting him stay till she is well."

The wagon rolled on, out of town to the main road, then north to Köslin. We were deposited at the train station. Some of the westbound routes were running once more, and the new Polish administration had prepared trains for our expulsion. We joined a throng of other Germans waiting to be loaded up and removed from what was now northern Poland.

Eighteen

I was miserable over leaving Onkel Otto behind, but I rallied in the train station in Köslin. I had to. With the incredible crowd on the platform, it might be hours before we boarded a train, and I decided I should make use of the time to forage for food. Once we were on the train, who knew when it would stop. Anna had packed some foodstuff, but there was no telling how long it would last. I was a clever ten-year-old, and our time in Swinemunde had taught me what I needed to do in situations like this. My role as food gatherer started now.

I tugged on Tante Anna's arm and said, "I'll be right back; I'm going for food." I thought she heard me. I left my canvas bag at her feet and rushed out of the train station into town. Polish settlers had taken over all the stores and shops and produce carts, and I found a woman selling potatoes who didn't glare at me when I approached her. I knew we couldn't communicate well, but I had something that communicated in any language. I held out two of the gold coins from my stash and her eyes grew wide. She bagged a good ten pounds of potatoes and held it out to me with questioning eyes: *That enough?* Well, it would be almost more than I could carry once I added it to my clothes sack back at the station. The coins were worth way more than those potatoes, but I didn't know that. I thought I'd struck a pretty good deal and hurried back to the *Hauptbahnhof* with my loot.

I was stunned when I got to the station. The platform was almost empty. That entire crowd had been herded into a long train of boxcars. Tante Anna, Oma, and Opa were nowhere to be seen. Up and down the line of cars, doors were already closed. I found my canvas sack sitting right where I had left it. I was in the Köslin train station, once again utterly alone. Only this time was worse. There wasn't even a social worker around looking for a farm assignment for me. The realization hit me in my throat, then my knees. I collapsed onto my canvas sack and sobbed. They'd left without me.

Then I saw a pair of feet standing in front of me.

"Little girl, what is wrong?" a voice said.

I looked up. The man was tall and he spoke German. He also had only one arm. I couldn't stop looking at his empty shirt sleeve, how the fabric hung loosely against his torso, how there was no hand where there should have been one.

"You have lost your parents?"

"My Tante," I said. "She boarded without me. My Oma and Opa too."

"Come with me; I'll help you find them."

I scrambled to my feet—not easy with my heavy layers. The man picked up my canvas sack with his one arm, and I picked up my potatoes. He asked for my family members' first and last names. We walked down the line of train cars, and he ducked into every door calling for Anna Arndt. Finally, at the fifth car, I heard Anna's voice shout back in reply.

The one-armed man guided me into the train car and through the wall-to-wall crowd in the boxcar. There they were: Anna and my Oma and Opa. The crowd itself held Oma upright. The one-armed man left me with them, wedging himself back out to the door.

Anna snapped at me: "Where were you?"

"I got food," I said, and showed her the potatoes. She was not pleased.

What a horror it must have been for Tante Anna when the crowd was forced onto the train and I was nowhere to be seen. For me, in that moment of our reunion, there was only this reality: Anna was upset and I wasn't sure why. I never thought to ask. Instead, I balanced myself on top of my canvas sack, between the backs and legs and hips of the other people wedged in around me, and sat as still and quiet as I could as the train crept into motion.

The next few weeks developed their own grueling pattern, their own blurred subsistence. Every running train was packed with people who looked like us. Every road was lined with others like us—every person wearing as many layers of clothing as possible, with small household goods and beloved items tucked in the folds; lugging packs and suitcases; and pulling wagons and pushing carts that held a few other valuables or a loved one who could not walk any further. We pitied the ones who wore little clothing or carried nothing—the ones who had heard no rumors, the ones who had not had time to pack a thing.

The first train took us only thirty or forty miles southwest, about seventy miles away from the new German border. Refugees were being shipped out of Pomerania by the thousands, and there weren't enough trains to ship us all. The trains that were running got stopped and delayed for hours in every town. Sometimes we disembarked and continued on foot. Following a rail line, we took trains whenever we learned there was one running.

Every day began with the challenge of toileting and finding food. Life became the complex management of all that used to be simple: intake, output, the hope of avoiding injury, the paltry mitigation of unavoidable injury, and walking onward. Sometimes when the train stopped at a station, it stayed the whole night. Sometimes we were sent out of the trains, and we slept in barns. Sometimes the train stopped for hours or days in a bombed-out city, and we walked among the ruins and found a dry place to sleep in an empty cellar. Sometimes we refused to leave the train and slept sitting up because Anna was concerned the train might carry on without us.

Once we jumped out of a stopped train car to find a barn to sleep in. Anna had tied a jar of molasses to my canvas bag, and as I leapt out of the train the jar struck the edge of the metal doorframe. I heard it crack and feared peeking at the damage. A quick glance down at the snow behind me told me everything. A fine line of syrup trailed behind me. Being refugees did not exempt us from mundane irritations. The obnoxious everyday mistakes still happened, but we had no time or means to clean or repair the matter. My one option was to keep going, sticky and dirty, our lone culinary extravagance leaking out behind me. By the time we got to that night's barn, the jar was empty.

Oma never slept well. She often cried quiet tears and said, "*Ich bin sehr müde.*" So tired. Every bone hurt, every muscle spent. She could not walk far, so we could not join the throngs on foot when the trains stopped. We could not leave the train and walk when the train traveled for miles at a speed slower than walking. Oma had nothing left. And yet, she kept on. She woke with us each morning wherever we'd slept, and she roused herself, rose to her feet to walk as far as needed to board the next train, to find the next shelter. We held our course, zigzagging south and west toward Berlin.

Our slipshod routine was punctuated by news: a rumor that a border was closing or opening, the tip to avoid the next village because occupying forces were particularly unkind there, an unfortunate delay because of track damage ahead, the possibility that another train line was running. News came by way of the line of other refugees, passed down the line like a ball or a fragile egg. Or it came suddenly—someone frantically running away from the next village and running up to our particular line or train car. Delivered by such an urgent messenger, it was usually not good news.

Whatever the news, these interruptions became a measure of time, more consequential than hiding in a barn at sunset and waking, still alive, at sunrise. News, even bad news, meant we might avoid a hazard, could alter our course towards a more hopeful end. News meant that, despite how we all conserved our energy for personal survival, people were still talking to one another. News meant there might yet be a destination that was safe, a location where a basic rule of law still reigned.

That was good, because there were so many threats along our journey. Not only from the occupying forces, but also from opportunists among our own people. Along with food-finding, shelter-making, squatting in brambles, and cursing a twisted ankle, shaking it off, and then walking on, the daily routine also included countless glances over one's shoulder. Every snapping twig in the woods could be a rogue gunman. Every sweet lady who offered to sell me food might take my coins and run. All news, even bad news, meant someone cared, meant there were still some decent souls alive. Someone valued our humanity just enough to inform us.

We arrived in Stettin about two weeks after leaving Seidel—two weeks to travel only one hundred miles. The trains were that slow, or completely stopped, that often. With Germany's east border pushed to the Oder River, Stettin was now a border town on the Polish side, but full of German refugees from Pomerania. We stayed there for a few days in a high school gym—a makeshift refugee camp and staging area for shipping us elsewhere.

The conditions were stable enough, even if it was both Russian and Polish occupied. Anna, Opa and Oma still had deep lines in their brows and sad eyes, but I felt somewhat relieved to settle in somewhere that seemed safe from thieves. I felt brave enough to walk about the town. While Anna and Opa helped build a little bed for Oma in a corner of the gym, I shot out the door. Anna didn't care; she was too spent to ask me where I was going. My stomach growled. I knew my role; if we were to eat, it would be best if I headed out immediately to find food. People were still, generally, more kind to kids. First things first, I needed to relieve myself before exploring the town. The surroundings were safe enough, but unsanitary; the "restrooms" were the frozen sport fields outside the gym. From the looks of the terrain, it was not going to be easy to find a patch of snow not already used. This was important to me, for I still had that heavy coin collection hidden in Opa's work pants. Even in our current circumstances, I had not yet overheard Anna or Opa comment on the missing coins, but they must have wondered who forgot to pack them. For my part, I wasn't going to admit to taking them. Not yet. Regardless, while I managed to keep the coins a secret, they reminded me of their presence every time I needed to relieve myself. As soon as I snuck my arms out of the suspenders of Opa's work pants, the sheer weight of the coins pulled the pants straight to the ground in a pool around my feet. Clearly, toileting at the Stettin refugee camp would be a challenge. I didn't want my pants touching the nasty ground here.

I surveyed the spacious facility, steeled my courage, tiptoed in, and found a not-too-wretched patch of snow. Between bending my knees just so and bunching the seams of the trousers into my left hand, I managed to relieve myself without letting the pants tumble onto the surrounding dirt and without thoroughly exposing myself. At least, in the latter regard, everyone at the camp was in the same situation. I fumbled with the heavy wool pants, wiggled back into the suspenders, and pulled my sweater layers and coat down over my waist. Good enough. This necessity cared for, I was off to explore the town.

I headed up the main road toward what seemed to be the town's center. Though the gym had been packed with people, the streets were empty. But the buildings were not bombed out, so I hoped I'd find a busy street with a shop that sold food. I could raid my coin stash then. Yes, I would return with something to eat, and Anna would be so happy. Better not let her know quite yet about the coins. I could tell her that I begged to acquire the food.

I'd walked only one block when I heard laughter across the street. Kitty-corner and behind me, two Polish soldiers pointed at me and shouted nasty sounding words. I noticed at that moment that my silver foxtail—the one usually tied snug around my overalls—had come loose. The tail dangled between my legs. I tried to tuck it into my pants, but the soldiers crossed the street, jogging toward me. Oh God. I broke into a run—around the corner, doubling back toward the gym—the foxtail swinging along behind me. I heard the soldiers pick up their pace, all-out chasing me. Their raucous teasing and laughter grew louder.

I pumped my legs as fast as possible. Despite all my extra weight, I outpaced those laughing soldiers and reached the gym a block ahead of them. Glancing back, I saw they hadn't given up the chase. I raced on through the building, edging my way around other families and their impromptu camps, to the far corner of the gym, where I knew Anna and her parents had set up sleeping mats. They weren't there. But our canvas sacks still stood under a folding table nearby. A few of Anna's and Opa's clothes lay draped on the table. They must have gone out to look for food themselves or left to help Oma use the back field. They'd be back soon enough. I heard the soldiers' boots near the gym entrance and dove under the table, crouching down behind our bags.

There was plenty of noise and distraction in the gym—families talking to each other, babies crying. The soldiers' taunting voices and heavy boots carried over the general din. I heard them walk a broad circle through the space. One of them cracked a joke, another laughed. Another said something brusque that drew the others off from the search—it was no use looking for one silly young girl in that haystack of humanity. The sound of their heavy boots receded. I peeked around the edge of the canvas sacks, confirmed they were indeed gone, and exhaled.

We'd stayed in Stettin for three days when we finally heard about a train to Berlin. That would bring us ninety miles closer to Melsungen. At the slower-than-walking pace of most trains, we'd get to Berlin in another three or four days. Anna had a cousin in Berlin. We could stay there, maybe rest for a few days before determining how to complete the last leg of our journey. Once in Berlin, we would surely be far enough back into German territory that travel would be easier.

When we boarded the train, Opa and Anna helped Oma climb the narrow stairs—Anna taking her mother's hands, and Opa standing behind, supporting his wife. More than sadness tugged at Oma now. She seemed so physically weak. Still, she settled into her seat and attempted a smile. We had real seats on this train, a pair of wooden bench seats facing each other, and we'd heard the rails were in good repair along the entire route. There should be no need to get off at any point to find another train.

"Everything will be better when we get to Berlin," I said to Anna once the train started moving. Anna offered no reply. She only stared at her mother's curled-up form.

Nineteen

Over the course of our journey, we grew accustomed to the occasional mugging. As we had nothing of value—at least nothing they could readily find—robbers only made a cursory survey of our goods, then hurried off. German rogues, Russian deserters, Polish thugs, the thieves could be anyone. Bad men, all of them. Whatever their original nation, they belonged to the kingdom of predators now. They often ran in packs, boarding stopped trains full of refugees. Unfortunately, the robbers had caught on that children often carried the jewelry. I went from feeling quite immune from their stares to realizing I was a target.

Our second evening on the train to Berlin, we pulled into a station and stopped for several hours. Sure enough, a gang boarded our car. I was sitting next to Opa, closest to the aisle. Oma and Anna sat across from us. My back was to the nearest door. So I saw the two men who boarded at the far end of the car, but I did not see the man who boarded immediately behind me. That one grabbed me. I yelped. Opa stood and leapt at my captor, but one of his buddies dashed over and punched my Opa in the jaw. He reeled and collapsed back onto his seat.

Meanwhile, the first man had a tight, wrenching grip on my collar. I would have screamed if I'd had the breath. The man held a knife to my chest. I stared at his coat and didn't breathe. I couldn't. He squeezed my neck tight, aimed the knife at my belly. Then, as if he were gutting an animal, he swiped the knife upward—not cutting my skin, but slicing through most of my clothing from waist to neck. He wanted only to find the flashy silver I must be wearing underneath all those layers. My treasure wasn't silver; it was Anna's delicate amber necklace, tiny honey-gold stones on a thin chain. I felt the necklace snap, felt the stones trickle down, nestling in the folds of my undershirt. The man did not hear the faint snap, did not see the thin frayed chain. He was looking for a brilliant flash of silver or gold. Seeing none, he scowled and tossed me back onto my seat.

Though my undershirt was not torn, my sweaters were a shredded mess. Opa's work pants and suspenders had not been in the knife's path, and thank goodness I'd left Opa's work jacket unbuttoned that day; it too was unharmed. I shook from both cold and fear as the gang slammed doors on down the line of train cars. Opa held me close, though he needed care himself. His jaw was horribly bruised. My Tante reached over and wrapped Opa's work coat around my ruined sweaters and cinched the old belt tight around the coat.

"Keep that coat shut all the time now," she said, "so you don't get cold." I was too shaken to even think of telling her about the broken necklace. The amber stones were safe at least; I could feel them snug against my skin under all the ripped layers.

We didn't make it to Berlin the next day. Or the day after. Oma was in trouble. Her breathing had slowed, and she often moaned in pain. She needed a doctor. Badly. We had no idea where we might acquire medical attention, but we knew we couldn't stay on the train. At the station in Angermünde, fifty miles northeast of Berlin, we got off. Together, Opa and Anna carried Oma out to the platform. I lugged two of our bags, and Anna carried the other two.

Volunteers at the station saw us and ushered us to Angermünde's refugee camp in the town's high school gymnasium. There, Anna settled her parents into a patch of empty floor space and ordered me to stay near them. She ran off to speak with officials, to beg for help, for supplies, for something, and Opa did his best to hold his wife, propping her up off the cold floor.

Anna returned with a man who was helping her carry a small mattress. There was no doctor available for anything other than the most acute injuries. For us, there was only this: a raggy little mattress. We could at least get Oma off the floor. I stood aside as Anna and the helper lifted Oma onto the rag-stuffed mat and draped a heavy wool blanket over her. The man left us.

Oma winced and arched her back. She didn't seem any more comfortable on the lumpy mattress. Opa, favoring his own back and knees, lowered himself back down next to his wife. I realized then what I could do to help. I walked to the head of the mattress, sat down, and propped up Oma's torso in my arms. Opa held his wife's hands, and Anna raced off once more to try to plead with a doctor.

We were, in that moment, entirely alone as a family. Yet all around us, the same sorrow visited other family groups. All around us, other families tended to their sick and dying—mostly the very old and the very young. No one wanted to be in Angermünde. Everyone there had been en route to Berlin. They were, like us, stranded because a member of their party had taken ill. There weren't enough doctors to tend to everyone. Certain cases had to be deemed lower priority, and ours was one of them.

I held Oma and remembered how she was before the war, back in Seidel, before the Russians. Since I was always on the run exploring the village and fields, I saw her only at the start of the day—when she sat peeling our potatoes by the wood stove—and then at our evening meal. Really, I knew remarkably little about Oma. But I knew this: she was the one who tempered Anna's frustrations with me. "Don't lay a hand on that one," she would say. "She's just a girl. A good little girl." Anna always sighed and agreed with her mother. Oma would always be there at the start and end of each day and whenever I was in a bind with Anna. I was sure Oma would feel much better with some good sleep. She just needed rest.

She slept for a little while, but then she woke and looked straight at me. "Call Anna," Oma said. "I need Anna. Now."

I gently laid her upper body back onto the mattress, then ran off to find Anna. I found her in the school kitchen talking to volunteers there. I told her to come quick, and we rushed back to Oma's side. The three of us sat with her. I returned to my post at the head of her bed. Once again, I wrapped my arms around her shoulders and let her rest her head on my chest. Opa and Anna huddled on either side of her, holding her hands and trying to keep her warm.

We held Oma like that for over an hour. Oma worked hard, continuing to breathe, but those breaths came slower and farther apart. Then they stopped. My arms still wrapped around her, I felt the change. Oma was gone. "Oma, Oma, Oma," I cried softly into her hair. Out of the corner of my eye, I saw Opa's hands entwined around her hands. I held her, and Opa held her, and we wouldn't let go.

Throughout the camp, other families crumpled under the same weight. For all of us, grief was eclipsed by the reality of what must happen next. As soon as a refugee was pronounced dead, an official informed the family of the common grave outside the town. The burial in the mass grave was free—and forever unmarked. Perhaps many of us wailed in the privacy of our own minds, but here, in a gymnasium full of the dying, most of the newly bereaved made not a sound. They watched in silence as the loved one's shell was carried away to be transported to the common grave.

Anna couldn't let that happen.

My Tante touched my shoulder. "They need to take Oma to another room," she said. "We will sit with her there."

Opa squeezed his wife's hands, then let them rest at her sides. He stood next to the mattress, his own hands hanging at his sides, his eyes down. Opa had no energy or words left; he had nothing. Anna had words though. And energy.

"My mother is not going into a mass grave," she said.

When refugee camp workers came to take Oma's body to another room, we followed them. They laid her body on the floor, and we stood around her. I kept crying, and Anna cried too. But then she composed herself and whispered to me, "Do not leave Opa's side; I will be back soon."

When Anna returned an hour later, she spoke with Opa. "I found the undertaker," she said. "I secured a private grave."

Her father looked at her. "Oh, Anna, how much?"

She shook her head and wouldn't answer. She must have used some of the bills she had set aside as starting-over money for when we got to Melsungen. The amount didn't matter; it was what we had to do. Anna alone attended the simple burial the next day. Opa stayed back with me at the refugee camp. They said this was for the best.

We missed the next train to Berlin and had to stay in Angemünde another two days. Those were two more days of food hunting. I had a new trouble too. I'd pretty much forgotten about the amber necklace that the robber broke. The weather was freezing, and I had no desire to undress and try to locate each little stone in the folds of my clothing. But those amber stones began to remind me of their presence. Pressed tightly against my chest, they had started to dig into my skin. I knew I should head outside to scavenge and beg, but the sores on my chest left me feeling achy and tired. Most of those two days in Angermünde, I lay on Oma's mattress in the gym.

If I lay on my back with my chest very straight, I could escape into a thin sleep; though the slightest shift shot sharp rays of pain across my skin. I lay stock straight and still and willed myself to sink into the mattress. I cried because my skin hurt. I cried because I was hungry. I cried because I was resting on Oma's mattress and she was not there. Anna and her father sat nearby. They were not hunting for food themselves, but they were not eating either. We sat in the gym and waited for a train to Berlin.

The morning of the third day, I realized Anna and Opa needed to eat something. Really. I left the gym to beg in town. It took me quite a few blocks to realize my right foot felt damp and colder than usual. Looking down, I saw that the sole had separated from my shoe. Cold and discouraged, I returned to Anna empty-handed. She stared at me.

"My shoe is broken," I said.

"Come," she said.

I sat down on the floor next to her. She unlaced the broken shoe, took it off my foot, tied the shoestring around the toe of the shoe, and then slipped the shoe back on my foot. The lace was long enough that she could loop it around the toe and back up around my ankle. It would do. We slumped together on the mattress.

Somehow, that day, we wound up back on a train to Berlin, once more on our way to Anna's cousin. Somewhere during that route, the sores on my chest began to sear.

"My chest hurts," I said to Opa and Anna. "It really hurts here and here."

They had far-off looks when I cried. They had far-off looks when I didn't cry. "We all hurt," Anna said. "We cannot stop until we are safe in Melsungen."

I stopped saying anything about the pain. I cried silently and winced with any jarring step or stumble, gritted my teeth when I lay down. There was no comfortable position. Eventually, even Anna looked at me funny and asked if I was well, but I'd trained my eyes to reflect her own far-off look.

Shortly before reaching the stop in Berlin that we needed to get off at to find Cousin Gerda's house, we crossed the Spree River. Anna leaned toward the window, looking out at the icy water below. Opa slept in the seat across from us, his head on his chest, rocking a little with the rattle of the train. Over Anna's shoulder, I could see the water flowing down there. Despite the cold, it still flowed. The train traveled at a snail's pace, so we had a good long look at the river.

I realized Anna was crying. Her back shook and she raised a hand to bat away tears. I leaned around her, looked at her eyes. My Tante's face was so drawn and hollow, like the faces of everyone on the ferry after we'd seen the explosion, after we all realized that this thing had really happened and there was nothing that could be done.

Anna turned away from me, looked back at the river. "Maybe I should jump in and be done with it all," she said.

It seemed the worst possible day for a swim. I figured that after such a wretched time, Anna might not be thinking clearly. I touched her elbow. "It's too cold," I said, kind and gentle, just as Oma would have said something kind and gentle to me if I wanted to do something ridiculous. Anna sniffed and swallowed and made a sound that was something between a sob and a laugh. She smiled at me and patted my hand. Good; she understood.

The train finally reached Berlin. In every direction we saw endless rubble fields—so much worse than in Kiel. We had no certainty that once we were in Gerda's neighborhood we would actually find her. But we were hopeful as we walked along her block; many of the row houses in that area were still intact. Anna knocked on her cousin's door, and what a greeting we received. Gerda and Anna spoke in rapid succession about all the hard things and sad things and about Oma passing away and about how amazed we were that Gerda was here, that her apartment was still standing.

Gerda welcomed us into her home, and as we walked into the living room, I saw the tall pine standing in the corner.

"You have a Christmas tree," I said, fascinated by the sparkling tinsel.

"It's still green," Gerda said. "As long as it is green, it will stay. I will keep it till next Christmas!"

Still green? I realized then how long our journey had taken. Christmas had come and gone during the early days of our journey. We'd been on the run for weeks. It was late January. I stared at Gerda's tree. I stepped closer and closer, till its boughs and sparkling tinsel were the only thing I could see. Nothing else could fit in my mind. Even the sores on my chest subsided.

"It is the best tree ever," I said.

Anna said nothing, but Opa agreed.

Gerda said we could wash up, but Anna and Opa were far too tired to do so. We would wash up in the morning. Then Gerda took me by the hand to her room and said, "You need a Christmas present, poor girl." She reached into her closet and took out a pair of high heels. They were brown leather and far too high for me to walk in comfortably, but I loved them. I also desperately needed a new pair of shoes.

"They're beautiful!"

"They're yours," she said. "I think you are about the same size as me."

I took the shoes in my hands. They were entirely impractical, useless for our journey. They were fantastic.

"Frohe Weihnachten," she said. "It's not right that you had no Christmas."

That night, we ate some bread and a little cheese and then succumbed to exhaustion on the living room floor. We woke early in the morning to Gerda rushing in from the front door—doubtless she'd been out looking for more food.

"The borders are closing," she said, her voice cracking. "You must go now. You might not be able to get out of the Russian sector again."

The Russian sector? What was that? Berlin was German. I knew that much. What was she talking about? Opa was immediately awake and alert. He and Anna seemed to understand this strange announcement and its implications.

"Why do we have to go?" I asked.

"We're in the Russian sector," Opa said. "We need to get to an American or British zone, and soon. We must not get stranded here." He stumbled over his words, looked at Gerda apologetically.

"This is my home," she said. "If it weren't, I would leave too."

Anna shook her head and said, "Will I ever see you again?" She hugged her cousin.

What on earth was going on? I couldn't understand Opa's explanation. Apparently there were parts of Berlin that were not German. But we were well into German territory now, weren't we? We weren't in Seidel, in the land that was now Poland. Still, I understood enough of the comparison between Russian and American soldiers. If one had to choose occupation by one or the other, Americans were the best option. British were a close second. Baffled, I followed my adults. In minutes, we gathered our belongings, donned our extra sweaters and coats, and left Gerda's house. Gerda walked with us to the train station. I stumbled along on the cobblestones in my new shoes, a few paces behind everyone else. At the station, a crowd was packing into a train bound for the American sector. There was no time for any kind and sweet goodbye. Anna purchased our tickets and we boarded immediately.

We stayed on that train for two days. It reached the end of its line at a checkpoint just east of Helmstedt, where we could leave Russian-occupied Germany and enter a region controlled by the Americans forces. The checkpoint was set up at the station itself, processing people as they got off the train. We waited in the line. When we got to the front, an official asked us for our papers. Opa presented his American birth certificate.

"I need papers for every member of your family," the official said.

"They have no papers," Opa said.

"We can't let you in."

"I'm American," Opa said, switching to English. "They're my blood relatives. My daughter." He spoke persuasively in American English for some time, but it was no use.

"We must get to Melsungen," Anna said. "We have family there."

This did not matter. The official shook his head. He sent us back to the platform. We were free to take any other train; any train that stayed in the Russian-occupied region.

A German train conductor approached us. He'd overheard us explaining our situation. "See that train," he said. "Get in the last boxcar. It will be disconnected soon; it's bound for a village west of here. When that boxcar stops, jump off. Cross the river outside town. You'll be in land under American control. There's no checkpoint, only a refugee camp; they won't be so strict."

It was just as he said. Our boxcar came to a halt near a small village and we saw the small river running along the tracks. The river was cold but shallow, and we waded it fairly easily. Anna and I helped Opa over the slick rocks. Together, we scrambled up the bank. At the top, there was a farmer's field, and in that field we saw the tents and the Red Cross flags. And an American flag. We had arrived, for all intents and purposes, in America.

Twenty

I'd learned by now that the pain in my chest was always worse when I had nothing else to think about. Worry or fear drowned out the pain most effectively. Now, safe in the American sector, the smell of food drew us across the field and the hope of clean cots and warm blankets filled our minds. The sores on my chest resumed their throbbing and burning, worse than ever. I wailed. Anna muttered a gentle curse and took my arm with her free hand.

At the tent, the Americans had us disrobe so they could coat us with delousing powder. After weeks of sleeping in barns, we were covered with the nasty bites. Anna and I went to one curtained-off area, Opa to another. I removed my outer layers well enough, but my undershirt was stuck to the sores. There was no removing it.

"Everything," Anna exhorted me. "You need to take off your underclothes too. It's okay."

"No, no, no," I said and crossed my arms.

She must have taken my resistance as modesty. Regardless, Anna had no energy to persuade a truculent ten-year-old to take off her clothes. She rolled her eyes and voiced some polite excuse to a lady official who stood near the curtained entrance. The lady smiled and shrugged. It was fine; they'd let me get the delousing treatment with my underclothes still on.

So I stood next to Anna and several other women while the American medic threw the white powder up and down our front and back sides. Then I scurried over to my pile of clothes and struggled back into them. I didn't get far; my chest hurt too much to shove my arms into my sweater sleeves. The powder had navigated under my shirt and stung wherever it touched my sores. I reached under the top edge of my undershirt, trying to brush it away. Anna bent down next to me, her brow furrowed.

"Brigittchen, what's wrong?"

"Nothing," I snapped. "I'm fine." She hadn't listened to me when we were on the road, hadn't listened when my chest first started to hurt. Now she wanted to help, and I didn't want her to touch me. She did though. She pulled back the top hem of my shirt and saw the red bloom, the upper edge of one wound. "What happened here?"

I pulled back. An American medic stood behind Anna. He must have been walking past and seen whatever it was that Anna saw.

"She is wounded?" he asked haltingly in German.

"Yes, I think so."

"No, I am fine!" I insisted.

The medic looked at me with a concerned smile. Seeing I would not follow him of my own accord, he picked me up and took me to the dispensary tent. I knew better than to resist, but I closed my eyes. I would not look at him. Anna followed, carrying the rest of my clothing bundle. The medic set me on a cot and poured a clear liquid on a white cloth. Gesturing, he asked me to remove my shirt, but I wouldn't. He tried to take the shirt off himself, but I clamped my arms down. He gave Anna a helpless look. She shrugged and shook her head.

The medic did his best to wash the edge of the wound, what he could see of it just under the top hem of my shirt. The alcohol stank and stung as it dripped down into the open sores below. I winced.

The man did all he could, then walked to a locked cabinet and returned with a bottle of pills. In scrappy German and gestures, he explained to Anna how many of the antibiotics I should take each day. She nodded, took the bottle, then helped me back into my shredded sweaters and coat. The sores bit back every time I stretched an arm into another sleeve. The medic left us—on to more pressing emergencies, and likely more grateful patients.

We found Opa and ate with him in the mess tent. Anna made sure I took one of the pills right away. For the next two days in the refugee camp, I swallowed those pills whenever Anna told me to, but the pain on my chest worsened. We had been traveling four-and-a-half weeks when we got to that American camp, and it would take another day or two to reach Melsungen. The Americans arranged for our train trip. I remember little of that leg of the journey other than the pain of the infected sores. I slept most of the way. Whenever I woke, I cried till I retreated back into sleep.

It was the middle of the night when our train arrived in Melsungen. A station attendant heard our story and led us to a heated storeroom where we could wait to connect with family. After weeks on the run, I found this humble shelter a great comfort—even more so than Gerda's apartment in Berlin. That dimly lit storage room felt like a little house, a safe place. I did not think of Oma. I did not think of Günther or of soldiers hanging in trees. I thought only of Anna and Opa and the warmth from the wood stove. Even the sores on my chest eased up. I reclined in a corner, leaning against a shipping crate, and fell asleep. Drifting in and out, I heard my Tante's voice speaking with the rail station attendant. The man hurried off into town to find Anna's husband, Richard.

Anna's husband arrived bleary-eyed, but smiling. My Tante saw her husband for the first time in over a year. Somehow alive. I'm sure Anna tried to rally, tried not to be too sad as she told him Oma was not with us. I'm sure she tried to look into her husband's eyes and feel thankful that they were together once again. I'm sure it was, on some level, a happy reunion. I tried not to spoil it. Really. But when I got up from the floor, the pain in my chest began to throb once more. Perched on a crate, I watched Anna and Richard through blurry, salty eyes. With no more strength to walk or stand or be brave, or at least be quiet, I cried. Loudly. The child who used to encourage Richard to head back to the war so she could have buttermilk soup once again, the odd little foster child who slept in Richard's bed when he was not around—that child—demanded his attention once more. Of course Anna was a little short with me.

"Get up," she said, terse and spent. "We need to walk a little farther."

I shook my head, cried even louder, and refused to move. Did Opa try to comfort me? Probably. But I was aware only of the pulsing, searing spheres in my chest. No I would not stand. I would not walk. No more. The pain took over and I would not move. Through the haze, I heard Richard's voice: "I will carry her."

The station attendant approached us and offered us the use of a wheelbarrow. Surely, it was both a compassionate gesture and a choice to preserve his own sanity—my crying had evolved into unrestrained screams at that point. Someone picked me up, toted me outside, and deposited me in the cold wheelbarrow. In this fashion, I was transported to Anna's in-laws. By the time we arrived, I'd settled back into muted whimpering.

I was hardly aware of the introductions. Richard was staying with his brother, Wilhelm, who owned a tree nursery on the edge of Melsungen. It was two in the morning when Wilhelm and his wife welcomed us into their house. Who knows what Anna said to explain my state to her relatives, but she managed to abbreviate the half-asleep handshakes and shuffled me into a back bedroom.

There, I stood before her and repeated my complaint from weeks prior, "My chest hurts so much."

Her hands were rough as she yanked off my coat and my tattered sweaters, then peeled the undershirt off—"Ow!" Anna stared. At least a dozen of the amber stones from her necklace were physically embedded into my skin, infected flesh simultaneously trying to expel and close up around the jewels. Everything was raw and weeping.

Anna fell to her knees in front of me. "*Oh Kind*," she said. "*Was hast du ausgehalten?*"

What had I endured? *Ausgehalten?* What a strange word. I did not endure anything. Endurance implies strength, a choice to face a hardship. Those five weeks since leaving Seidel were hardly about enduring. I existed. That's all. I existed because my body carried on, acquiring what it could from what sustenance we found. That is luck much more than brave and willful choice. I could not answer her question, but Anna's voice was kind, and it hadn't been for so many days.

I cried some more, and she cried. She removed the amber stones and washed the wounds as best she could. Anna still had some of the antibiotic pills from the American medic. She had me take one immediately. We borrowed a shirt for me to wear to bed. In the morning we'd wash our clothes. Oh, we'd finally wash our clothes—after five weeks of wearing the same layers, never once bathing. In the morning, we'd throw away my ruined clothes. Anna would find me new clothes; someone would have mercy. In the morning.

"Why are these pants so heavy," Anna asked as she fussed with my pile of ragged clothing. "What did you stash in your pockets?"

I didn't answer. I wasn't sure if I'd be in trouble, and it had been so nice to hear Anna speak kindly to me. I didn't want her to change her tone. She rifled through the pockets and found the bags of gold coins.

"Oh, Brigittchen," she said.

I looked at the floor. "You said to take only things that were very important," I said. "The coins seemed important, so I found them and took them with me." I braced myself for a lecture on stealing. What I got was quite the reverse.

"You have saved us," she said. She kissed my forehead and hugged me carefully, trying to avoid my sores. "We will be able to buy food. Things we need. We are saved, precious girl."

Dawn was not far off, but we slept long and deep. Anna slept on a guest bed with Richard, and Opa and I slept on beds in the attic. Mine was a baby bed, which I loved. It felt cozy and safe. We slept the hard and weary sleep of those who are homeless but finally safe. In the morning—perhaps much closer to noon—Opa, Anna, Richard, and Richard's family discussed our lot. They spoke of the government's help for people like us. The word for people like us was *Flüchtling*. Refugee. Now that we'd found Richard, he would head into town to get on a list for housing for his new family of four. Richard's brother, Wilhelm, was fine with sheltering one relative, especially a relative who worked at his business for a humble wage. But the house was a tiny three-room space. It was no unkindness; there simply wasn't room for all of us. We needed to find a home of our own promptly.

In the coming days, the sores on my chest began to heal and I felt more alert. I listened in to conversations and learned more about what it meant to be a *Flüchtling*. I followed Anna and Opa on their errands, and in every interaction in town there was a mix of care and caution. The west had been bombed out, every major city hit hard, and every economic center shattered. We Ossies—those from the former eastern provinces—flooded into the west, and the Wessies were not ready for us. Melsungen residents were quick to offer us food. But at the same time, parents discouraged their children from speaking with me. Charity was tempered by fear that we might ask for too much. It's the plight of any community that finds itself, by no choice of its own, host to a growing refugee population. Sometimes such host communities have very little to share to begin with; they're concerned with their own survival. It is no easy thing for either party. Regardless, we hit a stroke of luck that first week with Anna's in-laws. Having braced ourselves for perhaps weeks, maybe months, of cramped quarters and strained hospitality, Richard came home with good news. He'd reviewed a social services housing list and found a two-room apartment available in Röhrenfurth, a small village two miles from Melsungen. It was tiny, but the rent was low enough that Richard could afford it with his income from Wilhelm's nursery. We'd even have a little left over for food.

Part 3

Recovery
1946 – 1948

Survivors: Anna with her father and husband,
Richard, several years after the war

Twenty-One

Röhrenfurth

We settled into the two-room apartment in Röhrenfurth, a tiny village where almost every home had a farm connected to it—a lot like Seidel. One of the farmers owned several lots on a cross street, just a block from the main thoroughfare. He had built several timber-frame houses on that property and rented them out. We lived in the lower level of one of these houses; another refugee family rented the apartment above us.

Our front door opened to the main room, which housed our stove and sink, a table and two chairs, and the bed that Opa and I shared. A second small room served as Anna and Richard's bedroom. There was a toilet in the cellar underneath the kitchen, but no shower or bath. Once a week, we heated wash water in a giant soup pot on the stove. The pot was a donated item, one of several. Our landlord and several of his friends had compassion on us. They outfitted our kitchen so we could cook and eat. And they dropped off cuts of beef and pork and an occasional bag of potatoes so that we had something to cook and eat. No one in the region was wealthy, per se. The villagers and farmers gave what they could. Then their compassion ran dry. Who could blame them? The war had shattered everyone. Even a rural west German village was affected by the economic collapse.

There was some assistance for refugees. Anna heard about the care packages coming from America, and she signed us up to receive one. The box was full of canned goods and peanut butter—Anna had no idea what to do with that. Opa, the American, lit up at the sight. "Spread it on toast!" he said. The rest of us never quite acquired a taste for it, even on hungry days. But Opa regarded the peanut butter as a delicacy. The care package also contained donated clothing— dresses, slacks, a pink pullover that was a little big on me, but I loved it. The underwear was bulky as well, but it beat wearing no panties on wash day. After enduring our journey in tattered and filthy garments, everything in that box was a grand luxury.

We also received *Lebensmittelkarten,* ration cards, as we had in Seidel, which allowed us a pound of flour a month, a little sugar, and butter. The sugar was in limited supply, so it was not possible to bake anything extravagant. We had just enough to sweeten our barley drinks and porridge. Anna used our flour ration to make gravy and occasional biscuits. Always, always, there were potatoes. We could afford those. We boiled them, made soup with them, or fried them in a tiny bit of oil. Eventually, in warmer months, we would supplement these rations with *Sauerampfer*—a green that grew prolifically along the river. It was like spinach and could be eaten raw or cooked. Early in the spring, Opa took me down to the water and showed me how to identify the long sturdy leaves and pinch off individual leaves without uprooting the whole plant. That way it would grow more leaves and you could eat from it again in a couple more weeks. *Sauerampfer* jumped out of the dirt as soon as the ground thawed, and it grew all summer, so we had fresh greens whenever we wanted.

Anna enrolled me in school, and as long as school was in session, I never went completely hungry. Even if our cupboard was running bare at home, there was milk soup at school. Every lunchtime, my teacher scooped this out of big metal dairy canisters. Stamps on the cans let us know they were provided by a U.S. assistance program. It's true that the Allies were leery of providing wide-scale food assistance for all Germans, especially adults, but the United States did bring milk soup to every school. The soup was an oat porridge thinned with warm milk and a little sugar. Five days a week, I looked forward to that scoop, plop-slopping into my bowl. Dull cream slurry—it wasn't pretty stuff. But refugee and farm children alike, we all lapped it up, tilting our bowls to our lips to slurp up the last drops. That meal alone was enough to keep me up and at it for the day. My body had learned to make a little bit last.

I was ten, but I'd had only a year and a half of continuous schooling in Seidel. So I was placed in the second-grade classroom. The farm children called me *Flüchtling*, though they weren't unkind about it. Farm kids and refugees alike, we all had milk soup at lunchtime together. The farm kids also had lunch pails from home. They often tore off a scrap of sandwich or shared an apple with me. Their parents might be cool toward Anna or Opa whenever our family ran errands in town, but we children did not care about the distinctions between East and West Germany.

Because of my experience with Herr Schmidt, I was initially afraid of my new teacher. But this fellow was nothing like Schmidt. My teacher in Röhrenfurth was young and handsome, with warm eyes and brown hair. He spent as much time teaching us about music and art as he did teaching us reading and math, and his voice was always soft and loving no matter what lesson we worked on. He never shouted. He didn't have to; we adored him. For the first time, I found myself enjoying my lessons. I had no desire to skip school. That year, I learned to read in earnest.

Back at home, on the evenings and weekends Anna pieced together our family meals with the help of our rations, charity, and Richard's scrappy wage. We got by. Anna worked in the kitchen quietly, her eyes dark and sad. Sometimes I felt the heaviness too. Our minds no longer focused solely on survival and our bodies fairly well fed, we began to ponder what we had survived. I still thought of Günther and the ferry, and sometimes I thought of the soldiers hanging in the trees. Every day I thought of Oma and missed her. Occasionally I thought of my parents in Kiel, wondered if I'd ever see them again. Though I did not cry about them. I was ten and I'd lived with Anna and her family for five years. I knew them better than my own family. I didn't cry about my parents, but I did grieve for Oma. My Tante and Opa must have grieved their mother and wife and the loss of their home, but we never spoke of these things. I knew how to not talk about Anything, and it seemed that Oma and everything that we remembered about Seidel were now a part of the big Anything.

By spring, the wounds on my chest had healed well. The medicine from the Americans had cleared the infections and helped my skin stitch itself back together. My chest was polka-dotted with shiny pink circles where the stones had lodged in the worst. Since I wore my undershirt and a blouse or sweater all the time, and I was old enough to wash by myself, I was the only one who ever saw the polka-dot scars.

In the first months in Röhrenfurth, I kept to myself. After school, I sat for hours by the windowsill in the kitchen. But as my chest healed and as I grew accustomed to eating a little something every day, I got my energy back. I needed to get out and explore; our tiny apartment could not hold me. There was no need to ask permission. That much was the same as it had been in Seidel. We were safe once more, and I was free to come and go. I knew this because Aunt Anna did not even look up from the stove when I approached the kitchen door. She said nothing when I opened it and stood in the doorway looking up and down the road. So one Saturday afternoon, I headed out into Röhrenfurth alone.

It had rained the night before. There were deep puddles everywhere, and the air smelled like wet cobblestone and damp hay. I trotted down the street, down the hill toward the center of town. As I passed by houses and shops, I heard shouting. It came from the edge of downtown, where the main road crossed the Fulda River. The shouting didn't sound angry, not like soldiers or thieves. It was higher pitched, happy. Sometimes shouts, sometimes laughter. I picked up my pace, jogging toward the river.

What a sight. The Fulda had flooded its banks and swept up over the road. The street was under more than a foot of water, and with the water came fish. Three boys, a few years older than me, had waded into the street and were catching their dinner with their bare hands. The boys had buckets, several with twitching tails sticking out of them. I thought of soft potatoes and *Sauerampfer* and milk soup. The milk soup was so good. But, I had to admit, it did not come close to the prospect of fresh fish.

With no regard for my shoes and coat, I walked straight into the water. I yelped. So cold—but not as cold as a winter night outside, or a wet day in the back of a canvas-top truck. Not as cold as fording the stream to get to the American refugee camp. Not like those things at all. I wouldn't go in too deep anyway. The water lapped at my ankles, then my calves, my knees, soaking my dress and coat. This was as deep as I could tolerate.

My legs were so cold, but the fish were a marvel. The water appeared to be receding some, and now the trout and carp found themselves stuck and confused in the middle of our street. They leapt and fell on each other, darting shadows below the surface and slippery little flashes of light whenever they jumped. Dozens of them swam about my legs, glancing against my dress. I bent down, grabbed with both hands, and was successful on the first try. Hard to call this fishing—not in any sporting sense. The creature wriggled and struggled against my grip, but I held it fast with both hands. We would have fish—fish for dinner, maybe for breakfast too! It was a fine trout that would feed all four of us easily.

There were so many more still in the street. And how many days might I like to have fish with my plain potatoes? One was not enough. I tried to tuck my dinner into my coat at my waist to free my hands to grab more. But the slippery thing fell right out, splashed into the water, and got away. I laughed. Losing one hardly mattered; the street was teeming. If I had been wearing Opa's work pants, I could have shoved a fish down each pant leg. Too bad I was wearing a dress. Ah—but I had coat sleeves. This could work. I caught a second fish, fumbled with my coat, shimmying one arm out of one sleeve, then the next while holding tight to dinner with my free hand. Coat off, I tucked the fish into the right sleeve. I laid the bundle on dry ground, sloshed back into the water and acquired a trout for the other sleeve. Yes, these fish would make it to the fry pan.

Greedy, hungry, and, above all, smiling for the first time in months, I splashed back into the water to catch a third fish for good measure. I doubled the body of my coat around that one. With the fish securely swaddled, I clutched the soaking mess to my chest and ran the three blocks back home. My shoes squeaked and sloshed the whole way. What a surprise I had for Anna and Opa.

I tumbled into the kitchen, fumbling with the door with my left hand, holding the wet bundle against me like an infant with my right. There was Anna in the kitchen, Opa seated on a chair watching her. Both looked up and saw my dripping coat, my wet boots and dress. I spoke fast before Anna could utter a word.

"The river is flooded, and there are fish in the street!" I said. "I caught three for us to eat, caught them with only my hands." I un-wrapped the coat to reveal the trio. One was still gasping. This had to make Anna proud. Her eyes softened when she saw the carp and two trout. I really wasn't telling a tale to excuse my sopping clothes. Still, she had a hard time believing I caught them myself.

"Who gave them to you?" she asked. "Or have you got some more coins hidden somewhere?"

Opa was not so quick to doubt me. "I shall head down to the river and investigate this matter," he said. He gave me a quick wink as he brushed past.

I wanted to follow him back down the street and catch even more. No such luck. Anna stopped me. "We must get you out of those clothes before you get sick," she said. She set the coat-wrapped fish on the table and proceeded to peel off my soaked dress. It was one of two decent dresses, and it needed to be clean and dry in time for the school week—I hadn't thought of that. She stripped me to my skivvies, then began to rinse, wring, and hang my clothing by the stove. She sat me near the stove to dry as well, then turned her attention to cleaning the fish.

As Anna cleaned the fish, I told her about the older boys wading in the street with buckets. "I saw them in the water, so I went in too."

"Of course you did," she said. She shook her head at me, but there was a hint of a smile in her eyes.

Anna gutted two of the fish and set them in the cellar, hanging from the ceiling. The third we'd eat that very evening, just as I'd hoped. She sliced open the fish's belly. It was female; roe spilled out of her. We fried the fish eggs in the pan alongside the two big fillets, and the apartment filled with the smell of fish fry.

Opa returned, smiling. "The water is going down," he said. "There is certainly no threat of the flood reaching us." I hadn't thought of that and felt simultaneously troubled and relieved by a worry that I had not foreseen. Opa continued. "I saw some of the fish too. I think our Brigittchen might be telling the truth; she was there at an opportune moment. There are only a few left now—much harder to catch."

Richard came home from work, and we ate so well that night. Even our usual boiled potatoes tasted better with the fresh fillets. Of course, one needed to mind the bones. That only made the meal last longer. My coat would smell like fish for months, but I hardly cared. It made me remember the fine day when I'd finally managed to provide a few luxurious meals for my family. And Anna almost smiled.

Twenty-Two

Truth be told, I didn't miss my parents. My relationship with my biological mother and father had been so interrupted, such a staccato connection during the war years, I hardly knew them. When Anna and her parents and I fled Seidel, all I thought of was survival—finding food and a place to sleep each night. Every plan, every decision had a shelf life of about a minute, given that we never knew when a thief or soldiers or the weather might force us to change plans. There was little time for missing loved ones during that journey. In Röhrenfurth we finally had stable shelter, but we still needed to search for food and wood for the stove. When my mind wandered to the past, it landed on more recent thoughts—the frights and losses of the war itself, not the times before it.

If Mother or Father inadvertently wandered into my thoughts, they were swept aside easily by the thing in front of me in any given moment. It was summer, and Opa and I spent more time outside. He took me on walks through the village, and we sat by the fountain in the town square. We picked greens by the river. I felt at home in Röhrenfurth, just as I had in Seidel. My first home, Kiel, hardly existed to me. Instead, other things filled my mind: the fountain in the square, a boiling pot in the kitchen, new socks from an American care package, a carpet of *Sauerampfer* leaves by the river.

Yet, I did have a real mother and father somewhere. Anna did not forget this fact. Weeks stacked up into months, and the Red Cross and German infrastructure grew more organized. It was possible to find relatives in other cities, to learn whether they were alive and where.

"It's time to find your parents," Anna said.

I hadn't thought of this, that I might be sent back to Mutti and Vati. Years before, my Onkel Otto gave me to Anna to be her little girl because she didn't have a girl of her own. That was the arrangement. When the Russian front approached Seidel and Anna asked me if I wanted to go back to Kiel, I chose to stay with Anna instead. I wanted to. For all I knew, I was living with Anna forever. "Your parents need to know where you are," she said. "They ought to know you are alive and healthy."

Anna visited a Red Cross office, shared my address with them, and we waited for a reply.

Meanwhile, I continued my schooling, though these new thoughts of my other home, my real parents, became a definite distraction from my studies. The knowledge that Anna had contacted the Red Cross sparked a change in me. I began to wonder about Vati and Kiel and my baby sister, Elke. She would be three by now. I remembered them, imagined them. For the first time since my last visit to Kiel, I thought of my family often. I daydreamed at school. In my mind, I visited home to see my sister for a few days. Perhaps I could go to Kiel for a week or so, then return to Anna, where I belonged. Maybe Anna could come to visit me. I liked these thoughts far better than my memories from the war.

After school each day, Anna let me know if the mail had come. For weeks she apprised me: "No, nothing came today, but I hope we hear from them soon." I never asked Anna for these reports; she was eager to see a letter herself. Her excitement fueled my own. What a happy time it would be, the day my real parents came for me.

Trotting home from school one day, I saw the mailman walking along our block. I'd never pestered him before, but it had been over a month since Anna's visit to the Red Cross. I called to the mailman from across the street. "Have you got anything for me? For my Tante Anna Arndt?"

He rustled through his bag. "In fact, I do," he said, retrieving an envelope and holding it out for me.

What were the chances? I ran to him and took the envelope. *"Vielen Dank!"* I turned the envelope over in my hands. There was my mother's scrawl. I could read the words that made up the address. What was this? Mother's return address was in a town called Husum. Not Kiel. That was strange. The letter was addressed to Anna, so I raced home to let her open it.

"Tante Anna," I shouted as I ran up our steps. I shoved the door open. I was panting. Anna stood at the sink, and I blurted the news at her back. *"Meine Mutti hat einen Brief geschreiben!"*

She spun around and wiped her hands on her apron as she came to me. I handed her the letter, then sat on a chair, quivering. She opened the letter and summarized the highlights aloud. Mother was living in Husum with her mother and sister. She'd gotten her family out of Glogau before the Russians came through. The government assigned them housing in Husum. Father lived in a partially bombed-out apartment in Kiel for now. Once he had better work, he'd get everyone into a big apartment that fit the whole family. Elke was two and a half now and doing well. There was some big news too: I had a new baby brother named Rainer. Mutti said she could leave Elke and Rainer with her mother and sister for a few days and come and get me. She would write again soon to set a date for that. She was thankful to hear I was alive and well.

Anna finished the letter, refolded it, and tucked it back into the envelope.

She touched my shoulder. "You must be so happy."

I was. Actually, I was entirely consumed with the thought of Rainer. "I want to go home," I said. "I want to see my baby brother." This became my chant for the next three weeks. Just as Anna's writing to the Red Cross had awakened thoughts of my family, this actual letter from my mother multiplied my newfound homesickness. Every waking hour that I was with Anna, I made my longing clear. *"Ich will nach Hause."* I want to go home—and that meant Husum now. Wherever that was, I had a little brother there. We received another letter, this one from Father, confirming his whereabouts and Mother's plan to come get me. Anna wrote both my parents asking for an approximate date.

We waited for their replies.

Only two months earlier, I would not have been keen on the possibility of leaving Röhrenfurth. But the fact that I had a new little brother changed everything. I grew enamored with the fantasy of moving back with my mother, helping to care for Rainer. I could play with Elke too. I was sure Mother would see how much I'd grown, and she would love having me around. The war was over, and I had siblings. I was convinced I should be with them.

Anna, Opa, and Richard took fine care of me. I knew Anna and Opa cared deeply for me. Richard worked hard to provide for his household, which clearly included me. I had a home. And yet there was this other home, these real parents, who grew larger and more fabulous in my mind every day. I knew I was not really Anna's child, and that fact made me restless. I felt just safe enough to become highly imaginative, and in those imaginings, my other home called to me. Anna remained quiet on the whole matter. She listened to me prattle on about my plans and how much fun I'd have with Elke and Rainer. Anna listened, but did not say a thing.

Summer clipped along, and there was still no word from Mother. Our six-week school break began. My eleventh birthday came and went. School resumed. Then, one morning in late July, I woke to an urgent-sounding conversation. Richard was already at work. Anna and Opa spoke in hushed voices in the kitchen.

"How am I going to tell Brigitte this?" Anna said.

I kept my eyes closed for a while, but couldn't make out any other details; the whispers were too faint. I slipped out from under my blankets and perched on the edge of the bed, waiting. Anna's back was to me, but Opa saw me. He nodded in my direction, his eyes serious. Anna turned toward me. She was crying. She came over and sat next to me on the edge of the bed, one hand holding a telegram, the other wiping her eyes. She stopped wiping her eyes and wrapped her arm around me. Anna was always kind and decent to me, but she never hugged me. This was strange.

"Tante?"

"I need to tell you something, Brigittchen," she said. "Your Mommy cannot come to pick you up."

"Why?"

"She's passed away."

My lips formed the word "what," but no sound came out. I looked up at Anna's face. She was not lying, and I'd understood her words. Her sad red eyes told me that. I buried my face into her blouse and sobbed. Anna wrapped both her arms around me and held me. I could have wept for hours about this thing, about the woman I barely knew, but she was still my mother, and now she was gone—like Oma and Günther and the soldiers in the trees. I could have sobbed for days, but only a few minutes later Anna loosened her embrace and pulled back to look at me. She wiped my tears, dried my face with her handkerchief, and said, "You have to get dressed and go to school."

I took a big shaky breath and obeyed. What else was there to do? I got up and dressed to go to school, as if Anna had never said those awful things. Maybe if I went to school as if it was a normal day, when I came home everything would be fine. Anna would tell me she misunderstood the telegram, or I would find out I dreamed the whole thing. Mother is dead? The awful words wouldn't be in my mind anymore—because it didn't happen.

I dressed just as if it was any other morning. But I never made it to school. I opened our front door, stood on the second step down, and looked up the street. My feet were frozen. My knees felt funny. I sat down, held my face in my hands, and stayed that way all day long.

Anna had told me the truth. Mother was dead. Mother. We were never close; we'd had so little time together, and our rare moments were strained. But she was still my mother.

I was old enough to know that when a mother died, her children went to foster care forever because fathers couldn't care for children by themselves. I'd heard of these things. Mother was dead. That fact alone was heartbreaking, but what made me despondent was the thought that I might never see Elke or my father again, might never meet Rainer. My siblings would go to other families, and we'd never be together. That is the grief that fueled a day of tears. I sat and cried all day. Now and again, Opa or Anna opened the door and stood behind me, checking on me. Now and again, I looked over my shoulder and saw Opa sitting inside by the kitchen window, looking out at me. They let me be by myself. Mother was dead. There was nothing they could say or do to help; I knew that.

The sun progressed from morning to high noon to afternoon, and still I sat on the steps. Other children on my street began to appear, walking home from school. They saw me crying, and several came near me and asked what was wrong. "My mother, my real mother in Husum, she is dead," I said.

The children who heard me say this sat down next to me on the steps. The girls said things like, "Oh, that's terrible" and "I am so sorry." The boys only sat and stared, but their eyes were sad and concerned. It felt good when a couple of the girls patted my shoulders or my knees. They stayed with me like that till their own mothers called them home.

In the following days, I returned to school, even played with my friends. But now I was motherless as well as a *Flüchtling*. Believe it or not, no one bullied me for this. My classmates were kind to me on the day we received the emergency telegram, and they were gentle toward me at school too. But it was clear that I was different. They pitied me from a distance, and you cannot be close friends with someone whom you pity. After school, I didn't join in the handball games in the street. I sat on the steps and stared at houses and trees, at the children playing.

One day, Opa left his perch at the kitchen window. He opened the door, stood on my step, then took me by the hand. I shuffled along as he guided me to the sunny spot behind our house. He liked to sit and think there. He said the sun warmed his old bones. The afternoon light did feel good on a cool autumn day. No one could see us there, sitting in Opa's sunny patch. We didn't say anything. We just sat on the ground, leaning against the house and each other, feeling the warmth on our faces and arms.

I eventually learned that Mother died of diphtheria. Thousands of others like her fell to the combination of hunger, cold, and disease so prevalent after the war. None of us were eating incredibly well. Few had the resources to pay for a doctor. In school, I'd heard and read stories about what happens when a mother dies, how an older daughter sometimes has to become the mother to her younger siblings. She has to quit school so she can take care of them—cook and make sure they all go to school. I'd just turned eleven the month before; I was old enough. I could do this. I was sure of it. I'd go home and take care of Elke and Rainer and we would be a family together; we wouldn't have to go to permanent foster families. Knowing my mother had passed away did not squelch my fantasy of returning home, wherever that home was now. Instead, my daydream grew into a wildfire. My sister and brother and me—we three—needed to be with each other even more now that this awful thing had happened.

"*Ich will nach Hause. Ich will nach Hause,*" I said to Anna. I resumed my chant, reminding her of my desire at least once a day. I brought to this chant all my willful preteen insistence. I never once noticed how it affected Anna.

"We have not heard from your father," she said. "How can you go home if he does not come to get you?"

I didn't tell Anna about my plan to care for my brother and sister. I didn't want anyone to tell me this plan might not work. It would work; I could handle it. I'd take care of Elke and Rainer and save my family, and Father would be ever grateful. "I want to go home," I repeated.

She sighed. "I will write him again. That's all I can do."

Twenty-Three

Opa coaxed me outside for walks into the village to get food or to sit by the fountain. One weekend, he asked me to help him collect beechnuts in the woods. They were everywhere. Anyone could hike into the forest and harvest the nuts, then bring them into town to the grocery, where we traded them for other goods. The nuts were pressed into cooking oil. Opa commissioned me to help him; he knew I needed to do something useful.

We were off to the deep woods, across the river, west of Röhrenfurth. It was a long hike to where the forest began, maybe an hour, past farm fields and pastures. There weren't any nuts for us to harvest at the edge; other villagers had harvested there already. Opa knew of a grove much farther in that had not been harvested yet. I followed him on a narrow dirt road, winding between the towering trees. The canopy above was beginning to turn, every green leaf rimmed with gold. It was cool in there, under the spreading branches, but sunlight filtered in here and there along the road. Leaves and twigs crackled underfoot. It was good to be outside with Opa.

We each carried a woven basket for the nuts, and soon we arrived at the grove. I wasn't sure what to look for. Did we need to climb the trees to get to the nuts? The trees were giants—their smooth gray trunks rose high. Far above, their lowest boughs radiated outward and intertwined with each other. Their big round leaves fluttered in a slight breeze. There was no reaching even the lowest branches, even if I were to stand on Opa's shoulders. He stood next to me and followed my upward gaze.

"The nuts have already fallen," he said. "Look at your feet."

He bent down and brushed aside a few fallen leaves. There they were. The forest floor was littered with new beechnuts. I picked one up: a round little nut inside a soft fuzzy husk. The husk looked like a brown flower—four drab petals curled around, holding the nut inside. Harvesting beechnuts was easy work. I sat on the ground and swept the new-fallen leaves aside, then gathered nuts by the handful and tossed them into my basket. Opa did the same a few paces away. The baskets were good-sized, each one almost two feet long and five inches deep, with a sturdy half-circle handle arching over the middle. By the time they were full, we'd wandered far from the road. Pleased with the harvest, we lugged our baskets back toward home. We were scrambling down the ditch separating us from the road when we heard a truck approaching.

It was a military jeep. I hunkered down in the ditch next to my basket. "It's okay, Brigittchen," Opa said. "They're American. There is a base not far from here."

Maybe that was true, but I hadn't seen any soldiers in the area before. I wasn't so sure Opa knew what he was talking about. The jeep came to a stop, and two men in drab-green uniforms got out. One was the tallest, darkest-skinned man I had ever seen. I did not know that people could have skin so dark. With him standing on the roadbed and me crouching in the ditch, he seemed about twenty feet tall. I couldn't fathom how he managed to unfold himself from the cramped little jeep seat. I stayed in the ditch, my fingers tightened around the handle of my basket. I saw Opa at my side, shaking a little—not in fear though. He was laughing silently. At me. The tall man smiled, his teeth so bright against his deep brown skin. The two soldiers approached us and the pale man said *"Guten Tag"* to us. Opa said "Hello" *auf Englisch*, and he told them he was originally from Minnesota. The soldiers said some words that sounded like *Wirklich* and *Fantastisch,* and then the three of them happily chatted away in English. I had no idea what they were saying. My eyes were still wide with terror; I was sure the pleasant conversation was a ruse.

The towering soldier stopped talking to Opa and came closer to me, fishing around in his coat pocket with his right hand. Surely he was looking for a knife or a gun. Opa chuckled. He had no idea the big man was going to kill us. This was it. I was about to join Günther and Oma and Mother. The great man smiled again, pulled his hand out of his pocket, and aimed at me—*a Hershey bar.*

Chocolate. The international token of peace. I cannot say I felt a wave of immediate friendship. But the sweet was enough to loosen my hands and feet. I released my grip on my basket, stood, took one step toward the soldier, and snatched the candy away. Then I ran the whole way home. I could hear the men laughing till I was far, far down the road.

I ran all the way along the forest road, past the fields and pastures, and all the way through town. I stormed into the apartment and showed Anna the chocolate.

"Where'd you get that?"

"American soldiers in the woods!"

"Where is Opa?"

I gasped. "I left him with them!"

Not only did I leave him there, but I had no courage to go back and save him. Anna seemed nonchalant about the situation though. An hour later, Opa walked up the road, lugging both baskets of beech-nuts. No hard feelings on the matter. He was so pleased to have spent time with those soldiers, to get a little news from home, to speak his native language. The last time he'd spoken English was in the refugee camp, and none of us had felt like talking much back then.

I sat on the front steps while Opa went inside to show the fine harvest to Anna. I heard them laughing. Doubtless, he told her about how terrified I'd been, how I snatched the candy and ran. This did not bother me. It was good to hear Opa and Anna laughing. I held the unopened candy bar in my hands. With Opa home and safe, I felt I could open it now. I measured that chocolate bar out over the next two weeks, one tiny sweet piece per day.

A day after I finished the Hershey bar, I resumed my chant: *"Ich will nach Hause."* Anna was exasperated.

"What do you want me to do?" she said. "I'll write him once more, but how do we know if the letters even get to him?"

She did write him. I watched her. She wrote that his daughter was heartbroken and difficult and he must come and get me. I don't know if she had been as insistent in previous letters. She was plainspoken now. I watched her fold and place the letter in an envelope, paste a stamp on it, and mail it. My father would reply. I knew he would. He would come and get me and I would go home and be Elke and Rainer's sister-mommy. Elke was almost four and Rainer already two years old. They needed me. Everything would work out perfectly. I quit my chant and hunkered down, waiting for Father's reply. Every day I watched for the mailman.

Twenty-Four

Harvest came and went. Along the river, the first frost turned the *Sauerampfer* leaves brown and shriveled. There was still no letter from Father. Snow and cold rushed in, staking their claim on the ground, the air, and the walls and windows of every house. Another supremely cold winter. At least we were not living on the run. Every day we considered that fact, even if we did not speak of it aloud. Every refugee in Germany thought of this. It had been almost a year since our flight. At least we had the same shelter every day and night. At least we had food most days. How grateful to have these things. How sad to remember Seidel.

It was not quite Christmas when Father's letter came. He did not feel he had housing that was entirely appropriate for a child, but he would come for me. He was not sure when, but soon. He asked for us to please just allow him some weeks to save up for the train tickets. I was far too elated to pay attention to Anna's eyes as she read the letter, too thrilled to care that her mouth quivered at the last few lines. My father was coming for me! He would write again soon, letting us know an approximate date. "I'm going home!" I said. I said those words again and again, testing them, tasting the syllables—my new chant. *Ich gehe nach Hause!* I am going home!

Anna listened, expressionless. It made no sense why she couldn't be elated with me.

School stopped for the winter holidays. Father's letter implied it might be January before he could set a date to come and get me. I had little to do but keep warm indoors each day. I was, consequently, restless. Opa did not wish to run any errands in the bitter weather, and he'd grown very tired since the snows returned. He spent most of his days sitting by the south-facing kitchen window, letting the sun warm his bones. I sat with him as I worked on my homework, but it was hard to focus with thoughts of going home so close at hand. I stared at my studies and fidgeted with my papers. Often I set my homework aside and helped Anna with a small cooking task instead, peeling potatoes or stirring a soup. Anna was, as she'd been ever since we moved to Röhrenfurth, quiet most of the time. One evening, the week before Christmas, I watched her making our usual potato soup. She broke her silence to let me know that we wouldn't celebrate Christmas this year.

"We have no money for gifts," she said. "No ornaments and no tree. I am sorry, Brigittchen."

I told her that was okay. I didn't have any money for gifts either. Maybe we could have home fries instead of potato soup. Sometimes we boiled the potatoes and then sliced them and fried them in a teensy bit of oil. I liked it when we ate these home fries and milk soup; I never tired of that meal. Thinking of the ornaments made me sad though. I remembered the Christmases in Seidel, how Opa took me to the outhouse and the barn as if we had some urgent tasks there, and when we came back, Anna and Oma had decorated the whole living room. And they said Santa was responsible for the décor. We would have no Christmas this year because the ornaments were all in the attic of Anna's house in Seidel. Who knew who lived there now? Perhaps they were using our Christmas decorations.

"I will do this much," Anna said. "I have a little flour, and I've saved up some sugar, enough to make a cake."

That was more than enough to me. On Christmas Eve, there was a knock at our door. We opened it. It was one of our neighbors. He peeked at us through the boughs of the small pine tree in his arms. He'd seen that we didn't have a tree in our window and took it upon himself to cut one for us. And he decorated it too: a handful of delicate glass icicle ornaments hung from the evergreen's branches. The man helped us set the tree on our table, bracing it in a small stand he'd made. What a lovely thing! We wished each other *Frohe Weihnachten*, and the man left to celebrate with his own family. I sat and marveled at the little tree. It was nothing compared to our giant trees back in Seidel. But how the glass icicles sparkled, catching the light from the kitchen. After days of thinking we would have no Christmas at all, I decided this was the best tree I'd ever seen.

Anna pulled the cake out of the oven. It was a single-layer yellow cake with no icing, which was fine with me—I couldn't even remember the last time Anna had baked a cake. I sat with Opa, grinning at the tree and the cake cooling on the table. Richard was home, and he joined us at the table. We ate our dinner, and even the home fries tasted better with the smell of cake and fresh pine filling our apartment. After dinner and dessert, Anna had one more surprise for me. I cleared our dishes, and when I turned back to the table, there was a colorful box sitting there. Somehow, likely through the charity of a neighbor, Anna had managed to acquire a used board game as a gift for me.

"What's this?" I asked, and rushed over.

"It's *Mensch Ärgere Dich Nicht*," Opa said. What a funny name: *Man Don't Get Angry.* It had simple rules, which Opa explained to me. There was a symmetrical cross-shaped playing board with home bases for four players. The playing pieces traveled a path around the perimeter of the cross. Rolling the dice determined the number of spaces the playing pieces could move. I had never played it before, but I caught on fast and insisted that we play it over and over that night. Anna quit to go clean the kitchen, and Richard retired to bed. But Opa indulged me. He chuckled in defeat and agreed to round after round. I played till we were both nodding off. In the morning, I marveled that the game was still there, in its box on the table. So were the tree with its sparkling ornaments, and more than half a cake, covered by a dishcloth, on the counter.

I never tired of *Mensch Ärgere Dich Nicht*. After school resumed, I came home each day insisting on a round or two before or after dinner. It was my passion—sitting at the table with Opa and playing our new game. Beyond its inherent delight, I had one other reason for playing at the table hour after hour. My chair was by the window, where I could hold vigil looking down our lane. Any day now, my father should be coming. In January, we got another letter from him. He hoped to come for me within the month.

Twenty-Five

By late February, Anna and Opa weren't sure whether Father was still planning to come for me. But I knew he would. One Saturday evening after our potato soup, I sat at the table with Opa playing our board game. I always sat there so I could keep an eye on our street. At dusk, I noticed a lean shadow outside, a figure walking toward our home. As the man got closer, I knew it was my father, Hans Zobel. I could only see his silhouette and his measured stride, but it was him. I was sure of it. I abandoned the game, bolted out the door and down the front steps. Father stumbled when I jumped into his arms. He felt so thin, and I could tell he was shivering under his thin overcoat. But he was here, and he hugged me and hugged me and looked at me with gentle eyes. He was here to take me home, and everything would be good and we'd be a family again. I didn't want to let go of his embrace, but it was so cold out. I took him by the hand, up the steps, into the warm apartment.

Everyone was talking at once, welcoming my Vati and discussing the limited tickets he'd purchased and how he and I had to leave right away. Even Richard came into the room—he usually napped after supper. Their voices all rose and fell and rose. He was here. Vati was here. I buried my face in his coat and clung to his waist till Anna peeled me off. "You need to pack," she said. "You're taking the night train back to Kiel."

Anna went into her room and came back with the old army sack, the one we'd used to tote our most important things from Seidel. First I packed my beloved game: *Mensch Ärgere Dich Nicht.* It made a nice base in the bag. Then I pulled my clothing box out from under the bed in the main room and packed my two dresses, my skirt and blouse, and two thick wool sweaters. Then I packed the socks and the too-big underwear from the American care packages. While I stuffed the army bag, Anna told Vati to sit down, and she gave him a little potato soup. That was when she noticed his feet.

"Hans, you have no socks!" she said.

I turned away from my packing to see this. Vati nodded to Anna and continued eating his potato soup. His ankles were bare. They looked dry and gray and cracked. Anna's family and I, we were refugees from the east, but even we had a decent stash of donated clothing by now. I had more than one dress, and we all had a few pairs of socks.

Anna touched her husband's arm and pointed at Vati's feet. "This is unacceptable," she said. Richard gave a terse nod in agreement and ducked down the hall to their bedroom. He returned with a pair of his own socks. Father closed his eyes as he accepted the gift. He took off his shoes and slipped the socks onto his blue-gray feet, then finished his bowl of soup and stood up. He was ready to go. I pulled the cinch strap on the canvas sack; I was ready too. Richard patted my shoulder, and Opa gave me a hug at the door. The excitement of seeing Vati gave way to the realization that it might be a long while before I saw Opa again.

"Auf Wiedersehen, Brigittchen," Opa said. Till I see you again.

I hugged him again, but we couldn't dally. The train would arrive in minutes.

It was pitch dark as Vati and I walked to the station. Anna came with us to see us off, and the three of us waited a few moments in the cold on Röhrenfurth's miniscule station platform. A single light bulb hung above us. Anna looked at the platform and gazed up the tracks. Father shifted his weight from one leg to the other. Apart from the sadness in Anna's eyes, and the worry on my father's face, it was my happiest moment in years. I was going home to live with my Vati and my sister and my baby brother.

The train arrived. I smiled at Anna and said my goodbye: "Auf Wiedersehen." See you again. I was still certain we would visit each other. I hugged my Tante and pulled back and looked at her. It made no sense why her eyes were wet. Hadn't she wanted me to find my family? Wasn't this what everyone wanted? My sister and brother needed me. I was heading home to make things better for them.

Anna said her goodbyes to us and looked away. Then I took Vati's hand and we loaded onto the train. Peering down the aisle at the row of compartments, I noticed the doors were all closed, every seat full, and the aisle packed with people as well. It was what we called a *Bumelbahn*, a slow train, packed full and stopping in every single town on its route. Kiel was over 200 miles to the north; we'd be on this train long into the next day.

"We'll be standing unless a compartment comes available," Vati said.

We squished into the corner near the train car's entrance, by the first window in the aisle.

"Here, Brigittchen, this will do," Vati said, and set my tote next to his leg. "Sit on your bag and lean against me."

"Where will you sit?"

"I will be fine," he said and leaned into the corner at the end of the aisle.

Perched atop the canvas sack, I settled in, leaning against Vati. From atop my bag, I could see out the window to the platform. The train began to move and I gazed out at the dark station. There was

Anna, standing under the lone light bulb. All I could see was her face, the light shining off her tears. I realized then what she knew with certainty—I wouldn't get to see her and Opa again. I understood then, and I began to cry. My face pressed against Vati's coat, I looked up at him. I didn't say anything, just wept.

I was eleven years old; too old to be picked up and held, but I couldn't stop crying. Father did what he could—patted my head, rested a hand on my shoulder, and told me everything would be all right. I thought of Elke and Rainer, how they needed me to come home to care for them. Eventually that thought and the motion of the slow train rocked me to sleep. Father was taking me home to Kiel. It had to be a good thing. My real family needed me.

Twenty-Six

Kiel

The train stopped in every single village on the way, so it was morning by the time we finally pulled into Kiel. We slowed to a crawl at the edge of town as we rode past bombed-out buildings. I remembered what it was like to live in a city like Kiel or Swinemunde. It had been nice to live, for almost a whole year, in rural little Röhrenfurth, where all the houses and shops had never been bombed and still looked pretty. But I thrilled a little at the sight of Kiel's ruins, the hope of raiding them for treasure. Vati would be proud to find out how good I was at finding valuable things in the rubble.

When the train stopped and the doors opened, Vati threw my bag over his shoulder, held my hand, and guided me through the train station to a bus station. We boarded a bus, and I sat by the window, pointing and commenting any time I noticed an interesting building that hadn't been bombed or one that was equally interesting because it was a pile of rubble. Vati was gentle, but silent, largely ignoring my commentary. I caught on and stopped talking; who knew when he last had a full night of sleep. We needed to get home so I could tuck Vati into bed. Then we could talk in the morning.

The bus took us to a neighborhood a few miles south and east of the harbor called Elmschenhagen. There were rows and rows of brownstone apartments along every street here, originally built as housing for people who worked in the shipyards back before the war. I was not familiar with these streets; it wasn't where we lived when we first moved to Kiel, and it wasn't where my parents lived when Elke was born.

"Both of those places were bombed out," Vati said. "I found another place. It is a little better."

We got off the bus on Preetzer Chaußee and walked south on Reichenberger Allee. In this neighborhood, it seemed every building had been bombed. But between each bombed-out section, there were decent apartments. Father's gait slowed at one of the buildings. I heard children playing. They were near a frozen pond in a small park beyond another row house across the street. Vati approached a building whose north end was a rubble heap. The entrance, directly in front of us, was also partially destroyed. But the interior walls of the units on the south end appeared sturdy.

Father opened the main entrance door and I walked through. There was no ceiling. High up, the ragged edge of the original roof roughly sheltered the shared stairwell, but directly to the left, the building was entirely caved in. I looked up, scanning the edge between solid structure and rubble, shredded roof and blue sky. The original stairs were gone. Jagged remains of a landing protruded out of the wall far above, and a long, rough-looking set of stairs was tacked onto it, allowing access to a second-floor apartment. Roaming the ruins was one thing, but to live in them? Well, I'd done it in Swinemunde.

Father tapped the lowest step with his foot. "There were no stairs here when I first saw this place," he said. "I found these down the road. They were in a house that was completely destroyed and only the stairs survived. I dragged them over here to where the apartment was spared, but the stairs were destroyed."

Vati pointed under the wooden stairs at concrete steps leading down to a cellar. "See the strange door down there?" he said. "That is from a submarine. I found it in a bombed-out U-boat in the shipyard and dragged it up here."

I saw then my Vati's ingenuity, his resolve, and I marveled at the door and the steps. Father was the smartest man I'd ever met. I followed him up his salvaged stairs. He opened the door to our home. A short hall led to a kitchen and living room, where Father sat down on a bed while I explored. There was a bathroom with a working toilet and one more room—a bedroom in back. There were only a few boxes in that bedroom, no bed.

"The ceiling in that room is bad," Vati called after me.

The bedroom was closest to the bombed side of the building. A crack in the corner radiated across the ceiling and down the north wall. Water stains mushroomed out from the crack, bulging into blooms of peeling paint. I opened one of the boxes in the corner and recognized Mother's clothes, a few blouses that I remembered. I touched the fabrics, began to unfold one. It would almost fit me now.

"You don't want to sleep in there unless you like the cold," Vati called to me again, "or the rain on your head in the springtime."

I tucked the blouse back into the box and folded the box flaps shut. The room was indeed colder than the kitchen and living room area—and even those rooms were barely warmer than the outdoors at the moment. I left the useless bedroom and returned to Vati. He was hunched over a coal-burning stove that stood between the living room and kitchen. This was our heater. The gas stove in the kitchen also worked; we could use that for cooking. The apartment had electricity and running water and a working toilet. It was amazing how damaged a building could be and yet retain a portion that was intact and functioning. Vati closed the stove door and turned to me.

"You will sleep in the kitchen; it will be warm for you here," he said. "And safe." There was a small cot set up near the coal heater. He'd set my army sack on the cot. "I need to sleep some, Brigittchen," he said.

Vati showed me a loaf of dry bread in the kitchen and a little cold meat in the pantry. I could help myself while he slept. The next day was Monday, and he would need to go back to work right away. I ate and wondered where my siblings were. Perhaps they were staying with a friend while Vati went on his trip to get me. Surely he would tell me where they were when he woke up. I considered venturing outside, but it was awfully cold. Instead, I wrapped myself in the blanket on my cot and rested.

Later that afternoon, when Vati woke, he brought me to the apartment below ours and introduced me to our neighbor, Frau Müller. She was an older woman—older than Anna, but not quite as old as Oma was. She had salt-and-pepper hair and warm brown eyes, and she pulled me close and wrapped an arm around me. My real mother had never hugged me, and Anna only hugged me the day I got terrible news. I stiffened, my arms straight at my sides.

"Oh, sweet girl," Frau Müller said.

Father spoke to me: "Frau Müller will look after you while I'm gone during the week."

"Gone?"

"I need to work, Brigittchen," he said. "I have to go away to work."

Vati described the work that he had found and how he had to travel out of the city to complete it. Back before the war, many people left the countryside and moved into the cities so they could work in shipyards or munitions plants. Father himself had done that. But now the money one might find in the cities was worthless. A loaf of bread cost a few hundred *Reichsmark*. Ever since the end of the war, people had been leaving the cities and walking to farm villages to barter for foodstuff, exchanging the last of their coins, silver, porcelain, and jewelry. Some rural villages had become wealthy as a result, and farmers began remodeling their homes with their new wealth. Father worked for an Italian man who laid terrazzo floors. He spent three or four days at each job site and was paid in bread and meat and a little cash. The cash bought flour and soap and other necessities.

He explained that because he traveled to find work, and he had no wife, he could not care for Elke and Rainer by himself. He contacted social services to find foster families for them. My siblings were not in the apartment because they didn't live with him at all. They lived with two different families, miles away from each other. This was common after the war. Certain governmental services were still functioning, and fostering programs were vital to care for so many orphans and children from families with no income and children with only one parent.

This was quite the change of plans. I would not be playing mommy to my siblings. Vati and I would not even have time to walk around the neighborhood or play games in the apartment. I would live with a stranger instead. Still, if there was one thing the war taught me, it was that nothing in life happened as you hoped it might. Sometimes—maybe most of the time—you had to work incredibly hard to get the thing you really wanted.

Vati looked at me, rested his hand on my shoulder. "You will be a good girl while I'm away," he said.

"Yes, Vati," I said. "I will be good." In my mind I vowed to get my siblings back. Mother was gone, and I didn't know if I'd ever see Anna again. But I would find Elke and Rainer. It was the whole reason I came back to Kiel—to get my real family back together.

Father had to leave before sunrise the next day. He settled me into Frau Müller's apartment, then headed out into the dark morning.

Frau Müller's place looked just like ours, but it was warmer, and I learned that their bedroom did not have any leaks. She was married and had two grown daughters who often stopped by and dropped off food and coal. Frau Müller's husband was sitting on the couch when I arrived. He seemed small, his back tight and hunched, and he struggled to lift his head and look up. But he did do just that and smiled at me. He was injured in the Great War—not the most recent one, but the one that happened years before I was born. Frau Müller explained this and said that, no, her husband was not able to play or walk with me around the neighborhood.

We ate Brötchen and butter for our breakfast, and I thought I might head out on my own to poke around the bombed-out south end of our building. My new foster mother informed me that I ought to go to school instead. Of course. This was no holiday. As the sun came up, Frau Müller bundled me in my coat and walked me out to the sidewalk. There she introduced me to several neighborhood children and instructed me to follow them to the school. Off I went.

That week, I learned the nuances of my odd new life. I was back in Kiel, but rarely saw Vati. I was happy to see him when he came home, but preferred sleeping at Frau Müller's, where the coal heater was always banked and she wrapped me up in about ten blankets every night. I came to Kiel thinking I would become a sister-mommy to my little sister and brother, but instead a stranger was caring for me. I had never been hugged so often, and soon I began to hug her back.

When I stayed upstairs with Vati on the weekends, he slept a lot—though I couldn't figure out how. I sure couldn't sleep so soundly. Despite sleeping in all my clothes, I often woke to the cold grabbing at my arms or legs, to the sound of the wind whistling and sifting through the windows. I rolled into my single wool blanket, pulling it tight and willing myself back to sleep. Sometimes I dreamed of the soldiers hanging in the trees. It was harder to fall back asleep when that dream came to me. I reminded myself it was only a dream. The war was over, and a good, brave girl was not scared by such things.

Twenty-Seven

During the week, school took up my days. The makeshift classrooms were in an old barracks, and it was mercilessly cold in there. The warm milk soup every morning took the edge off. My teacher, Frau Chech, was strict—not anything like my music-loving teacher in Röhrenfurth, though not mean-spirited like Herr Schmidt either. I learned early on that there was one topic that could upset her immensely. She wore a sweater that had holes in it. Everyone had sweaters like that, but Frau Chech had woven and criss-crossed multicolored thread to mend the holes. It seemed she had stitched many more of these colorful patches than necessary to make them look intentional. I stared at her sweater one morning, contemplating it. There had to be at least two dozen of these colorful fixes broadcast all over the sweater.

She caught me staring and snapped. "What are you looking at?"

I looked down and apologized, though I wasn't clear on my offense. Didn't a good student always look at her teacher? At lunchtime, my classmates told me that Frau Chech snapped at them for the same thing. She was decent as long as you didn't stare at her patched-up pullovers. She knew when your gaze drifted to her torso. One needed to look at her face or hands or her desk or the blackboard; then all was well.

At the end of each school day, I walked home as fast as I could. I could see my breath in the school, but outdoors was colder still. Though there were other children in my neighborhood, the weather kept us inside most evenings. Sometimes Frau Müller had enough food to share a supper with me; sometimes she asked me if Vati hadn't left me a little something upstairs. When she asked this, I knew her daughters had not visited recently and that her pantry was getting bare. Downstairs in our cellar, I might find a cut of cooked beef or pork keeping cool and a bag of potatoes. Father often left me Brötchen, a little butter, and a few more potatoes in our kitchen pantry. I also found a jar of sugar in a cupboard and used it to create the easiest and most satisfying meal. It was too much work to fix a potato. The far more attractive supper was this: rip off a scrap of bread, spread a little butter on it, and dip the whole thing in the sugar jar. Sugar bread.

There were a few levels of hungry. Mostly, I sustained myself on sugar bread at home and milk soup at school. Sometimes a slice of sugar bread was not enough. I might trouble myself with tearing a few bites of cooked pork from the cellar. If I was still hungry after that, I endeared myself to Frau Müller or a classmate's family and joined them at their table for a more substantial soup. If that was not possible, I did go to bed a little hungry. But my bed at the Müller place was warm. That made up for a lot. I felt a little bit hungry most of the time, but not starving. It was all right.

At the end of each week, Father returned. He carried a mesh bag full of meat, which he cut and wrapped in newspaper on our kitchen counter. He sorted the cuts. He would cook one or two for us, and we would eat this over the weekend and store the leftovers in the cellar for me to pick at through the week. The rest of the meat went back into the mesh tote. Every Saturday he left with that bagful of meat and came home an hour or two later empty-handed. A few weeks in, he explained the situation with the meat as he worked in the kitchen.

"This meat is payment to the families who care for Elke and Rainer," he said. "It's the best I can do for now."

Father had never told me outright that my siblings were not going to live with us. Though I'd caught on well enough.

"Will they ever live with us?"

"We would need a bigger apartment, wouldn't we?"

"I guess so."

Trimmed and wrapped and neatly stacked, the foster families' meat was ready to go. "There aren't many apartments available right now," he said, and set the last wrapped cut into the tote. "Even if I had the money for one."

The shipyard's union had built the buildings in our neighborhood, and for the time being squatters' rights continued to rule there. But in other parts of the city, renting required cash—a lot of it. I'd heard about that. Given the paltry number of livable apartments, landlords charged inflated rents. Still, I was heartened at Vati's insistence on paying Elke's and Rainer's foster parents. The gesture fed my hope. Father had not agreed to outright adoptions.

When Vati went to deliver these payments to Elke's and Rainer's foster families, he usually made the trip alone. On one occasion, he allowed me to come with him when he visited, and so I met Elke for the first time since she was an infant, and my brother for the first time ever. They were four and two years old, respectively, and regarded me with understandable shyness. I got to see my brother, but we didn't even touch. He was too scared of me to let me pick him up.

Elke lived with a woman named Hanna Nüncke on a farm a few miles outside of Kiel. This was too far for me to easily walk on a school-day afternoon, but Rainer's foster family, the Bolls, lived on Innsbrucker Allee. That was close to us, a few blocks north of Preetzer

Chaußee, the main thoroughfare from our neighborhood into Kiel. I could find his house easily and visit without my father knowing. Once a week or so, I stopped by the Bolls' place, and after several visits, Rainer began to recognize me, began to smile when he saw me, and began to let me pick him up. Frau Boll did not mind if I played with my baby brother in their living room or walked with him along the sidewalk on warmer days. This was good. Rainer needed to know me, since someday we might live together like a real brother and sister.

I did not talk about this with Vati, did not ask any more questions about Elke and Rainer. If the war taught me anything, it was that there were certain topics about which one mustn't inquire. I should not ask about this Big Topic, because there was nothing that could be done. It did not matter that I was willing to take care of my siblings. The fact remained that, for now, Father could not find enough work to feed and clothe and house all three of us. I kept my dream to myself. It would happen. I was convinced that someday I would be able to take my siblings to live with me in the apartment on Landskroner Weg.

Twenty-Eight

I had arrived in Kiel when it was still winter, so my primary obsession each day was the pursuit of warmth. Cold ruled as soon as I was out of Frau Müller's blanket cocoon. Sweaters and tights and layered dresses and thick socks could keep a body only so warm. The true pursuit of warmth began with acquiring coal, and our shipments were somewhat unpredictable. In Elmschenhagen, the coal line was on Preetzer Chaußee, about five blocks away. The shipments came in massive truckloads. If I got into the line early, I might glimpse the mountain of coal towering above the queue. If I got there late, the coal mountain was decimated. It took only an hour or two for the neighborhood to assimilate the coal deliveries. I usually heard about the coal line as I walked home from school. There were always people chattering about it up and down the street: "The coal is in; we must go quickly." I quickened my pace, got home, grabbed our empty bucket and a stack of Reichsmark, and rushed back out the door.

My boots hindered me from running the whole way. The soles were beginning to separate. I'd gotten the boots from the American care package back in Röhrenfurth, and the soles on this pair were beginning to separate just like the old shoes that fell apart during our journey to Melsungen. I relied on Anna's old fix, tying a spare shoelace around the toe of the shoe to keep the raggedy thing together. I arrived at the coal line soon enough and took my place at the back.

When walking to and from school, one successfully fought the cold by moving fast. Standing still in the coal line, the cold became a living, breathing creature. It froze nose hair and seared faces and immobilized toes and fingers. The handle of the metal bucket was so cold it burned, even through my mittens. Depending on when I got there, dozens or hundreds of neighbors stood in line ahead of me. All those people, but never a sound. Years later I would meet others who had stood in that very line, and we would wonder how we'd never met each other. No one spoke in the coal line; we didn't even look at one another. The cold pinned our lips shut. There were only two sounds: the squeak of the snow under our feet as the line shuffled forward and the swish-crunch of coal being shoveled and poured into metal pails.

By the time I reached the front of the line, I could barely remember what I was doing there. I fumbled with the bucket and stabbed at the Reichsmark bills with stiff fingers. Sometimes the coal seller, who often felt sorry for children in the line, gave me a few extra coal scraps above what I'd paid for. Bucket topped off, I hauled it back home. It was only enough for Vati to start a small heating fire to take the chill off each morning when he was home. It wasn't much, yet the bucket threw my balance off as I slogged home. Every half block or so, I shuffled the load from one side to the other. Once home, I stashed the scuttle next to our stove, ready for Vati when he got home. Then I scurried downstairs to the Müllers, where the heating fire was always banked up warm. Doubtless, the warmth from the Müller's heater rose to our empty apartment and kept our pipes from freezing.

During the war, I learned to scavenge. After the war, I learned to wait in lines. Vati entrusted me with a bundle of bills and our *Lebensmittelkarte* so I could join any line I saw during the week. I was his lookout since he was rarely around when shipments arrived. The coal line was only the beginning. There were milk lines and bread lines and lines for flour. There were lines for sugar and lines for butter. Sometimes lines formed for something more exciting—soap or hand lotion. When lines formed for a rationed food, one needed to show the *Lebensmittlekarte* and have it stamped. Lines started outside small storefronts and roped down and around several blocks. Walking home from school, I'd see a line and hop in back without knowing what the line was for. Sometimes the woman standing ahead of me did not know either. We waited and found out. *Oh, I can see, it's butter; that's good! Ah, it was soap, but there is none left now.* I always stayed on the line when there was food involved; who knew when we'd have such a thing again.

Feeling greedy once, I purchased a whole liter of milk on a Monday, brought it home, and promptly forgot I had it in the pantry. By the time Father returned, the milk had turned sour. The first time this happened, Vati said, "When you have leftover milk, pour it in shallow plates so it sours well. Then sprinkle it with sugar and bread crumbs and eat it." The next time I bought milk early in the week, I tried this experiment and found it quite tasty. There were no solutions for the other perishables that I hoarded and forgot in the pantry. Sometimes I left potatoes on our counter till they turned soft. This became more of an issue as the weather warmed. Vati did not say anything when he discovered these finds.

"It's okay," I told him. "If the food goes bad, Frau Müller gives me more of her bread."

Vati stared at me and shook his head. He began bringing meat to Frau Müller each week, in addition to his food payments for Elke's and Rainer's foster parents.

Winter was not forever. Grass grew in rough patches, bursts of tenacious green among Elmschenhagen's stone grays and sooty reds. After school one day, I saw Frau Müller digging in the dirt in front of our building.

"What are you doing?"

"I think we need a garden, Brigittchen," she said. "Would you like to help?"

Would I ever. Frau Müller had saved flower seeds from before the war. She had not planted anything the year before. Who could think of gardens the spring after that worst of winters? But in the spring of 1947, she decided it was time. She showed me the seeds in folded paper packets. She'd scrawled the names of the plants on each one. "I am not sure they will sprout," she said. "But we must plant them to find out."

I followed her out to the dirt patch near our walk, and she explained how to plant the larger seeds a little deeper and the smaller ones not so deep and how to pat the soil firmly on top of them. She used a trowel to scratch a furrow into the dirt, pressed a line of seeds into the ground, then closed the furrow up. She handed me the trowel; it was my turn. That whole evening, I worked alongside her. We planted small mounds and rows. She knew which seeds grew which color and which plants became tall and which ones crept along the ground. I couldn't imagine how she knew all those things just by looking at a speck of a seed.

In truth, I did not wait in eager anticipation for those seeds to germinate. In fact, I forgot about them. In the lengthening days, the sun woke the ground and warmed all the children on Landskroner Weg. Winter had been a nasty jailer, and summer meant freedom. Long, bright evenings permitted lengthy handball games in the street. We played till late, and I realized how hungry I was only as I sauntered home at sunset. Walking home one evening, a couple weeks after Frau Müller and I planted the seeds, I saw the first sprouts in the dirt patch. Two more weeks and they were leafing out. Frau Müller plucked out some of the young plants. She said this had to be done, that a good garden had to be thinned early on or the plants would not have enough nourishment.

Summer break was coming. We would get six weeks off, and we could play handball all day if we wanted. For the time being, I still had plenty of liberty outside of school hours, just like back in Seidel. Frau Müller shook her head whenever I came home late at night. Anna had always looked at me that way too; I didn't think anything of it. I roamed our neighborhood. Instead of poking around in barnyards and farm fields, I rummaged through bombed-out apartment ruins. It was more like Swinemunde in that regard, only without the Russian soldiers—that was a nice improvement.

The scavenging was slim pickings. Most of the ruins had been looted for over two years. There was nothing valuable left. Certainly no food. I ran into other neighborhood children scrambling around in the rubble heaps. Now and again there was a find—a glass or mug unbroken or only lightly chipped. The finder took these rarities home to show to mother. I shared my finds with Frau Müller. Most of the time, the neighbor kids and I gathered and compared the prettiest shards of stained glass and broken ceramics. When we grew bored with that, we started our handball games.

On a grand whole, living with Vati and Frau Müller was a really successful arrangement. I couldn't understand why Father looked at me with more and more concern each weekend. With that sideways furrowed brow—the look he gave me when the milk turned lumpy. He began giving me that look more and more often. Spoiled milk, rotten potatoes, dirty knives and plates, coal dust on the floor. The state of the apartment was hardly a bother to me, and I spent more waking hours in the place than he did.

It mattered to Vati though. One day during my summer break, he spoke with me in a serious tone. "You need to go to Hanna Nüncke's to be with your sister," he said. "Frau Müller is getting too old to look after you."

I liked Frau Müller, but this change wasn't bad news to me. I grew excited about seeing Elke. I'd had a chance to visit Rainer regularly, but hadn't seen Elke much at all. It was time to get to know my little sister. It would be one more step closer to finally getting my siblings together.

Twenty-Nine

Hanna Nüncke did not like me. My new foster mother adored Elke, who was three and a half at this point. Elke had been Hanna's little girl for almost two years. But me? I was a scrappy kid, just turned twelve and hardly housebroken. I knew how to scavenge and fend for my own, how to eat anything readily available, how to climb and scramble and escape. I was also decent at begging and adept at making a single dress last for weeks at a time. I did know how to read well, thanks to Frau Chech, but I could not sit still long enough to read anything outside of required schoolwork. Hanna took me in only out of pity for my father. She insisted on the stipulation that the arrangement was temporary; he would need to find a more permanent home for me elsewhere.

Granted, it wasn't an easy living situation. Hanna lived with Emil, her man friend, who had a small farm two miles south of Kiel—out in the countryside, but not exempt from the air strikes during the war. The original estate had been flattened. Hanna and Emil built a square, one-room cottage as a temporary shelter until they could rebuild the original farmhouse. The four of us slept on two twin mattresses shoved together—Elke in the middle of the pile. My sister was a tiny snip of a thing, but she kicked all night, running in her dreams. None of us slept well.

Despite the cozy sleeping quarters, I perked up well enough each morning. The property reminded me of Seidel, and I fell into my old routines—climbing in barns, jumping from haystacks, running through muddy fields. There was a massive canning garden and berry bushes along its perimeter. Elke was allowed to pick the gooseberries, but I was not. So of course I hid in the berry bushes waiting for my sister, and we ate every berry we picked. Who would know?

It was the middle of summer break, and those first few days at Hanna's opened up like field flowers. But when I came home dirty and wanting to play with my little sis, Hanna was not pleased. Her hands were harsh when she scrubbed me, and she shook out my clothes with an undisguised violence. Onkel Emil was not like that. He walked with Elke and me through the meadows in the evening. My sister chased the chickens and ducks, I chased Elke, and Emil joined in chasing the whole menagerie. It was almost like being a family. I lapped up my moments with Elke and Emil, and I gave Hanna a wide berth.

When school started, Hanna seemed relieved to be rid of me during the days, and yet she made it hard for me to leave the house. I had to walk two and a half miles to get to my school back in Elmschenhagen, my Vati's neighborhood, which was the closest option for me. To arrive on time, I needed almost half an hour to jog the whole way there. Hanna woke me at half past seven and kept me at home till I had no more than ten minutes to get to school. I ran at breakneck pace each morning and still arrived late.

Once I slid into my seat, I made up for my tardiness by being as attentive and helpful as possible. One morning, I had a fine idea of how I might appease Frau Chech. I could assist with the milk soup distribution. The two dairy canisters holding the soup were so large, and there was always a little bit left. It seemed wasteful—did Frau

Chech throw the leftovers away? I could tell that if everyone received a full scoop rather than a scant one, we'd use up all the milk soup and all the students would be happier too. Right before we were called up for the breakfast line, I raised my hand and asked Frau Chech if I could help serve. She squinted at me, but answered in the affirmative. I strode to the front of the room and took my position at the soup vats, ladle in hand.

Frau Chech hovered over me. "Remember," she said, "give only one scoop." She lined up the class, then returned to her desk.

My classmates looked at me with big eyes as I poured brimming scoops into each bowl. One by one, they sat down and slurped the extra-large servings. When about half the class had passed through the line, I finished the first vat and switched to the second. Perfect. When there were only eight more students left, I still had plenty of soup. It seemed so anyway. But after three more children, I wasn't so sure. The ladle rasped against the bottom of the canister. Maybe I hadn't estimated this so well. The next two classmates looked crestfallen when I gave them three-quarter scoops. I stared into the deep container. It was empty.

Perhaps I could conjure up another half scoop by scraping the sides thoroughly. The room was silent. No one was supposed to speak when they were in a meal line, so the last three students said nothing. But they grew restless, shifting their weight from one foot to the other, leaning around each other to look at me. I caught their fidgeting out of the corner of my eye. They knew what had happened.

Frau Chech spoke up, "Brigitte, is something wrong?"

I couldn't look up. Her shoes tap-clicked on the linoleum as she approached. She stood at my side, surveying the situation.

"I told you not to do that," she said. "I told you not to give too much!"

I dropped the ladle into the empty canister, then shuffled back to my desk. Three of my classmates and I would not get any breakfast because of my mistake. Silent stares fell heavy on my back and head. Students whispered to each other. Frau Chech took the four empty bowls, left the classroom for a few minutes, then returned. She was able to gather leftovers from the other classes, and scraped together decent servings for my three classmates and a small portion for me as well. I did not help with serving milk soup ever again.

Mostly I focused on getting to school as minimally late as possible. Every afternoon I reminded Hanna of that conundrum. "Frau Chech is mad at me for being tardy."

"That is unfortunate," she said.

But, every morning, the same thing happened. Hanna kept me at home, fussing over my clothes, insisting I take longer to eat—until I had only minutes to get to school. The more I complained about the matter, the longer she delayed my departure in the mornings. I continued to run as fast as possible every day. After about three weeks of this frustration, I told Father about it. He stopped by every weekend to drop off a few pounds of beef or pork. We rarely spoke at length; he dropped off the foodstuff, patted me on the head, then trudged back to town. I did not relish the thought of adding more weight to his heavy steps. But I could hold in the concern no longer.

He had just set foot on the drive to leave. Hanna was inside; she would not hear me. "Vati, wait," I said. He turned to me and out tumbled my story.

"Every morning this happens?" he asked.

I nodded. "She must not understand that I need to get to school on time," I said. "Maybe you could talk to her?"

Vati's eyes looked weary but kind. "I will see what I can do," he said.

I doubt Father spoke with Hanna. Her habits certainly did not change. But the following weekend, Vati let me know that social services had found someone else who could take me. A week later, I moved back to the city, to the home of a woman named Frau Grotjan. This meant saying goodbye to Elke, but I wasn't too worried. I would ask to visit her sometimes; surely Father and Hanna would let me do that much. Perhaps in another year, when I was thirteen, Vati would get a better job with more money, and we would get a bigger apartment. Then he would see that I was old enough to take care of Elke and Rainer myself, and we would be a family then.

Thirty

Frau Grotjan was a war widow. She and her husband had been wealthy before the war. Technically, she still had plenty of money, but the Reichsmark wasn't worth a thing. Frau Grotjan's one remaining asset was her home. She still had her apartment in the city, with upholstered furniture and a piano in the sitting room and paintings on the walls. Fine wooden scrollwork embraced the soft cushions on the chairs and settees. The living room and bedroom were enormous, and none of the rooms leaked when it rained. I had no idea how this new foster would treat me, but at least she had plenty of room for a guest.

The day Father dropped me off, I stared at the stone steps outside and looked up the full height of the three-story brick building. There were six large homes inside, three on each side of a wide central stair. This whole block in downtown Kiel had somehow remained intact—un-bombed, pristine old architecture. Frau Grotjan's home was on the top floor. She welcomed us, her fine arms opened wide. Father patted my head and left, and Frau Grotjan showed me around her home, apologizing for the one hardship of living there: we had to walk down four flights of stairs to the lower level to get to a washroom with working toilets. That was fine by me; it reminded me of going to the outhouse in Seidel.

Frau Grotjan had a nineteen-year-old daughter named Gisella. She was already grown and lived in her own apartment, so my foster mother lived alone in that grand flat. I was more than happy to be her surrogate little girl. Frau Grotjan and I stood in food lines together, and we scavenged coal together. It didn't matter how much money a person had; everyone had to do those things. I slept on the chaise lounge in her bedroom. When the nights grew cooler, she pulled the chaise next to the heating stove and banked pillows and down comforters around me.

Gisella visited us on Sundays. My foster sister had warm eyes, just like her mother, and brown hair to her shoulders. She played the piano in the sitting room while I watched transfixed: how she could play such music, and have her own apartment, and live on her own. Sometimes Gisella invited me to sit next to her on the piano bench. She taught me a few scales and one short tune that I learned to play exceptionally well. Over and over. I played that tune when Frau Grotjan and I were alone in the flat. She sat and listened, as enrapt as if I had been a concert pianist.

After summer break, I resumed my studies at a city school in a building that was formerly a hospital for wounded soldiers. The large recovery wards were now classrooms. I was twelve, but this was only my fourth full year of school. Each morning before I headed out the door, Frau Grotjan entrusted me with a bundle of several hundred Reichsmark and a *Lebensmittlekarte* in case I might notice a line for a food item on my way home.

I always stood in line when I heard there was a meat shipment, but meat disappeared fast. Whenever I got close to the front of a line for meat, the butcher was cleaning up and grumbling, "We're out. Go home!" Frau Grotjan and I were successful enough with lines for bread, butter, and flour, and thanks to Vati, we still had meat regularly. Every two weeks, he stopped by to deliver food from his work for the farmers. We ate the meat first, then saved the bones for making soup. Frau Grotjan made noodles with our flour ration and added them to the soup. Once my father brought a massive beef roast. It was better than a cash payment. There was no refrigerator; we had to cook the entire thing. After several hours, Frau Grotjan hefted the steaming slab out of the oven, onto the table, and sliced it. We had roast for dinner that night and for every meal the following day, and then ate stew the rest of the week.

Autumn passed. Winter blew in. It was coal-scavenging season, and fetching coal was a far less loathsome task now that Frau Grotjan accompanied me. Instead of walking to a coal seller, we went straight to the rail yard nearby and gathered the scraps littering the ground. Coal shipments disappeared so fast in the city, and Frau Grotjan's home was large and cold. It was far more efficient to heat the place by stealing coal scraps than waiting to buy a single bucket's worth.

We hurried to the rail yard early every morning, before the sun was up. In the predawn light, we could see the dark streak of coal on the ground under the conveyor belt. As coal transferred from train car to transport truck, the smallest pieces shook and sifted off the belt to the ground below, painting a black track in the dusty snow. That was where we joined our neighbors, scooping slivers of coal into tin scuttles.

Sometimes I scrambled into empty coal cars and threw down any briquettes that I found. These were precious. About a foot long, they gave good lasting heat. One or two were enough to keep us warm for a day. Whenever possible, we gathered more than we needed, since we never knew for certain when we would have decent scrap-picking again. When we got home, we set the intact briquettes by the coal heater and scattered the small pieces out on old burlap sacks to dry. Inevitably, muddy snow got tossed in the scuttle along with the coal. Eventually the fuel dried out well enough to burn. Frau

Grotjan thanked me and said I was a good and helpful girl. I was important, just as I was when Anna's family relied on me to find food in Swinemunde, or when I snatched the fish out of the flooded Fulda River.

For a time, I was warm enough and ate just enough and felt entirely safe wrapped in Frau Grotjan's feather throws at night. But as winter waned in early 1948, I learned that I would be leaving her. Vati had a surprise for me. He wanted me to move back with him.

Thirty-One

Every other weekend, Vati walked to Frau Grotjan's to deliver his meat and potato payments. On the weekends that he didn't come to us, I walked to him. It took me about two hours to walk from downtown Kiel to Elmschenhagen. I walked straight through the city, past produce shops and butchers and pharmacies, some with long lines, some brimming with shiny, empty shelves. I walked past the Bahnhof and up into the hilly neighborhoods east of the harbor. Once I got to Vati's, I planned to spend a few hours with him—or at least in his neighborhood. On most visits, he was too tired to talk much, so I played with my old friends or said hello to Frau Müller and ate a little bread at her table. Then I woke Vati to give him a hug and walked back to Kiel.

But one such visit in February was different. Vati was awake and dressed and eager to talk to me that day. He asked me to take a walk with him. We headed out and strolled in the cemetery south of his place. It was beautiful, even in winter. The late winter sun warmed us as we walked under the bare trees. Their limbs sparkled with melting snow. We stopped by a still-frozen pond.

"I have met someone," he said, "a woman named Martha."

Vati's eyes were wide and clear, and he fought a big, silly grin. I nodded. I knew from stories at school that this was the other way a father could keep his family together when his wife passed away and the oldest girl was not quite old enough to mother her siblings. He continued, "We will get married soon, so you need to meet her."

I nodded again. Father, usually so solemn and tired, was excited about his news. But I felt nothing. If the war had trained me in any way, it had honed my soul for passivity, for letting events happen. With painful happenings, if one railed or cried or shouted, often the bad happening only hurt more. Fortunate happenings were fine and good, but one could not hold them too tightly; for they would be gone in an *Augenblick* as well. I surely had no ultimate control over the major events in my life—painful or pleasurable. So when Father spoke of Martha, of how I'd leave my sweet foster mother and live with another stranger, I felt no concern. I felt nothing at all. As far as happenings went, there were no soldiers or bombs involved, so it couldn't be too bad. I would acquire a new mother. I would live in Father's apartment once more—not tomorrow, but soon; maybe in a couple months, in April.

"First I want you to meet Martha and me for dinner at her home next weekend," Vati said.

He explained which bus I ought to take the following Saturday and the stop where I should get off, and he pressed a stack of bills into my hand to cover my bus fare. I agreed to all these things and then asked if I could head back home to say hello to Frau Müller.

The next weekend, I followed Vati's instructions. He was standing at the bus stop to meet me when I got off in southern Elmschenhagen, and he showed me the way to Martha's rented room. Father rang the doorbell at a two-story brick and plaster house. A petite, not-very-pretty lady opened the door. She had reddish hair and an expression like she'd tasted something sour. My real mother had been such a beautiful woman; surely this was not Martha but the owner of the house. I tried not to gape. I gaped. She looked me over, her eyes expressionless.

"Martha," my father said, "this is Brigitte."

I immediately smiled. She didn't.

"Come in," she said, not a hint of hospitality in her voice.

Her room held a bed, a couch, a round table—all three of us fit at the table well enough—and even a small hot plate so she could cook in there. She shared a bathroom and kitchen with the owners of the house, but otherwise had all that she needed in that one room. It wasn't too bad. Martha had a job doing secretarial work and domestic tasks for an Englishwoman. The lady paid in cash, and it certainly wasn't easy to find such decent work or housing, for that matter. Martha did not like her situation though.

At one point, as we ate our potatoes and roast, Father explained how he'd like me to come and stay with Martha on the weekends from now on. "Soon Martha will move in with me," he said.

Martha stared at her plate, but her lips softened into what could have passed for a smile.

"Brigitte, you will move in with us as well," Vati said, "and we'll be a family."

"Finally," I said, and Martha looked away from us both.

I concluded she must be very shy.

Winter thawed into spring, and, per my father's request, I spent every Saturday night with Martha. He wanted us to get to know each other. Frau Grotjan, who understood from the start that I would not live with her forever, hugged me and wished me well each Saturday morning. She knew this was the best possible situation for me; I was getting a new permanent mother. Bus fare was not a luxury we could afford regularly, so I often walked to Martha's each Saturday morning. It was hard to say exactly what I was supposed to do once I got to Martha's place, but Vati said I must go there every weekend. So I did.

When I arrived, Martha would open the door and stare at me, as one might examine a piece of questionable meat. After a shallow breath or two, she stood aside and let me in, her face still blank and strange. Sometimes Vati arrived a few minutes after I got there. Sometimes I had to wait an hour or two. When the latter occurred, I'd sit on a chair across the room from my mother-to-be. We talked a little, about the weather, which had either given some impression of warming or had grown mercilessly cold once more, or we spoke about dinner, which was potatoes and whatever meat Vati would bring us, usually pork or beef. Then we'd sit in silence. Martha would leave her rented room to peel our potatoes in her landlord's kitchen. I sat quietly. It was like hiding from soldiers. I knew how to do that.

When Vati arrived, Martha would set the roast in the oven, and we'd head outside. The three of us took walks down to Wellsee, a nearby farming village, or a park that had a pond and trails around it. Vati and Martha walked hand in hand, and I ran ahead. In the evening, we'd have our supper together; then I'd lie on the bed while Vati and Martha sat on the couch, talking late into the night.

Eventually, Vati would say, "Well, I should go."

Martha would walk out with him, then return a few minutes later. She'd stare at me in her bed and sigh. Regardless of her preference of sleeping mate, she got into bed with me. There was only one bed in that cold room, and we would be warmer if we shared it.

Martha was a war widow. Vati told me that. They'd both lost a spouse. That explained how she and Father had connected. Maybe it explained Martha's moods too. She wasn't like Anna. Nothing like Frau Grotjan. But neither did she yell or pound on a desk like Herr Schmidt. She only gave me that scrutinizing gaze. Adults generally seemed to be one of two molds. If Martha was not the wildly ill-tempered sort, I believed she must be the sweet and friendly type.

Deep down. Father liked her a lot, so she must be. We were off to a good enough start. Martha was just shy. If I was quiet and helpful whenever possible, she'd warm up to me. I was sure of it.

Our Saturday visits lasted through the rest of February and all of March. The awkward afternoons were occasionally interrupted by visits from Martha's sister Ellie. A few years older than Martha, Ellie smiled at me and talked constantly. Even Martha's stern lips softened when Ellie walked in. I had discerned several unspoken rules in Martha's presence—mostly related to silence and the complete stillness of limbs and facial muscles—but those rules dissolved on Ellie's arrival.

"Come, Brigitte," Ellie said, and took me by the hand. "Let's go out and window-shop in Kiel."

Martha said nothing as I slipped from my perch on the chair in the corner and followed Ellie out the door. Off we went for two or three hours, down to the shops by the harbor. There were, in fact, some windows to shop by then. Slowly, slowly, clothing stores and jewelers had set up a few storefront displays. We stopped at a window full of women's and girl's dresses and shiny saddle shoes and Mary Janes. Ellie pointed to a pleated skirt. "One of these days, when I have money, I'll get you that," she said. Ellie was a waitress, and, like Gisella, she lived on her own. Anything was possible.

My aunt-to-be was soft and warm like Gisella and even more chatty. On days when she kidnapped me, I forgot all about Martha's perplexing manner. Vati had arrived by the time we got back, and I gave him a full report of our expedition. Once we sat at the table, Martha's strange stare reminded me that it was time to be quiet again. Dinnertime was when adults spoke to each other. That was clear. I wanted my new mother to like me. Having a mother at home might be my best chance at getting Elke and Rainer to live with us. I ate my food in perfect silence, determined to impress Martha, even if it killed me.

Part 4

Reconstruction
1948 – 1954

Thirty-Two

I t was spring, but still cold at night, when I moved back to Vati's place. Martha and Father were not married yet, but they would be soon. My mother-to-be had already settled in, and she showed me the new arrangement: she and Vati had the bed near the stove in the living room, while I would be in the back bedroom—the one that leaked rain and cold. This meant I got my own room though, and that seemed a kindness on Martha's part. If the dripping ever got really awful, I was permitted to drag my cot into the kitchen. And I could always wrap an extra blanket around me to keep warm. We did have a few more blankets now that Martha had moved in with all her things.

One Saturday during that spring, Vati and I took a walk through the cemetery. It was a lovely cemetery, with giant willow and beech trees and ponds and gardens. Even in early spring, when everything was gray sticks and wet dead leaves, at least there were ducks in the ponds and little shoots of grass. I hoped Vati would tell me more about Martha, but I had a more pressing question.

"I miss Elke and Rainer," I said. "When can we have them stay with us?"

Father's mouth tightened in the slightest wince.

I tried to soften my request. "When I'm fifteen maybe?"

"Ja," he said in his tired voice. "Then."

His response was hardly convincing, but I said nothing further. I didn't want to trouble him. We walked quietly for a while, then Vati continued.

"Your mother died," he said. "If she hadn't died, we'd all still be together. It's her fault."

"What?"

"She didn't take care of herself."

We stopped under a hulking leafless beech tree and Father told me a story I hadn't heard before about something that happened when I was three years old. "We had big windowsills in our first apartment," he said, "and you climbed onto one of them, hefting my family Bible with you. Then you sat at the open window and tore pages out of it and dropped them out the window." He smiled at the thought. "You must have liked how they fluttered to the ground."

"Did you watch me do that?"

"No, I was working at the shipyard."

"Where was Mutti?"

"She was across the street at a party," he said. "She left you there alone. With an open window."

Martha was not like that. She took care of herself. She was very clean, and she did not do foolish things. Vati wanted me to be respectful and grateful for this new mother he'd found for me.

Slowly, I learned a little more about Martha and how she met my father. During my stay with Frau Grotjan, Vati had been so tired on the weekends in part because his work was exhausting, but also because he stayed out late in the evenings. Kiel was resurrecting. There were restaurants and cafés that hosted dances on Friday and Saturday nights. That was where he met Martha. He learned that this woman had a long walk home from the café, so he let her stay at his place. Father was thoughtful like that. They spent their Saturday nights with each other until Vati decided it was time for Martha to meet me. Then she began spending her weekends with me instead. Martha's silence toward me was a fairly clear expression of her thoughts on that swap, but I continued my crusade to show her what a well-behaved and friendly girl I was. She liked my father an awful lot; she would come to favor me too. I was sure of it.

At first, things looked promising. Martha stitched a blue-and-white-checked dress for me out of an old curtain, and when a friend gave her a pair of blue leather shoes, she gave those to me as well. Her eyes were blank when she gave me these gifts, but she did give them to me. It seemed like progress. Martha cooked for me. She boiled and fried potatoes and roasted all the meat that Vati brought home each weekend, and I ate dinner pretty much every day. Once or twice, she also walked me to Elmschenhagen's new school, where I would finish off my spring classes. I walked with her, not talking. She liked things quiet. Or to be more precise, silence was the state least likely to provoke a frown. So I listened to the crisp tap of her steps as we walked, and I looked forward to class in a building that was not an ice-cold military barracks.

School was a nice break from studying Martha. The new school building was well heated. Between that and the spring weather, I felt decently warm each day. It was so much easier to concentrate on lessons and eat milk soup slowly and talk to the other children at lunchtime. I excelled at reading, slogged through arithmetic, and read German history books, which only went as far as 1930. And I met Regina. She lived barely a block away from me, so it only made sense that we began to walk together to and from school. Sometimes we dallied on our walk home and strolled through the cemetery, noticing the newest flowers—the recent reds and yellows exploding in the gardens. During one of our cemetery strolls, we told each other about our families.

"My father was shot when the Russians came through," Regina confided. She escaped her town with her mother and sister, and they made it to safety in West Germany. But Regina's mother died after the war, just as mine had. "I live with my older sister now," she said.

I told her how my real mother got sick and died after the war. "Now my father is going to marry a woman named Martha," I said. "She lives with us, and I'm not sure that she likes me."

Eventually we spoke with each other about our war experiences. We'd both stayed in bomb shelters. We'd both scavenged for food. We'd both lost parents. Regina had also witnessed a *Tiefflieger* attack—American planes strafing an entire train. It had looked like a military convoy. But it wasn't. Not entirely. Several of the cars held civilians. I told Regina about running from Russian soldiers and about Oma dying. But I never mentioned the soldiers in the trees. I never talked about Günther. I did tell her more than I'd told anyone else. She understood it all. I'd never had such a friend.

I rarely went home immediately after school. There were walks with Regina. There were ball games in the street. There were still rubble heaps to explore. I didn't expect to find anything of value anymore, but on one such expedition I did. Pushing aside a stack of collapsed shelves, I found a few books lying compressed between the heavy boards—all pages present and surprisingly undamaged by fire or rain. They were the *Elke* books, a series written for girls my age. I'd heard of them. There were four books in the series named after the four seasons. They followed the life of a girl from childhood through her adulthood. How sweet that they were about a girl who had the same name as my sister. All four of the books were there under the shelves. What a find! I stuffed them in my school bag next to my chalk tablet and graph paper and hurried home.

No matter what diversions I entertained, once I got home, Martha greeted me in the kitchen with narrowed eyes and a glance at the clock. Those first weeks together, she hadn't said anything aloud about the issue, so I figured things were mostly fine. But I must have taken extra long poking around in the rubble where I found the *Elke* books. I walked into the kitchen, and there was Martha.

"Where have you been!" she snapped.

"I found some books in one of the bombed-out apartments," I said.

"You're lying."

I'd always been mischievous. Adventurous. But a liar? I wasn't even sure what she meant; I'd just given her an honest confession. "They're *Elke* books. They're in good shape," I said, and stared at my shoes. Martha should at least be pleased that I was still a good scavenger. That skill came in handy.

"Where were you really?"

"I was out walking with Regina," I said. I wasn't a child who was prone to lying, but the line rushed out of me, smooth and simple. Martha's disbelief drew it out. She needed it, and there it was.

"Why didn't you tell me that to begin with?"

"I don't know. I'm sorry."

"You shouldn't spend time with her. She's an orphan. She lives with her sister."

I couldn't see how this disqualified Regina for the role of best friend. I also discerned that questioning Martha's logic might be hazardous to my health. "Okay, Mutti," I said. "I won't."

A second lie. Or at least a promise I had no intention of keeping. The words lingered dry and ashy in my mouth. I went to my room to wait for dinner. No longer excited about reading my new books, I hid them in my suitcase and lay on my cot, my eyes tracing the path of the crack in the ceiling.

There was a cold snap that spring. We needed heat. Martha did not go with me to gather coal as Frau Grotjan always did. She sent me to Preetzer Chaußee alone. That was fine; I remembered how to get there from my first months with Vati. I headed out to the coal seller's, came back with a full coal scuttle, and set it by the heater. As always, we needed to be careful how much we used. Instead of lighting a heating fire right away, Martha said she was going to spend the evening wrapped in her blankets on her bed to keep warm, and she advised me to do the same.

For the next week, I watched for coal lines every afternoon on the way home from school. I knew the system: always buy coal when it's available; you never know when you'll need more. At home, it was cold enough that I was permitted to drag my cot out of the cold bedroom and into the kitchen, close to the heater. Apart from a wordless dinner with Martha, I retreated to my cot to keep warm. I began reading my *Elke* books, and they were a fine escape. In the first book, Elke was a young, sweet girl like me, but she had a real family, both a mother and a father who lived with her. I pulled my blanket tighter and lost track of time reading that first book in the series, the one titled *Spring*.

I knew Martha was bundled up in her own bed in the living room, keeping warm just like me. So I was surprised on the third or fourth day of this routine when I heard her footsteps approaching the kitchen door.

"What are you doing?" she snapped.

"I'm keeping warm," I said. "You wanted me t—"

"You're reading."

I looked at her, confused. Was reading a bad thing?

"You're lazy, aren't you," she said. With no further explanation, she returned to the living room, to her own blankets.

Despite Martha's assessment of reading being a lazy girl's activity, I finished *Spring* in a matter of days and began *Summer*, in which Elke was a grown woman and had fallen in love with a good and gentle man. She was getting married. I would give anything to be the woman in that book. Elke lived with people who loved her. Reading her life made me long for my own sister, of course, and made me think of Rainer too. Those thoughts were often cut short as my reading binges grew shorter. Martha would listen for the rustling, the turning pages, and I'd hear her throw her own blanket to the floor and rush to my door. *I was lazy. I was impossible. I was just like my mother. I needed to quit reading and go scrub the kitchen floor.* We had no soap, at least none that we could spare for cleaning the floor. No scrub brush either. So I ground away at the red-tile floor with water and a cloth rag. The grout was perpetually gray and the tiles dull. It never got clean.

After several evenings of that particular rant and punishment, it wore me thin. After school, I ran into our neighbor Frau Müller in the stairwell, and she asked how I was faring. "Really," she said and touched my arm. I remembered how Frau Müller took care of me when I first moved back to Kiel. I told her then, just a little bit.

"My new Mutti, Martha, says I'm lazy for reading when it's cold," I said. "She makes me scrub the kitchen floor if I read."

"That's ridiculous," Frau Müller said. "I have an idea. Come visit me after dinner."

I managed to carry out that request without incurring too much suspicion from Martha. Frau Müller pulled me into her apartment, excited. "Look what I have," she said, and fanned a stack of pages torn from magazines. They were chapters from installment books. "And come see what I made for you."

My neighbor took me by the hand back out into the hall and guided me down to the basement to a nook under the cellar stairs. She'd stacked blankets and pillows under there. Dusty blue light filtered in from a window in the washroom nearby—just enough illumination to read. Frau Müller set the stack of magazine pages on the floor next to this nest. "Any time you want, come down here and read," she said. "Bring your own books too."

I hugged her.

"My sweet girl," she said.

Whenever I wanted to go down to the reading nest, I could give Martha the excuse that I was visiting Frau Müller. She usually begrudged me that liberty. My neighbor would help me keep peace with my mother-to-be. It was perfect. I curled into the blankets, and Frau Müller left me there contentedly reading the first chapter of an installment novel.

For better or worse, Vati and Martha were getting married. March thawed into April, and April drizzled into May. My mother-to-be said she and Father would get married any day now. This and the warmer weather lightened both our moods. I had no idea what to expect of the wedding itself. Having never attended such an event, I pictured it as something like a birthday party. I needed to get them a gift. I knew that much. Over the past month, I had gathered and stashed a small roll of Reichsmark from the change I got from purchasing coal or bread or milk. It would be enough to purchase a fitting wedding gift.

The first Friday in May, I was playing handball after school when I overheard a few women chatting about a drugstore in central Kiel—there had been a shipment of Nivea cream. That could be a fantastic wedding gift, a little luxury none of us had since before the war. I left the handball game and raced home to grab my Reichsmark stash. Vati was home. He and Martha were talking in the living room, and they didn't even look up when I dashed in and headed right back out the door. Perfect. I walked to the downtown drugstore; I couldn't waste any money on bus fare.

I walked fast, picking up my pace to a jog, down Preetzer Chaußee and into town, past the harbor and the bombed-out shipyards. I knew about the drugstore that the ladies had mentioned. We had an *Apotheke* in Elmschenhagen, but its shelves were always bare. The shop in downtown Kiel was well known because it was one of the few that could fill prescriptions reliably, and it was finally getting shipments of other sundries too. I needed to get there fast. I arrived at the shop. No line. That was a bad sign. I walked right in and approached the woman standing behind the counter.

"I heard you have Nivea cream," I said, still catching my breath.

"I'm sorry, we don't have any more."

"My father is getting married."

"That's lovely, but I really have none left," she said. "The shipment was so small. I'm sorry."

I scanned the shelves behind the counter, searching for anything else that might be a suitable gift. Other disappointed people had beaten me to any consolation prizes. Only a few apothecary jars remained. I held my tears in till I was out the door. It was late when I got back, but Vati and Martha didn't think anything of it. When they were together, Martha didn't mind my disappearing for hours at a time. I ate a piece of sugar bread and went straight to my room. They would never know a thing about the surprise they never got.

Thirty-Three

The next day, Martha woke me early in the morning and told me to get dressed. She wanted me to run an errand for her. I dressed fast and ate half a Brötchen. This was my chance to impress her.

"I need you to go to Pretz to the butcher there," she said. "Ask him for soup bones; he always has plenty. I want us to have a decent soup."

"Yes, Mutti," I said. She told me where the butcher shop was and gave me money for the soup bones and the train fare, and I rushed out the door, elated over my mission. She and Vati still hadn't told me the date of their wedding, even though I asked Vati at least once a day whenever he was home. I couldn't understand why they never told me, but I was a good girl and never argued, just waited patiently. And Martha trusted me enough to get the soup bones, so things were really looking up.

I got on the train at the station south of our cemetery park. It was about a twenty-minute ride to Pretz, where I disembarked and found the butcher's shop on the Hauptstraße right near the station. Confident and walking tall like Gisella or Ellie, I headed in. Just to the right of the ordering counter, there was a table draped in newspaper. A few bloody roasts sat out on the table, soaking the newsprint. So there was meat available. Yes, this shop did some good business.

The butcher stood behind the counter, his apron streaked with both fresh and dried blood. He had a kind, round face.

"Do you have any soup bones?" I asked.

"Oh, my dear. I ran out yesterday."

He looked so sorry for me. Too sorry. His eyes were sweet and pitying. Far too sweet. I was going to cry right there on the spot, and I shouldn't. Without a word, I turned from him and walked back to the station. I studied the cracked leather of my shoes and drilled each step into the sidewalk, pounding the tears away. I had to think. I was returning home with no soup bones and a wasted round-trip train ticket. There had to be something I could get for Martha. For Vati. For the wedding.

I took the next train home and watched the farm fields give way to houses, then storefronts that held apartments up above—all of them occasionally crumbling into piles of dusty stone and brick. I got off at Elmschenhagen station and walked past the cemetery. I needed to think. The cemetery park was in bloom. No more winter. No more cold snaps. I was four blocks away from facing a serious situation. Martha would be furious when I came home empty-handed. All the trees had leafed out and flowers grew by the ponds and in the grave plots. Bulbs and hedges and bushes and trees all shouted their loud colors. I would have found them quite pleasing if I wasn't in such a fix. All those cheery flowers.

Flowers. Of course. My father had acquaintances—two sisters who owned a villa near the railroad station—they wouldn't mind if I pulled a few sprigs off their giant lilac hedge. I headed to their property. The lilac stems were thick and green and it took some wrenching, but soon my arms overflowed with the purple blooms. I bent my face into the bouquet and breathed. Peeking over the blooms, I made my way back to our neighborhood, up the hill to our apartment building.

As I rounded the corner to Landskroner Weg, I saw Martha and Vati walking hand in hand, coming from the other direction. We met in front of our building. Martha was smiling, really smiling—a good sign. She'd be in a fine mood and wouldn't mind about the bones, and she'd love the flowers instead and say they were even better than soup bones anyway.

"We're married," she said, sounding joyful, but something else too—victorious. Father's smile was more embarrassed than pleased. He looked away.

"What?" I said.

"We're married," she repeated. "Where are the soup bones?"

"I…you…what?" They'd gotten married? They got married while I was in Pretz?

"We met with a justice of the peace. We're married. It's done," she said. "Where are the soup bones?"

"The butcher didn't have any," I said into the flowers. Then, in a rush, before she could reply and before I might cry: "I got you these flowers for your wedding present."

"You didn't get any bones?" she said. "I don't believe it."

I held the bouquet out for her. She snatched it, tucked the whole bunch under her arm, and stomped up to our apartment. Father looked like he was about to say something. He didn't. He turned away from me and followed Martha into the apartment.

Thirty-Four

The lilacs sat in a pail of water by the living room window for a day, then wilted. I should have known; lilacs never last long once cut. No one said anything more about the flowers. No one said anything about the soup bones. Or the wedding. After that weekend, Vati went back to work, I went to school during the days and played handball in the evenings, and Martha worked at her secretarial job. Vati and Martha were married. This was significant, and yet it wasn't. It hadn't changed anything. Nothing changed. But something had changed. Something shifted and tilted. Something slipped in Martha.

Most every evening, I ran outside to escape the tension in our apartment. I played with the neighbor boys and girls out in the street till late. We stood in two lines of six, facing each other. We had no handball net, but drew a line in the dust and bounced a rubber ball back and forth. The rules were simple: don't catch the ball, only bounce it back. If you get hit, you're out. We played for hours. We laughed and played till dusk, when neighbors leaned out their windows shouting, "Will you please shut up!" We played a little longer, till the shouts became really insistent.

I got home dusty but pleased. Hungry too, but I knew how to feed myself if I missed dinner. Initially, Martha scowled at my dirty clothes. Then she began calling me in before the handball games were over. Her voice cut through our laughter: "Brigitte! Get in here. Now!" If she found bad stains on my dress, she'd tell me to clean the kitchen floor. "If you don't do it, I'll tell your father and he'll take care of you." This was effective. It was the greatest terror I could imagine—that she might turn Vati against me.

There were tight folds that formed in her upper lip when she was about to shout. I grew adept at watching for that, at changing the subject, or backpedaling whenever her upper lip scrunched up. I set about learning all I could about Martha. I tried asking her about her family once, but her response was, *"Das geht dich nichts an!"* It's none of your business! I tried telling her a little about my mother, and she scowled. There had to be something she liked, something I could do for her that would make her pleased about having her very own daughter. She had family in our neighborhood. I'd met her sister Ellie, but saw little of her since moving back to Vati's. Martha's father, Adolph, lived nearby, not far from my school. We all went to Adolph's house once when Martha's brother, Willie, was visiting. Willie told me that he and Martha had one other sister who was stuck in East Germany. Maybe that explained why Martha was angry all the time.

Another clue came to me in the unlikeliest fashion. In June, the Reichsmark was phased out and the Deutsche Mark began. Every family received sixty Marks to start out. Around that time, Vati spoke with Rainer's foster parents and asked if Rainer might come back to stay with us. The couple vehemently refused. They told him, "You can have him back only if you pay us for every expense we've incurred caring for him." They knew we had only the allotted sixty Marks. They knew it was an impossible request. Father told Martha and me about this and never spoke about it again. Martha, on the other hand, stewed. Slowly, slowly, I caught on. Martha had wanted a boy.

During my summer break—between striving to get home before Martha began yelling for me and trying equally hard to keep away from her during the day and making sure I still had time to scrub the kitchen floor every evening—I retreated more and more to my back bedroom. During those retreats, I lay on my cot listening to the sounds of construction outside. The neighborhood resounded with the sound of hammering and shoveling and the ka-thwump of debris being tossed into trucks. While hiding in my room, I also became intimately familiar with the contents of the boxes that held my real mother's things. By August, I confirmed what began as a fleeting suspicion: Mother's things were disappearing. By then, most of her clothes fit me, but Martha wanted them out. A blouse, a skirt, a sweater, another blouse—the boxes grew lighter every day.

I couldn't hide all the clothing, but I stashed a few shirts. Then I took all the photos I could find and hid them in the bottom of my suitcase. They were portraits of my real mother and baby pictures of me and a photo of all three of us—mother, father, daughter. I would not let Martha disappear these things as well. I hid them in my suitcase beneath a pile of underwear and socks.

By the end of break, Father's salvaged stairs were gone. We had a new sturdy wooden staircase with a solid landing outside our apartment door. Granted, the roof was still missing and the north end of the building remained a rubble heap, but the stairs were nice. Reconstruction projects were completed as funds were available; the largest rebuilds would need to wait a few more years. When school resumed, I learned that we had also graduated out of the milk-soup program. There were plenty of bakeries up and running now. We could all get cheap bread for breakfast. Each morning, I hurried down our new stairs, raced to the bakery to pick up Brötchen, ate one roll, dropped off the rest at home, and got out of there. I missed milk soup but was happy to be at school. It was good to not have to sneak out of the house, good to have a fully justifiable reason to be gone during the day.

Martha developed a new aggravation. She began to time my arrival home each afternoon. She claimed it took only ten minutes to walk back from my school. It took, honestly, about eighteen. So I began to run home. It still took me twelve minutes, and she was waiting for me at the door. She began with lengthy lectures and the ongoing accusation that I lied about why it took me so long. A few weeks into this, the slapping began.

No one had ever hit me before. My real mother had often ignored me. Anna was, at times exasperated, but never violent. Hanna Nüncke did not like me, but she never struck anyone. And Frau Grötjan adored me. In my mind, violence was the strict domain of people who hated us—thieves and gangs and the Russian soldiers and the Polish people who made us leave Seidel. Slapping—like punching and stabbing and strangling and shooting—was something that happened between enemies during a war. Not between people who shared a house together. Even the bullies in Seidel had only tossed verbal taunts. The first time Martha slapped me, I could not comprehend the words in the lecture that followed. I stared at her in awe, incapable of understanding her shouts. Her lectures always ended with a grand declaration, which I did hear and perceive in full. Most often, the final words were, "You are just like your mother!" But the first time she hit me, she resorted to her second favorite endcap, "If you don't listen, I'll have your father take care of you!" That one frightened me the most.

After the hitting began, whenever Frau Müller saw me in the stairwell, she asked me if I was okay. She spoke with palpable heaviness, stopping me, searching my eyes. I told her I was well, thank you. I knew she could hear Martha's shouts; the Müllers lived right below us. But I feared what Martha might do if she discovered that I spoke about her to neighbors. She'd turn Vati against me. I knew she could. He liked her so much, he'd believe anything she said. So I did not tell Frau Müller about the newest development, and I certainly said nothing to Vati. I did confide in Regina. She could do little but pat me on the arm. She listened and believed me, and her belief sustained me.

I decided once to visit Martha's father on my way home from school. I would get home late. But as soon as I told her where I'd been, with her own father as witness, she'd have to be pleased. Adolph's house was north of Preetzer Chaußee, near my school. He rented a room above a closed restaurant, a bedraggled stone building. Willie, Martha's brother, said that their father drank too much, but Adolph seemed like a decent fellow when I first met him. So I stopped by. I knocked on the door and heard Adolph's shuffle step and the tap of his cane as he approached from inside. He'd hurt his leg in the war. The door opened, and Martha's father smiled in surprise. "Come in, come in!" he said, standing aside.

His rented room appeared to be the living room of the house. Like our living room, it was crammed with furniture one might not expect, including a table and a bed. Adolph stood leaning on his cane in the little bit of open floor space and said it was so good to see me, and he gave me a hug with his free hand. I thought this was pleasant until the hug didn't end when it should have. When I pulled back politely, he kept his right arm around me tight and pulled me over to the bed. I followed, but my feet moved like lead, not sure what was happening, not sure whether he was being kind and I should not be rude.

"Brigitte, you're old enough for this now," he said, sounding hurt by my reticence. He sat down on the bed and pulled me onto his lap. His clothes smelled musty and sour, and his hands reached around my abdomen, up the sides of my chest. I leapt up. He grabbed my arm. I was old enough to know what he was up to. I was old enough to know what it meant when Anna said thirty Russians stepped on my friend Heidi. I knew about those things now. I yanked free of Adolph and ran across the living room, out the door, and all the way home. To Martha.

As I walked up the stairs to our apartment, I wondered whether I should tell Martha what happened. She'd be more likely to believe that I'd been out walking with Regina—she'd slap me, but I was getting used to that. The lecturing rarely lasted more than a half hour or so. Then I could retreat to my room for the evening. What would she say if I told her the truth? What would she do? I trudged up the last few steps and across the landing. I would tell her. I only wondered how, what words. She was waiting for me in the kitchen, her upper lip creased. She said nothing; her eyes alone demanded the explanation. So I told her.

"I am late because I went to your father's house," I said. "He made me sit on his lap and he tried to grab my breasts."

Martha stared at me. The folds in her upper lip softened, and she blinked. There was a sound Martha made when she didn't believe something. It wasn't a word, just a noise in the back of her throat. "Tcheh," she said and waved her hand like she was batting away a fly. That was all she did when I told her about Adolph. She turned away from me and began washing a dish in the sink. She did not care that I was frightened and angry. But she did not hit me, and she did not rage at me for lying. She did not yell at me for anything that evening.

I remember the sound of Vati and Martha's first loud argument, but not its content. It was a Sunday night, and I hid out in my bedroom. Whatever the fight's focal point, they were sure they needed to determine a winner before father left for work the next day. The shouting lasted at least two hours after dinner. They did eventually settle down, did eventually turn quiet. I waited a while before I felt safe leaving my room to use the toilet. The lights were off in the living room. They were asleep.

In the morning, I thought maybe everything was fine because the house seemed quiet. I walked out of my room, ready to head out the door to buy our Brötchen, but I got to the kitchen just in time to see Vati brush past Martha. He slammed the apartment door behind him. The house had been quiet only because they were refusing to talk to each other. I heard his footsteps down the stairs, across the second landing, down again, and out the front entry. As soon as the door shut, Martha turned to face me.

"He left without saying goodbye!" she shouted. "It's all your fault! All of it!"

I needed a moment to think about this, to decide whether there was a suitable reply. Likely there wasn't. She left me no time to rationalize my own defense, invent a fresh lie, or even perceive why she was about to rail at me. Martha grabbed the rug beater from the wall by the kitchen door. It was a lovely thing, the rattan woven into a Celtic-looking knot. She grabbed it and spun toward me. "I'll teach you!" she screamed.

I jumped away from her and ran into the living room. She swung at me once and the rug beater grazed my back. She raced after me, back through the kitchen. I was headed for the door. She couldn't possibly chase me down the street like this. Just as I escaped the apartment, the rug beater came down hard on my right shoulder. The impact doubled me over, leaving my back a much more convenient target. I struggled upward, grabbing at the doorframe, still heading for the stairs. Martha was a lunatic, shouting and slamming the rug beater on my back. I had almost reached the stairs, almost made it. A blow came down as I set foot on the first step, and down I went. I rolled. There was the ragged roofline above me, the flash of sky, and there was Martha leaping down the stairs two at a time.

She didn't stumble. And she didn't care that I had fallen. I was sprawled on my side in the corner of the next landing by Frau Müller's door. Everything hurt, I couldn't breathe, but I could move. A little. I had to get up. I gasped and pushed up with my arms and saw Martha above me winding up with the rug beater. Immediately I coiled my head into my arms into my legs. There was nothing more to do but let her run herself down. I'd take what I could with my back.

A door opened, and the rug beater stopped its whistling descent. Frau Müller. "What's going on out here?" she demanded. She sounded disgusted. Angry. In the space between the crook of my elbow and my thigh, I saw Martha's legs racing back up the stairs. I unfurled and watched my stepmother sneak back into our apartment, without a glance back. Frau Müller hurried to my side.

"What did she do to you?"

I looked up at her but said nothing. I said nothing as she lifted me to my feet, as she checked me over for cuts. I said nothing as she drew me into her apartment. I said nothing as she wrapped me in blankets and laid me on her couch and told me to rest. She asked me once more, "What happened, Brigitte?"

"I don't know," I said, and they were the truest words ever spoken.

I don't know how long I cried. I don't know how long I slept. Maybe an hour. Maybe a whole day. When I woke, Frau Müller was there watching over me. "I want to report her to the authorities," she said. "You need to see a social worker."

I came wide awake and sat up. "No," I said. "No, no, no. Please don't tell anyone." I pleaded with her. I couldn't tell her the worst of it, how if anyone reported Martha to social services, she'd only turn my father against me. If I told Frau Müller this worst possibility, she'd only try to do something about it. Then the worst possibility would happen. This was my greatest fear: that Vati might be persuaded I was a liar. I feared that more than the lectures and the slapping and now the fine twists of the rattan rug beater. "Please don't tell anyone. Please don't," I said over and over.

Frau Müller argued with me, but not for long. "If anything like that ever happens again, I'm going to social services," she said.

I agreed to this, our compromise.

I did not run away that day or even the next day. I returned to Martha and she ignored me. Not kind. Not unkind. Never penitent. Only mute. She did not look at me or speak to me for three days. When she finally spoke, she ranted and slapped me on the face as usual, but not as hard as before. Her heart wasn't in it. But my back hurt and my face hurt and I was tired. I was tired even in the morning when I'd had enough sleep. I felt tired as soon as I arrived home after school.

It wasn't any one thing that sent me running. It was a thousand things. Martha needed things to be clean. Vati liked that she kept herself and the apartment so clean. Her clothes were always clean and pressed, her hands always scrubbed. My real mother died because she didn't do these things. Not a wrinkle on Martha—except for her upper lip. I was never clean; my dress was dusty from playing outside. Martha said I had better learn to clean or she would teach me a lesson. I had dirt under my nails from handball and floor scrubbing. Martha said if I didn't do as I was told, she would tell Father to deal with me. My shoes were always dusty. If Father yelled at me, I would die. I destroyed my blue leather shoes walking in puddles, and I didn't care about my hair. If Father hated me, I would have no one. I was so boyish. Martha wanted a boy. She wanted Rainer. She despised me.

Many nights, I dreamed that my real mother was alive. She showed up and saved me. Or I found her. There she was all of a sudden. She had her own apartment, and I moved in with her. She'd been trying to find me all along. Mother would come and save me, and we were happy together. And then she'd disappear. All of a sudden her body began to fade, like an angel that drifts away. As she disappeared, Mother would tell me: "I'm sorry. I couldn't help it. I had to leave." I'd wake from these dreams with the deepest ache, wishing I could fall back asleep and call her back to me.

One weekend, Vati was not able to come home, and I was stuck with Martha. I left. Ran the whole way to my sister's foster home, to Hanna Nüncke's. Anything had to be better.

One of the family photos Brigitte saved from before the war

Thirty-Five

It was November, cold and rainy, almost snowing. Still I ran. My sister's foster mother, Hanna, was not happy to see me, but she was not angry either. "What?" she said, stunned to see me at her door. "What are you doing here?"

"I don't want to be spanked anymore," I said. My voice cracked. I had to tell her just enough so she'd let me in, but not so much that she would turn me in to social services.

Her scowl melted. "What's this?"

"Martha spanks me all the time, and I don't know why."

"There are no busses this time of day. Did you walk the whole way here?"

"Yes."

Hanna took me in. She fed me and she let me sleep with Elke. My sweet little sister had her own bed now, and it was so much easier to share a bed with only her and not the whole family. How good it felt to curl up next to my sister that night. Hanna wrote a letter to Martha. There was no way around this; my stepmother would come for me, and who knew what would happen then. But Hanna did let me stay with her while we waited for Martha's reply. I didn't feel very much like playing and exploring the farm, and it rained most of the time anyway. Hanna, surprisingly, did not insist that I go to school. Instead, she sat with me during the cold, rainy days and tried to teach me how to knit. She was ambitious, I was attentive, and we had a lot of time on our hands. Her first project for me was a pair of finger mittens. She gave me a ball of green wool and two pairs of knitting sticks—you needed four total to knit the fingers. I caught on quickly and knitted for hours each day. I decided that the mittens would be a gift for Martha. I almost missed home. Martha hadn't been as bad since that very worst day. Maybe things could get better.

After four days, my stepmother showed up. I knew this would happen, that I couldn't stay with Hanna forever. It was time to go home. Really, where else could I go? I hid the knitting project under my extra clothes in a tote I'd brought with me. The mittens needed to be a surprise. Martha took me home on the next bus and didn't say a thing the whole way there.

Back home, Martha was decently civil with me for two whole days. Father got back, and neither Martha nor I said anything about my running away. Surely it was a near miss for her. What would she have said to Vati if he had come home and I was gone? A few evenings after Father returned to work, I resumed my knitting project. My cot was in the kitchen because the back bedroom was leaking from all the rain. I waited till Martha went to bed. I waited a little longer till I was sure she was asleep, then turned on the kitchen light, sat on my bed with my blanket around me, and began knitting. The mittens were taking shape. I'd already finished the palm, thumb, and grown two slender fingers for one hand. I just needed to finish the last two fingers, then make a perfect mirror copy of the first finger mitten. Not fifteen minutes had passed when I heard footsteps. I shoved the project under my blanket.

"What are you doing?" Martha snapped.

"Nothing."

"Why is the light on? What's under your blanket?"

I had no energy for lying. Not even a sweet lie, a good girl's lie to preserve a surprise. "They're mittens," I said. "I'm knitting mittens."
"Let me see!"

I grabbed the mitten parts, the fistful of yarn, and tossed it all on the kitchen table. "They were going to be your Christmas present."
"Oh," she said. She flustered. She had no words. No threats.

I saw Martha realize I was telling the truth. I saw her stumble over her own anger, her own habit of hating me. Like a woman who trips on the sidewalk and looks around to see if anyone noticed, Martha looked to either side of the room before meeting my eyes once more.

"Well, keep going then," she said. "But turn the light off soon. Work on those during the day."

She left the kitchen, and I turned off the light. I left the green wool mess on the table. There was no way I'd ever finish the project. This hardly mattered. Martha noticed the unfinished mittens and caught on. Two days later I saw her working on them in her own bed. She finished the mittens and wore them proudly that whole winter.

Christmas 1948 was fast approaching, and I had no gifts for either my beloved Vati or my frightening stepmother. Unhappy relationship or not, I was a good and sweet girl, and sweet girls gave presents to their parents at Christmastime. I had once again saved up a small handful of coins and bills from change at the coal line and at the bakery. It was easy to find a present for Vati and not too expensive either. I bought a pair of men's socks and knew he'd love them. He needed them badly. He always needed socks.

Martha was another story. What do you get for a woman who hates everything you do? On the way home from school, on a day when there were no coal lines to stand in, I passed by a secondhand shop and saw a single *Sammeltasse* cup and saucer in the window. It was a fine pair—the white porcelain cup with gold flowers embossed on the side and a gold stripe around the lip, and the matching dish. Usually these were given in sets of six or eight. But who could find intact sets of porcelain three years after the war? It was impressive to find a complete cup and saucer pair. Even more surprising was this: I went into the shop, inquired about the cup, and found out I could afford it.

I don't remember a thing about how Vati and Martha received those gifts. I don't remember gratitude or sullenness or false smiles or any gifts for me. I don't remember Christmas of that year, because New Year's Eve stands out too starkly. New Year's 1949 would seal in my mind certain conclusions about Martha. I would not bother to buy any heartfelt gifts for her ever again.

Thirty-Six

Martha had only two friends that I knew of, the Steiners, a couple who lived just down Landskroner Weg, a few blocks from us. Heinrich Steiner was from Swinemunde and so was Martha. Their shared hometown was apparently one very strong bond. The Steiners invited us and a few other friends over for New Year's Eve. Vati said I was welcome to come along. I could stay up with the adults until midnight, then I would need to go home. I'd never been to a grown-up party before and found it entirely vague and dull. I sat on the couch while they drank beer and cracked jokes that made no sense to me. Still, the notion of being there, of seeing what happened at such an event, seemed a privilege. We all wished each other a Happy New Year at midnight, and then Vati encouraged me to bundle up and head home.

Back in our apartment, I didn't feel like sleeping. I was too excited thinking about the party, even though all the conversation had been beyond me. Keeping my clothes on, I curled up in the blankets on my cot and read. I had just settled in when the doorbell rang. I climbed out of bed, thinking Vati and Martha were locked out. Opening the door, I was surprised to see not Vati, but Herr Steiner. As soon as the door was a few finger-widths open, he leaned into it, pushing it the whole way open. He smelled like alcohol, and he leered at me, not unlike Martha's father. I jumped aside, ran into the kitchen, and put the table between him and me. He stumbled after me, dodging around one side of the table; I ran to the other. Around we went. "Go away," I said. "If you don't get out of here, I'll scream!"

For whatever reason, that was enough motivation for him to leave. He didn't run. He didn't say anything. He just turned around and walked out. I locked the door and sat stock-still on my cot, shaking. Father and Martha found me there an hour later. I was crying, and Vati asked me what was wrong, so I told him what happened. "I'm scared," I said.

Vati was very upset and said, "I will go and see him tomorrow and ask him what he thought he was doing."

"Yes," Martha said. "This needs to be investigated."

The next day, Vati summoned Martha's friends to our apartment. I was in my bedroom when I heard them arrive. Martha called me out to the living room. The Steiners were seated on the couch. Vati and Martha sat at the kitchen table, and they had me stand in front of them, facing the Steiners.

"So, what is this about?" Heinrich asked.

"You came and chased me around the table last night."

"And what time was that?"

"Right after the New Year's party."

"That can't be," Frau Steiner said. "That's not possible. He was with me the whole time."

The Steiners stared at me. Behind me, I heard Vati get up from the table. "That's enough," he said to the Steiners. "You may leave now."

And they did leave. Martha walked out with them. Everyone had decided to paint me a liar. The wife had to be lying. Maybe Vati believed me, but he didn't stand up for me, not exactly.

Martha followed the Steiners out to the stairwell and shut the door behind her. I heard their voices on the other side of the wall, the low tone of the man's voice, saying something serious, and then Martha's heartfelt agreement. Then lighter words. Then laughter. Father left the next day. As soon as he was gone, Martha gave me a few good wallops with the rug beater for falsely accusing her dear friend. And for being just like my mother.

From then on, I lied about everything. I lied to defend myself and I lied for no reason. I lied because a lie was apparently more believable. Only lies were truth to Martha. Really. I lied to test this fact over and over. Always, always, this woman preferred to believe a lie. I could tell her the truth: *I ran all the way home from school,* or *I already scrubbed the floor this morning,* or *Herr Steiner tried to assault me.* She did not believe these things. But if I claimed I had stopped at a girl-friend's house or window-shopped the pastries at the bakery—when, in fact, I had done nothing of the sort—these things she believed. She believed every lie, and some lies were less likely to earn a slap on the face than the truth. Only one lie angered her. She didn't want me to visit Regina, so I quit saying I had done that, whether it was true or an invention.

For my own entertainment, I crafted more and more inventive lies. In my lies, I stood in a line for meat, but the butcher ran out. In my lies, I spoke with a teacher after class. Or I took an extra-long walk through the new snow in the cemetery. In my lies, I carried out errands on Wednesday that I'd actually completed on Tuesday. In my lies, I had many friends and I spoke with every single one of them on my way home. In my lies, I was happy and healthy and fine.

That winter, Father's boss found work for him in Kiel. He began laying terrazzo for businesses and a handful of residences in town, and he came home each night. His daily presence meant fewer beatings; Martha didn't dare do such things in front of him. She had only an hour or two after I got home from school in which she could safely execute her tirades. In the evenings, Vati and Martha occupied themselves with their tiffs over finances, and I retreated to my books.

I couldn't use Frau Müller's book cave when it was so cold out and got dark so early. So I read while curled up on my cot, and as long as I could hear Martha and Vati's bickering in the next room, I could read uninterrupted. Frau Müller regularly restocked my supply of installment-novel chapters, which were like candy to me. My staple, though, continued to be the *Elke* series. I had finished reading *Summer* and *Fall*. Elke was married and had children of her own. She was a sweet-spirited mother, just like her own mother. Elke's child was soon an adult and falling in love and marrying. What elusive things, these fictional mothers who combed their children's hair and spoke kind words to them. This had to be something that only existed in books, but blunt reality made the reading no less soothing.

Thirty-Seven

I lost my edge. Having Father around more often made me feel safe. So safe, I broke my own rule of not telling too much to Frau Müller. One Saturday, I stopped at her apartment to say hello. She hugged me and invited me in for a little bread, and I never said no to food, so we sat a while and talked.

"Are things any better with your stepmother?"

"A little."

"How is that?"

"Vati is home now and that helps," I said. "Nothing has happened that is as terrible as that one day. But she still yells at me." I tore off a chunk of dry Brötchen and chewed it slowly. "Martha says I'm just like my mother. She says that all the time."

"How can she say that? She never knew your mother. Did she?"

"No."

"So maybe the next time she says you're just like your mother, you could tell her that. Just say to her, 'You don't know my mother.'"

Frau Müller wanted me to stand up to Martha. I'd never considered the thought before. It was a fantastic idea and an inarguably perfect point. She'd seen pictures of my mother, but that was all. How could she, in any objective fashion, compare me to a woman she'd never met? I tucked the comment into my mind, unfolding it now and again: "You don't know my mother." I repeated the words to myself over the next few days. I wanted to be ready with them at the right moment.

That moment came a few days later. The three of us sat at the kitchen table drinking malt coffee after dinner. Martha drank hers out of the Sammeltasse cup that I gave her for Christmas. She sat across from me, and Vati sat to my right. It was a remarkably amicable moment, almost like a real family. But the conversation soon shifted from Father's latest flooring contract to whether the living room floor had been swept recently. I insisted it had; Martha said it hadn't.

Martha's upper lip scrunched up. "You're just like your mother," she said.

I had never felt so glad to hear it. "You don't know my mother," I said, savoring each word.

"Don't you ever talk to me like that!" she shouted, and simultaneously launched herself forward, leaning over the table to slap me. Her less-than-graceful performance did little damage to me—but the Sammeltasse cup went flying off the table. It hit the floor and shattered. She said in triumph, "That will teach you to say things like that!"

Martha breathed hard, ready to hit me again, but I sat composed, hands folded in my lap. For once, Vati spoke up.

"Enough already!" he shouted. "Don't ever do anything like that to Brigitte again!"

"She does things like that all the time when you're not around," I said.

Martha dropped her hand to her side. Then the real fight began. Vati and Martha raged at each other the rest of the evening. I slipped away into my bedroom, and they shouted on and on about me and about my mother and about money and about any other topic that ignited well. I knew I was in trouble. I knew Father would leave in the morning without saying goodbye. I knew Martha would blame me, would hit me with the rug beater. Yet I lay on my bed both fearful and pleased, smiling at the crack in the ceiling, at the cold wind pouring through the crumbling plaster.

The next day, I told Frau Müller what had happened. I told her how I said the words she told me to say. I told her how Vati was there, how Martha exploded, and how Vati yelled at her all evening. I told her how Martha beat me again after he left.

"I'm going to report her now," Frau Müller said.

"No. Don't do that. Vati doesn't know how bad it gets."

"He's supposed to know."

"He'll hate me for making her so angry."

"I doubt that."

"She'll only beat me harder," I said. "She will. Please, don't."

Frau Müller had no reply. She kept quiet.

Vati kept quiet too. He never again asked me about the hitting. He saw Martha hit me, and he did not approve of it, yet he still left me with her. The hitting continued. Martha slapped my face harder and more often. She yelled louder. From the start, I had assumed that if I was good and obedient, she would eventually stop. The slapping and the rug beater and the lectures, these things were my fault—just as Martha said. That spring, looking forward to my fourteenth birthday, I began to question these assumptions. I began to wonder whether my actions affected her at all. I began to dodge her slaps. I found reasons to stay outside each afternoon and evening. I avoided her. Of course, sometimes my disappearances only intensified her anger.

Mostly, I learned the way of silence. I learned to open the squeakiest door without letting it squeak, how to tread creaky floorboards without making a sound, even how to chew food quietly. Life with Martha revolved around inaudibility. As long as I made little noise, she might not look up from stirring a pot of stew. As long as she did not look at me, she might not think of me, might not recall how I did a poor job of scrubbing the floor the day before or how I caused all her arguments with Father. As long as she did not think of such things, she did not yell. As long as she did not yell, she probably would not hit me. Silence was the safest room in the house.

There is, in an odd fashion, no relationship so close as the one between a child and her abuser. Fear spurs her to observe the other with the keenest attention. It was my avocation, watching Martha. I went to school to learn reading and math and science. I came home and learned Martha. At an age when other girls daydreamed about boys, my mind wandered to Martha. She was my obsession. She would never adore me. I saw that now. But I still believed I could prevent her worst rages. I studied her, becoming an expert at what made her eyes turn steely, what made her upper lip crinkle: lateness was the worst trigger; reading in bed and talking about my real mother tied for second. Leaving a light on even a minute past bedtime was up there as well. It was like trying to keep your balance on an obstacle course of wobbly little stones spaced far apart. Like balancing on the rubble in bombed-out ruins. I could do it. Most of the time. Every day I slipped at least once. But if I made it through an evening and Martha had shouted at me only once at suppertime, but never actually hit me, that was a very good day.

I was not yet entirely jaded. Occasionally I still made clumsy sentimental attempts to leap across the chasm, to connect with her. Once every two or three months, brilliance came to me. I dreamed an idea: an extra cleaning task, a compliment about her skirt, a bouquet from Frau Müller's garden. Once provided, the token would surely make Martha's eyes glisten. The mirage of her someday pleasure fueled every gesture. I did try.

Thirty-Eight

Early in the spring, Martha commissioned me with spring-cleaning our apartment. It was a Saturday, and she and Vati were heading to Kiel to run errands. They planned to be gone all day. "Dust and sweep everything, and clean the windows and scrub the floor again," she said. "You need to show that you can clean well so you can be a decent *Hausangestellte* someday." Martha had a plan for me now; I was to be trained as a maid. At the time, my skill level was lacking. The grand spring-cleaning of 1949 was my chance to prove myself.

I took it seriously, staying indoors all day despite hearing my pals playing outside. I swept and mopped the floor, sponged coal dust off the floor around the stoves and the windowsills and bookcases and door handles, and scrubbed the windows till they gleamed. Then, even though it made me shudder, I took out our rugs, hung them on the clothesline, and beat them with the rug beater. When I was done, the kitchen floor still looked impossibly grubby, but every other surface shined. I knocked on Frau Müller's door and asked her to come up to inspect. I didn't want to take any chances.

She touched every surface and looked at her finger to see if there was dust on it. She walked from room to room, then declared, "I don't see a hint of dust. Martha must approve when she returns. She has to; the apartment is shiny clean."

Martha, of course, had no such glowing summation. She said the place was still filthy, especially the kitchen floor. "When you are done with sixth grade next year, I'm sending you to the farms to learn to clean," she said.

This was in reference to a government program that transplanted undernourished children in the cities to farms, where they might put on weight, in exchange for them providing free, or very cheap, labor. It was inspired by the programs that shipped us out of the cities during the airstrikes. There was nothing attractive about this option. I would finish sixth grade by the time I was fifteen and wanted only to carry on with my schooling, to complete middle school. Martha knew that. Vati knew that. But Martha insisted that school was a waste. Housekeeping was the only job I could aspire to, and I obviously didn't know how to do it. Vati capitulated to Martha's judgment; the post-war economy was hard for young women, and Martha clearly wanted what was best for me.

A few weeks after my botched apartment scrub, I discovered another opportunity that might better demonstrate my resourcefulness and attention to detail. I had noticed several families in the cemetery cleaning and weeding, tending their loved ones' graves. This was a common thing, to tidy the graves of loved ones in time for Easter. I knew Martha was a war widow; Father had told me about this and once told me the name of her first husband. But Martha had not gone to the cemetery to tend her first husband's grave, though I knew he was buried there. All my own loved ones' graves were far away, including my real mother's. She'd been buried in Hennstedt, southeast of Husum and almost fifty miles away from us. It didn't seem right that none of us were taking part in this tradition. After school one day, I headed to the cemetery and found the grave of Martha's first husband, Herr Schlappkohl. It was a modest plot. The gravestone was about an arm's-length wide and six inches tall, a thick slab lying flat on the ground. On it was etched the man's name and years of birth and passing only. No inscription or any other information. Martha had never planted a garden around the stone, as was typical around the other plots in the park. A plain gravel walk led up to the grave from the main path. At the very least, she could have kept this path clear. She hadn't. Tall weeds had already taken root. Sticks and damp leaves blanketed the stone. The grave looked abandoned.

I could do this for Martha. I could do this to show her I really cared about keeping things tidy. I could do this no matter what she said. I could do this because it was right. I sank to my knees in the gravel and began to weed, just like Frau Müller in her flower beds. I piled the pulled weeds, then brushed aside the windblown debris covering the stone. A large hedge ran along the edge of the graves. I gathered up my weed pile and leaves and sticks and tossed the whole mess into the hedge.

At other graves, the memorial stones were encircled with evergreen branches. I wrenched a few short boughs off a pine tree nearby and set them around Herr Schlappkohl's stone. There. Standing back a few paces, I looked at the gravesite. It looked good. Not stunning, like the more elaborate plantings nearby, but certainly not neglected.

At home, Martha started her interrogation before I'd even stepped across the threshold.

"Where have you—"

"I cleaned your husband's grave," I said before she could gain steam.

"Oh?" For a second, she almost softened. Almost flustered, like the time with the mittens. But she caught herself and narrowed her eyes. "I'll go down and take a look for myself," she said, obviously skeptical that I'd been to the cemetery at all.

It wasn't a long walk. Martha left and returned fifteen minutes later. "You left a few twigs on the pathway," she said. "If you can't do a better job, stay away from his grave."

Sometimes I spoke with Regina about Martha. Sometimes I spoke with Frau Müller, though I was careful to avoid telling her about anything real serious. More and more, I retreated to my reading. With warmer months and longer daylight in the evening, I returned to the book cave under the cellar stairs. I had good light there for an hour or two after dinner. I finished the last book in the *Elke* series, the one titled *Winter*. At the end of that volume, true to the way of things, the beloved Elke died. My book friend joined Günther and Heidi and the soldiers in the trees and my real mother. Reading of her death made me feel as empty and hopeless as when Oma's body went still in my arms. My book sister was gone. All I had left were Frau Müller's silly installment novels. They would have to serve until I left home in another year, until I was shipped to a farm to learn what really mattered.

Thirty-Nine

That summer, I turned fourteen—a non-event, as all my birthdays had been since moving in with Vati. At that time, I also learned that Hanna Nüncke's man friend, Emil, had died. The farm where he and Hanna lived had been entrusted to Emil's handicapped brother, and Hanna was made homeless. She moved to Elmschenhagen and, wonder of wonders, rented an apartment not far from us, only three blocks from Rainer's family. The news of Emil's death was sad, but any grief I felt was fast swept aside by the realization that my little sister now lived in Kiel. Theoretically, all three of us siblings could spend time together. My brother and sister had never even met each other.

I redoubled my efforts to spend time with Rainer. He was four and the shyest little boy I'd ever met. I stopped by his house at least once a week and walked with him up and down the sidewalk. On Saturdays, there was an outdoor market at the end of his block. We often walked there, and I held his hand and pointed to all the goodies. We had just started getting shipments of bananas, and these exotic fruits sat next to the oh-so-familiar potatoes. At another booth, colorful imported jackets hung in a row. A baker stood by his display of bread and pastries. The Deutsche Mark had been around for a year, there were marvelous things for sale, and slowly people were beginning to make purchases again. The square was a busy place any time we visited. Rainier held tight to my hand.

I began visiting Elke too. I spent time with each sibling separately, as I had a suspicion that not only had they never met each other, but they had never even been told of the other's existence. I also suspected that all the parents involved might not appreciate my uniting our trio.

Martha begrudged me the time for the visits, and Rainer's foster parents held a similar chilly attitude whenever I showed up. The Bolls had been prickly with me ever since they told Vati he would have to pay them back for all of Rainer's care if he wanted his son back. I caught on that the Bolls feared that Rainer might begin to like me too much, that he might beg to be with his blood relatives instead of them. My sister's foster situation was also delicate. Despite Hanna's kindness when she taught me how to knit, I never felt sure there was any stable rapport with her.

I plotted, in secret, to arrange for my brother and sister to meet in the market square. I still believed we Zobel siblings needed to be together. Even if we didn't live in the same house and we only met now and then, maybe if I stitched us together in that way, everything in my life would feel a little more stitched together. We didn't live in the same apartment when Elke and Rainer were babies, but we could be pals now.

On a Saturday in July, I made my move.

First I picked up Elke. My six-year-old sister was not entirely unlike myself at that age. She had sandy blond curls and wore darling skirts, but she was still the little spitfire who used to kick me while running in her sleep. Hanna once told me that Elke wouldn't sit still in school and, like me, sometimes simply left the classroom in the middle of lessons. Hand in hand, we walked down her street, turned a corner and headed toward Rainer's block.

"Elke," I said, "did you know we have a brother?"

"What?" she said. She saw that I was serious. "Really?"

"Yes, we have a little brother named Rainer, and he lives with a different foster family really close by."

"I have a brother?"

"Do you want to meet him?"

Her eyes got big. "Yes, of course!" she said. She got excited, dancing and skipping all around me.

Off we went to the market, Elke skipping at my side. I asked her to wait at the edge of the market near the first shop on the corner, just out of sight of Rainer's house. I trotted over to his home and fetched him for our usual Saturday jaunt down the block. He walked along in his white knee-high stockings and shorts, a tight grip on my hand. So far, so good. Out of earshot, I knelt next to him and said, "Rainer, did you know we have a sister?"

Of course he had no idea. And, of course, he wanted to meet her—but showed a little less enthusiasm than Elke. He grew nervous as we approached the square. There she was, standing at the edge of the market crowd. We approached, and I presented them to each other.

"This is our sister, Elke," I said. "Elke, this is your brother, Rainer."

Elke stepped toward us, and our brother hid behind me. My sister stopped mid-step and smiled, waved, and held out her hand. See, little guy, no threat here.

"He's really shy," I said. Eventually Rainer ducked out from behind my legs and smiled at Elke, then looked away—at the ground, at my skirt, at anything other than her. There were no hugs, no loud elation, but there we were. The Zobel siblings had finally met, all three of us standing within a pace of each other.

"*Guten Tag*," Elke said. "*Guten Tag, Bruder.*"

Rainer finally looked up long enough to give Elke a little wave, then stepped backward, leaning away from me, tugging on my arm. I took him back to the Bolls' house, then returned to the market and walked Elke back to Hanna's. Not bad for a first meeting. My sister and I laughed at how shy Rainer was. That was fine. It took me a little while to befriend him; Elke could do likewise.

In the delight of the moment, I failed to tell my brother and sister that they must keep our meetings secret. Sunday afternoon, I tried to visit Rainer again. No one answered my knock on the front door. I went around to the backyard. Only the chickens were out in the yard.

Right then, Frau Boll threw the back door open and shouted at me, "What are you doing here?"

"I just wanted to visit my bro—"

"I don't want you coming here anymore," she said. "Rainer isn't here anyway!"

I looked up at the loft window and saw Rainer up there, standing on his bed to peer out. I waved to him. He didn't wave back. He looked sad.

"If you want, we can just play in your yard and—"

"No! Rainer is ours. He belongs to us! You may never see him again. Get out of here!"

I left. I had little choice. By the next day, Frau Boll had informed Martha of my dastardly escapade. Martha held the same opinion as Rainer's foster mother and took it a step further. I was told I was not allowed to visit either of my siblings ever again.

Forty

When you were told something, you obeyed without question. That was how a good German girl had to be. My dream of reuniting my siblings was fully shattered the day Frau Boll yelled at me. Martha took Frau Boll's side, and that was the end of the matter. At first, I thought about Elke and Rainer all the time, but it was too sad to ponder the impossibility of the matter. Mostly, I willed myself not to think about it. I thought of school, and I thought about Martha's latest accusations, and I thought about Frau Müller's installment novels. I thought about leaving home soon to begin my training as a maid. I did not let myself think too long about my brother and sister. Ever.

That last year before shipping off to a farm, I had one more escape in addition to my book cave. I began confirmation classes at Maria Magdalena church on the other side of the cemetery. Every Saturday afternoon, I walked through the quiet memorial park and joined about twenty other boys and girls my age in the church rectory. The pastor taught us the Lord's Prayer and verses from the New Testament and the finer points of Lutheran catechism. Neither Martha nor Vati attended church, and they made no requirement of me to become a confirmand. I attended the classes purely because most of my school classmates were there. The Confirmation ceremony would deem us adults in the church's eyes, which sounded awfully attractive, even if our parents and teachers did not agree with the assessment.

On the whole, the religious learning was lost on me. I memorized the bare minimum needed to ensure I would be confirmed, along with my friends, shortly before my fifteenth birthday. Still, I always sat right in the front row—because I finally could. Back in Seidel, I'd never been permitted inside the church. In Elmschenhagen, I was endlessly fascinated with the grand stone structure and its rectory buildings. Hardly religious in heart, I was devout in attending the Saturday classes and Sunday services purely because I was finally allowed to see the architecture up close. Every Sunday morning, I sat alone in the dappled stained-glass light. I loved the church, the building itself—the iron scrollwork on the heavy wooden door, the slender silvery organ pipes standing sentry at the back of the sanctuary, the glass panels in yellow and green, here and there a flash of magenta or blue. I liked the echo of the sanctuary, the resonance when the congregation sang hymns about incomprehensible wonders. I liked the quiet of the park on the walk there and back.

At the Saturday confirmation classes, the pastor taught on a single catechism topic, then gave us homework. During the week, we were to read certain scriptures and write short reports summarizing the previous lesson. I told the pastor that I did not own a Bible and he gave me a New Testament. I savored this reading, for I loved reading in general and owned very few books. And when Martha heard the pages rustle and came to investigate, she stood stock-still if she saw it was the New Testament in my hands. She didn't dare reprimand me for reading that.

As I learned about God, I could have grown angry with him. I did not. I'd seen violence and rage and I'd been abused myself, but I'd never seen any other human direct their anger at a deity. Essentially, I didn't know God-rage was an option. To rage at God, I would've needed to feel that God had neglected me. To feel neglected, I would've first needed to believe in a God that was somehow inherently involved in human life. I had, at age fourteen, no reason for such a thought to manifest in my mind.

Despite the horrors I'd seen and survived, I remained profoundly naïve to some significant matters. One was the notion of making my own decisions. Decision making necessitates a sense of rightness and wrongness. I did understand pain. I fled, when I could, from discomfort. But I never knew I could take any greater action, make any decision rooted in a drive higher than base survival: fleeing from pain, finding food when hungry, hiding when in need of shelter. Even after the war, with fairly consistent food and shelter, living with Martha ensured that my horizons stayed small. I never thought that I might be able to choose a different way of life. Or that God himself could have dealt me a better hand. So I wrote my reports each week, repeating the pastor's teachings on lofty words like *incarnation* and *salvation* and *sanctification*, but I wrote these essays in the same way I parroted mathematics rules in school. I didn't understand and certainly did not take any of it personally.

The Jesus stories were fascinating reading material—a man who walked on water during a storm, touched a dead girl and made her start breathing again, and multiplied a few loaves of bread to feed four thousand people. The Gospels had been presented to me as a factual account, and I believed the Bible's stories were true. But I never wondered why such miraculous happenings did not occur in the present day. I memorized the Lord's Prayer, but it never occurred to me to pray.

Some war survivors grow accustomed to the constant, moment-by-moment bafflement. Long after the war is over, some still live in awe-filled passivity. Maybe that is how I looked at the wonders that the church presented to me. I read the stories, but gave them little further thought after I closed the book.

Still, here is what the church was to me, and it is no small thing. Church meant quiet voices. Whether during confirmation classes or Sunday services, the voices were soft, reverent, hushed, like the voice a mother uses when she's trying to keep a baby asleep. Even when the pastor projected his voice from the high pulpit so everyone could hear, the echoing hall required syllables so precise and careful that they could be mistaken for a whisper. This was rest for my ears, and I never wanted to leave when class or service ended. Teaching and music and sermons cascaded over me, gentle poetic language soothed me, even though I paid little attention. The pastor's voice was a benign balm after a week of cutting critique.

On the way home from class each Saturday, I walked through the cemetery at dusk. I had no fear, for the paths there had always felt as peaceful as the church sanctuary. I had survived a war; the dead did not frighten me. Everyone in the neighborhood regarded the cemetery as a fine place to stroll. Perhaps a little fear would have been wise. One autumn evening as I walked home, a man walking from the other end of the park approached me. He stopped me at a trail juncture and hailed me, asked me where I was headed. I told him I was headed to Landskroner Weg.

"You don't know where you're going," he said.

What a strange thing to say. "I always take this route," I said. But he'd startled me, and I second-guessed myself. He was tall and well dressed, wearing a suit coat; I wondered if he knew something I didn't know. Perhaps he lived in my neighborhood and had seen me before. Perhaps I'd made a wrong turn in my daydreaming.

"I know a better way," he said, pointing to his left. "Follow me."

Utterly foolish and programmed to obey, I followed. We walked side by side on the trail briefly, but soon I slowed down. He slowed down as well till he was walking a little behind me. This seemed strange. I stopped. That was when he attacked—grabbed me by the shoulders and shoved me to the ground behind a hedge. I thought he was about to kill me, had a vague sense he might do something worse. I closed my eyes in fear.

Right then, a man shouted: "What's going on over there?" It was the farmer who worked the land adjacent to the cemetery. He raced over, waving his arms and yelling. The rapist leapt off me and ran away, and the farmer hurried to my side. Strong, kind hands picked me up. I was shaking and crying, for the most part uninjured, but my legs didn't want to move. My rescuer waited while I caught my breath, and then I followed him out of the cemetery.

At Landskroner Weg, I thought I could get myself home all right, but the farmer insisted on escorting me the whole way home. "Please don't walk alone through that cemetery anymore," he said. "It's too dangerous."

At my apartment, I thought I could see myself in, but my rescuer insisted on speaking with one of my parents. This seemed like a bad idea to me, but I was too shaken to explain the Martha situation to a total stranger. The farmer knocked on my apartment door, and my stepmother answered.

"What is this about?" She looked from me to the farmer and back to me.

"Your daughter was attacked in the cemetery," my rescuer said. "I was able to scare the man away, but she really should not walk there alone."

He meant well and thought I was safe. After he left, Martha lectured me for my foolishness. If I ever walked through the cemetery alone again, no one would save me. I deserved what happened to me. If I didn't get attacked again, she'd teach me a lesson herself. Martha's approach to parental instruction usually sent me in the opposite direction. This time, despite her distortion of the farmer's sound advice,

I followed it. The cemetery paths were my favorite walk, and I did not let the assault drive me away. But from then on, I only walked that route when I had friends with me, and I no longer dallied after class till I was the last one out. I never saw the attacker again in the cemetery, but I did see him once more in town. Martha and I were at an outdoor market, and I saw that awful creature across the square. There was no mistaking him; he was wearing the same suit coat.

I grabbed Martha's arm. "That's him," I said, and pointed. "That's the man who attacked me."

Martha looked and ascertained we were looking at the same man, the same coat, same height. "Tcheh, I don't believe you," she said, and pulled her arm out of my grip. "Look at him. He's a good-looking man!"

I was accustomed to Martha's disbelief. It shouldn't have rattled me. But it did. I left her side and wandered into the market crowd, all the while keeping an eye on the man. Martha be damned—I wanted to know where that bastard lived. I followed him through his morning shopping and stalked him, one cautious block behind, as he left the square and headed home. I had to follow him. I couldn't not follow him. He carried a basket full of bread, like any other fellow walking home from market. Maybe Martha was right. Maybe it was the wrong man. He turned a corner and I saw, for a moment, his profile. No, it was him. I watched from behind a hedge as he turned up a walkway to a brick house. I didn't know why I followed him. I had to. I had to know. I knew now. I hated knowing. I wished I had never followed him. Wished I could remove the knowing. This was a street I often used when I walked to our bakery. Now I'd think of that terrible man any time I walked past. This was terrible. No, it was good. It was good to know. I could watch for him. And I did from then on. Every day on the way to the bakery, I stared at his house and passed by fast. By some strange grace, I never saw him again.

Forty-One

Halfway through that final school year, I became entirely despondent. Regina and I drifted apart when she got confirmed a year before me. I hadn't seen Elke and Rainer in over six months, and I hadn't spoken much with Frau Müller lately since there was nothing new to tell her. Every day was the same old trap at home. Without hope of reuniting my family, I wanted to leave, to live on my own. Yet I had no skills to do so. I wanted a quiet home of my own. At the very least, I wanted to come home to no one yelling. Wanted to go to middle school. Wanted a home where my parent—real, foster, or otherwise—told me to continue school. Instead, I had a stepmother who put all villainous fairy-tale stepmommies to shame. I had a home where I feared, if not for my life, certainly for my sanity.

I held the crying at bay till late at night after Martha was asleep. Tired and alone, the sobbing began. I wept many nights in a row, grieving my real mother and my brother and sister. And I longed for Anna. Finally—why hadn't I thought of this sooner?—I wrote a letter to my foster Tante. I'd always struggled to discern the bounds of Anna's love for me, but she cried when I left. She'd been genuinely sad. Martha hated me. Anna did not. Martha wished I did not exist in her world. Anna might be able to make that possible. I wrote Anna a long letter, telling her all about Martha and how she slapped me all the time. I wrote about the time with the stairs and the time with the mittens and the man who attacked me in the cemetery. I wrote all these things and asked, "May I come back to you?"

I signed and folded the letter, slipped it into an envelope, and sealed it shut; then I asked Martha for a stamp. "What are you mailing?" she asked, sounding more curious than unkind.

"A letter to Tante Anna," I said. "I want to say hello to her, to wish her well. I haven't seen her in so long."

"I don't have a stamp," Martha said. "But I can mail it for you."

I handed the envelope over, believing I could trust Martha to do this one thing. She was harsh, but she hated liars. Surely she would not lie herself. Martha took the envelope. I never heard from Anna. I brought the matter up several weeks later, and my stepmother said, "You know Anna doesn't want you. There is no point in bothering her."

The spring of 1950 brought me delight and fear in equal measure. Two weeks after confirmation Sunday, school would end. Two weeks after that, I would head to my first farm assignment. But that looming deadline did not dampen my excitement on the second Sunday in April when I stood at the front of the church with all the other confirmands. Morning sun filtered in through the stained glass; five towers of gold and green and peach light embraced our group in the sanctuary's alcove. We spoke serious-sounding vows, and the pastor presented each of us a certificate declaring us confirmed as fully accountable adult members of the church.

Both Vati and Martha came to watch. Martha was not herself. Martha was smiling. She hadn't been her usual self for three weeks leading up to confirmation. She had become, in an *Augenblick*, profoundly maternal—beginning with the challenge of finding a decent dress for her confirmand. As if it were her new passion and greatest happiness, she set about acquiring a dress from an American care package. What she found was a saucy black cocktail dress with a plunging neckline. It required significant modification to pass as suitable attire for the event at hand. Martha went to work, pulling the seams on the top panels, fashioning a bodice out of lavender fabric, taking my measurements repeatedly, and piecing it all together. It fit me well when she was done. I had nothing but white knee-high stockings, which made the final ensemble a bit patchwork. Still, it was the finest dress I'd ever worn.

Between seamstress sessions, Martha spent her free moments in town planning the food for the party. Beyond a handful of friends from the neighborhood, I had no idea who would be there. This was Martha's domain, and she'd grown secretive about the guest list. I didn't want to ask any questions that might break the strange spell over her. My stepmother seemed honest-to-God pleasant in those preparation weeks.

At home after the service, Martha set out an incredible spread: a cake and hot chocolate, bread and butter, and several types of cold cuts and cheese. We had never eaten such extravagant fare. I watched Martha set out the food. I would have helped, but my head began to throb. The headache started while we were still in the church, but it hadn't bothered me then. At home, watching Martha bustle about, the pain intensified. "I'm afraid I have a bad headache," I told her.

"*Schade*," she said, without looking up from the sink. Too bad.

The guests began to arrive—first a few neighborhood friends. Then the real surprise. Hanna Nüncke arrived with Elke, then Herr and Frau Boll with Rainer. I hadn't seen my siblings in almost a year. Between hugs, I rubbed at my temples and tried to smile, tried to appear delighted.

Everyone was complimenting Martha on the food and thanking her for arranging such a lovely party. What a sweet woman she was. Martha lapped it all up. Everyone was happy and congratulating me, and I stood there in pain. It pounded a persistent rhythm behind my eyes. Initially, I tried to join Elke and Rainer and my friends in the kitchen, where they ate cake and played *Mensch Ärgere Dich Nicht*. I brought that silly board game all the way from Röhrenfurth, and I finally had enough friends in the apartment to play it. I'd never had a significant headache before in my life, and this was the worst timing ever for a first migraine. I tried to eat a bite of sandwich, tried to smile, but the headache heightened with all the noise. It hurt so bad, I couldn't keep my eyes open. The kitchen light hurt. Color hurt. Laughter hurt. I wished I could close my ears. And there were my siblings, and for once, Martha was letting me see them. And everyone thought Martha was sweet and fabulous for throwing this party, and all the adults were in the living room gabbing as if they were one big kind-hearted family. And my head was ready to launch itself off my shoulders.

I slipped out of the kitchen, shuffled down the hall to the back bedroom, closed the door and lay down, holding my hands over my eyes and listening to the laughter rise and fall. My friends and siblings were too involved in the game to notice me leave. Eventually I returned to the kitchen and tried to join the board game, tried to eat a little more. I spent the rest of the party volleying back and forth between the bedroom and the kitchen, rallying just enough to say my goodbyes and thank-yous when everyone left late that evening.

Martha and Vati looked at me then. *Schade*, what a shame. It was a shame, the fact that I had such a headache, today of all days. "It must be from too much excitement," Martha said. Vati nodded. So did I. It was a sensible explanation.

Forty-Two

Sagehorn

Three weeks after my confirmation, I boarded a train for my first farm assignment. I had a whole morning on the train to ponder what awaited me. The Wilkens Farm was about a hundred miles away in a village called Sagehorn, not far from Bremen. It took about four hours on a train that stopped in every village on its route. By the time I arrived in Sagehorn, I'd decided the farm assignment could be a good turn. After all, when I was shipped to Seidel, I wound up with a decent family, and it was great fun exploring a farm.

At the Sagehorn train station, a social worker identified me by the tag clipped to my coat and introduced me to Herr and Frau Wilkens. The woman seemed cheerful as we left the platform. Their property was just down the road from the station. Our first afternoon was pleasant. They showed me around their house and milking barn, introduced me to their six-year-old son and a daughter who was only two years younger than me. I had the afternoon off. Frau Wilkens informed me that my chores would begin the next day.

The next morning, after our bread and jam breakfast, Frau Wilkens summoned me. Still pleasant in tone, still smiling, she told me to wash the dishes. After that, she would bring me outside to learn my farm tasks. I did as I was told. Washing dishes wasn't so bad. I could handle that.

"Follow me," Frau Wilkens said when I was done in the kitchen. "I'll show you how to milk the cows."

Back in Seidel, I found the cows a teensy bit frightening. But I followed my new boss. I knew refusing to try wasn't an option. There were three stalls in the small milking barn, and three bovine rear ends stuck out into the corridor. Behind their dirt-spattered tails, a drain ran the length of the barn. A stack of clean straw stood in one corner at the far end of the structure, a pile of soiled straw in the opposite corner. Still smiling, still pleasant, Frau Wilkens stopped near the door and picked up a metal pail and an odd wooden disk with a single dowel protruding from its center. A milking stool. She directed me to the first stall and said, "Watch me first."

She seemed unconcerned about her proximity with a beast that could kick her into next week at any moment. But the cow, eyes half open and chewing her cud, seemed equally nonchalant. Frau Wilkens set the pail under the cow, balanced herself on the one-legged stool, and grasped the two udders closest to her. I stood to her side watching and couldn't quite see how she had grabbed the teats, but how difficult could it be? My boss squeezed each udder alternately, and streams of milk rang into the pail. I stepped closer, less scared of the cow, genuinely interested. I'd be able to tell Vati I learned to milk a cow. That was something.

"Watch how I draw the milk down and then squeeze," she said.

"Yes," I said. I had no idea what she was talking about.

"Your turn now."

She held the milking stool for me while I cautiously took a seat. There was no time to ponder the inanity of a one-legged stool. Frau Wilkens was waiting. I grasped the two udders in a rough approximation of my boss's demonstration and squeezed. Nothing happened. I squeezed them one at a time. I squeezed them at the same time. Nothing. Frau Wilkens scrutinized my hands, repositioned them.

"Draw the milk down, then squeeze."

"Yes, Frau Wilkens."

I followed her directions. Tried to. Still, not a drop came out of the cow.

"Squeeze harder!"

"Yes, Frau Wilkens."

I kept trying, but to no avail, and at that moment Frau Wilkens permanently lost her smile.

"I'll do it myself," she said. "Your hands are obviously too weak. You'll muck their stalls instead."

So, from then on, every morning while Frau Wilkens or another farmhand milked the cows, I used a pitchfork to expand the pile of manure-speckled straw and lay fresh bedding in each stall. During my first week at the farm, I learned a few new tasks each day. By the end of the week, I'd learned the rhythm of my new life.

I woke at five in the morning and set out bread and butter and marmalade for the family and their Polish workhand, Jan. He'd been a POW laborer placed with the Wilkens during the war, and, like some of our POWs in Seidel, he found the circumstances better than the hungry life he'd had back home. He'd also acquired a German girlfriend. So he and his lady friend lived in modest lean-to quarters attached to the storage barn. Like me, the Pole received room and board for his labor. Unlike me, he received a small cash payment each month as well. Silent and bleary eyed, we all ate breakfast together.

Afterward, everyone scurried off to their respective chores. I stayed on in the kitchen to wash dishes. Then I hurried out to the milking barn to muck stalls, then back to the house to make beds, and then back to the kitchen to scrub the floor—I was damn good at that. Though the Wilkens' kitchen floor was concrete and looked even grimier than Martha's floor no matter how I leaned my whole weight into the sturdy scrub brush. After kitchen cleaning, I gave my own hands and arms a good scrub so I could begin peeling potatoes. That took me through to prepping the midday meal—the large meal in German homes. Frau Wilkens helped with the cooking, which usually entailed boiling potatoes and warming canned pork on the stove. I always ate my fill; the Wilkens family did not begrudge me that. The social worker had written down my weight at the start of my service term: ninety-two pounds. The whole point of my stay with them was for me to weigh more at the end of six months. And so I was never hungry, though the sheer workload kept me thin. After lunch, I beat rugs, swept the rest of the house, cleaned the front sitting room, helped hang wet laundry, and helped Herr Wilkens cut peat bricks when needed.

The latter required long-handled spades. I worked with Herr Wilkens and Jan, the three of us switching tasks occasionally. One of us jammed a spade into the ground, cutting the outline of a rectangular brick; the other two leveraged the bricks out of the ground and stacked them in long, squat rows to dry for several days. It wasn't the highest quality peat. We didn't dig very deep, and we dried the fuzzy turf that grew on top along with the clay-like peat underneath. But it met Herr Wilkens' standards for decent wintertime heating fuel. At least the dried turf caught flame quickly on a cold day, even if that meant it burned fast as well. Once dry, Herr Wilkens loaded the bricks into a wagon, and his draft horses hauled the load to the storage shed. I got backaches from that work, but working in the field meant a break from Frau Wilkens' glaring supervision.

After completing miscellaneous afternoon chores, I peeled more potatoes for dinner. Our evening meal consisted only of potatoes. I sliced them into cottage fries and fried them in a cast iron pan. By the time I was done scrubbing the evening dishes, it was seven o'clock. I sat on the porch or walked in the garden with Jan. He had seen how Frau Wilkens scowled at me, and he likely felt sorry for me. He asked me simple questions and I replied with answers like: *Yes; no; certainly warm today; yes, the breeze is nice.* I had no idea how to speak with a man; most of my encounters with men outside my family had been horrifying. Jan and I spoke about absolutely nothing, but who knew what our little walks in the garden looked like to others. His girlfriend glared at me anytime I sat next to her on the porch.

I shared a room with Renate, the Wilkens' daughter. She, too, did not like me much. This was primarily because I once rescued her brother from what I believed was an unjust punishment. I had no idea what he'd done wrong; I walked in on the situation in the kitchen right as Frau Wilkens shouted, "That's it. Down in the cellar!" Her son was hollering to begin with and cried even louder at those words. The cellar door was right there in the kitchen, and Frau Wilkens opened it. "Now!" she said. The boy continued crying but obeyed, climbing down the steep steps. His mother watched his descent. As soon as his feet touched the dirt floor, she slammed the door shut. The screaming reached a whole new decibel level at that point. It had to be pitch black down there. Frau Wilkens left the kitchen and headed outside to milk a cow or something. She didn't even look at me as she rushed past.

I knew I shouldn't do a thing. This was none of my business. I could get in serious trouble if I intervened. I approached the cellar door. I could hear that the boy had felt his way back up the stairs. His crying was just on the other side of the door. I knew he wouldn't let himself out; he was too scared of his mother. So I opened the door.

His sister, Renate, saw me do this and immediately ran outside shouting, "Muttiiiiiiii! Brigitte let Horst out of the cellar!"

When Frau Wilkens returned, she had, surprisingly, calmed down. She sat with her son and spoke with him about never again committing the offense that sent him into the cellar. He sniffled and nodded. Then my boss turned to me. A world of ifs passed between us. She might hate me, but I was sent there by a government program. We both knew that a social worker would check on me. We both knew the social worker would interview me and ask what my farm family was like. I was sure she wanted to send me into the cellar next. But she didn't. She shook her head and went back outside.

Horst became my little buddy from then on, but his mother and sister despised me. I could do nothing right. And while I had plenty of practice with that sensation, it grated on me more at the Wilkens' house. This was my first farm assignment since Seidel. On some level, I'd hoped that just as Seidel had been a respite from my real mother, perhaps the farm in Sagehorn would save me from Martha. It didn't. I was so useless that I couldn't even milk a cow. I couldn't peel potatoes fast enough. I couldn't clean anything well enough or fast enough, and one time I even managed to clean too thoroughly.

We had no laundry starch, so on one occasion Frau Wilkens filled a small pot with water and dissolved a palmful of potato starch in it. She soaked a blouse in the cloudy water, then wrung it out and took it outside to hang on the clothesline. She didn't return for quite some time. Meanwhile, I cleaned the kitchen, and when I got to the pot, the starch had settled at the bottom. Knowing I had received sturdy rebukes for leaving my cleaning partially done, I picked up the pot and poured it out in the washroom, then gave it a good scrub and dry and put it away. At that moment, Frau Wilkens came back into the kitchen holding another blouse.

"Where is my starch water?"

"I thought you were done with it... I washed the pot."

"What were you thinking? You wasted my starch!"

I understood how to use care in rationing goods. We all did. But the two teaspoons of cooking starch were hardly worth a Pfennig. She griped at me as she refilled the pot, added fresh starch, drowned another shirt, squeezed it out, then stomped out the back door. I mopped up the filmy drips behind her. She never once hit me, but the constant verbal whipping was almost as exhausting.

Every two or three weeks, I received an afternoon off from cleaning and farm tasks. Frau Wilkens sent me down the street into the village with Renate in tow. My boss lady gave me enough money to purchase two tickets at Sagehorn's theater. On those afternoons, Renate became my best friend. She must have not known that her mother gave me the money for the tickets, and I had no intention of telling her. We saw our first British film in that little theater—*The Third Man,* with Orson Welles. I couldn't read the German subtitles fast enough to grasp the plot of the murder mystery, but it kept me perfectly terrified. I thought Welles was creepy. The theme song that played every time he came on screen lodged itself into my mind and kept me awake long into that night. Still, an afternoon at the theater beat peeling potatoes or cutting peat. No matter how scary the film, I was grateful to live inside a completely different world for an hour or two.

At the end of August, four months into my six-month term, a social worker checked on me. Herr Wilkens had received a letter announcing her visit date, so he and his wife had several days to prepare me. Wasn't I in fine shape, considering no one ever hit or starved me? Didn't I get to eat as much as I wished at every meal? I had my own bed and got good sleep every night. And hadn't I learned valuable cleaning tasks, which would help me acquire a decent job or a reasonable husband in a few years? I couldn't argue with any of that.

The social worker arrived carrying a briefcase, and she walked about the property asking Herr and Frau Wilkens questions. I kept at my work in the kitchen until the social worker asked to see me in private. In this case, private meant that Frau Wilkens stood in the hall outside the kitchen; I knew she was listening in to everything I said. So I claimed that all was well, that I was treated fairly. The social worker nodded and made a few check marks in her notebook. Then she met once more with Herr and Frau Wilkens, shook hands with them, and left. I stood on the porch watching the lady walk down the drive and then turn left at the road to return to the train station. We were the last house on her round in Sagehorn, and she was heading back to Kiel.

Herr and Frau Wilkens had already left the house to work in the barn. I was alone. I dashed down the drive, racing to catch up with the social worker and caught her just before she arrived at the train platform.

"Wait!"

She turned. "Brigitte," she said. "Is something wrong?"

"Everything is wrong," I said. "Everything!"

She took a step toward me and touched my shoulder. I began to cry. "Do they hurt you?" she asked.

"No, but they hate me," I said. "I know they do."

"Listen, can you make it through two more months? Only two months? There is little that I can do for you right now."

Couldn't I go back home? Couldn't she end my term early? But then what? Home wasn't really any better. I took a deep breath and nodded my agreement. Two months. She waited for me to compose myself, then sent me back to the farm to be a good girl and do my best.

Forty-Three

Kiel

Father was happy to see me when I got home from the Wilkens Farm in late October. He touched my arms and said, "You're still skinny though."

I shrugged. I'd eaten well, but I'd worked awfully hard. I told them about my jobs, about scrubbing the kitchen floor and mucking stalls and making breakfast and making beds and making lunch and washing dishes and peeling potatoes and cutting peat.

"You may live with us for a while," Martha said. "I found you a job in Kiel."

The job was at a small grocery downtown, not far from the *Hauptbahnhof.* They needed an employee who would wash used milk bottles and prep them for refilling. No experience needed. At least I wouldn't be required to do the actual milking or muck the cow stalls. It sounded like a nice change. It was paid work too. I visited the employer and explained my experience—I knew how to clean absolutely anything—and he hired me that day.

Heading into that winter, I became a professional bottle washer. Unlike any other cleaning task I'd ever completed, I gained some recognition for this one. My boss at the grocery noticed that I was attentive to detail, I arrived and departed each day in a timely fashion, and was a generally reliable little cog. He noticed also that I had a decent face. So he promoted me to sales. By early 1951, I was the milk seller at a large slaughterhouse nearby. My boss drove me there with fifty bottles of milk every morning. I stood just inside the business entrance hawking the milk till the crates were empty. Then I was free to return to the grocery on foot to deliver the money to my boss. I always sold through my supply and never had to request a ride back to return unsold bottles. For the first time in years, I felt successful, just as I had when I scavenged food for Anna or when I found coal for Frau Grotjan.

One of my regular customers did not work as a butcher. His name was Max, and he had inherited his father's scrap-steel business across the street. He had acres of salvaged steel, and his company melted it down and resold it for all the reconstruction projects. Apparently Max had seen me arrive with the milk crates each morning. It was convenient for him to pick up a bottle each afternoon, shortly before he headed home for the evening. He also enjoyed chatting with me. We spoke about his job, and he asked which grocery I worked for. I told him.

"When do you get off each day?" he asked.

"About four o'clock."

"You live nearby?"

"No, I take the bus to Elmschenhagen."

I did not catch on that he was interested in me. I answered his questions as I had answered Jan's questions—factually and with as few words as possible. I hoped that giving him plain answers would satisfy him and he would, perhaps, have less to say. This did not happen.

After a few weeks of these little chats with Max, he appeared at the grocery store at the end of my shift. Martha had drilled into me that men only wanted one thing, and based on the assault I'd survived, the nature of that one thing was horrifying. But I was not afraid when I saw Max waiting for me on the walk. Did I mind if he walked me to the bus? No, I didn't mind. What harm could come? We were in the middle of a busy city street.

So we walked the ten-minute walk to the bus station. We spoke a little about his work—it was going well—and mine, which was uneventful. Most of the walk, I looked straight ahead, watching my step, but I caught a couple glances at him, actually noticed him for once. He was sandy blond and wore a long, black leather jacket. It was the kind of jacket one owned only due to great wealth or good black market connections. Or both. He was an attractive young man in his twenties, but I felt no interest in him—mostly because I felt no interest in men in general ever since the assault in the cemetery. Regardless, Max had a kind face, and I did not feel afraid in his presence.

At the station, we shook hands and said our see-you-in-the-mornings. Then I was off to catch my bus. Max showed up to buy his milk the next day and escorted me again the following afternoon. This continued for months. I was sixteen, and I had never had feelings for a man—there had never been time for such things. Honestly, I didn't feel especially drawn to Max, but I did begin to look forward to our walks. I did enjoy the sensation of having a new friend. That was as far as my heart could reach. Sometimes we walked a little too slowly and I missed my usual bus. This was not of any great concern. The busses ran regularly now. It was only another ten or fifteen minutes before I could catch another.

I didn't know that my late arrivals had caught Vati's and Martha's attention. Things had been unusually peaceful at home. Apparently it was because they were scheming. Father, not Martha, confronted me one evening.

"Who was that man with you at the bus station today?"

"What?"

"I've followed you several days now. Who is that man who walks with you?"

"That's Max Hartmann. He buys milk from me every day."

Both Vati and Martha bombarded me with a litany of the bad qualities of the Hartmann family. Vati asked me the young man's name, but it was clear that he and Martha had already thoroughly researched the matter. They only wanted to hear me confess it myself.

"He wears a black leather coat," Father said, with great scorn.

"Max's father had an accident and he had only one hand!" Martha chimed in.

"Now his father is dead."

"His mother too; she killed herself!"

"Max and his sister are orphans. You should not associate yourself with such people."

That last zinger made no sense. None of Vati's and Martha's declarations about Max's family seemed rational. Most appeared to be, if anything, good reasons to feel a little sorry for another person.

"Besides," my father continued, "you are too young to be dating him."

At least that one held water. I was sixteen, and I estimated Max was in his early twenties. However, we weren't dating. Really. I didn't feel that strongly about him.

"I've found a new job for you," Martha said. "You will be a maid at Wulfshagen Manor. You'll leave in two days."

"You will go to work tomorrow morning and quit," Father said. "Come home right after you tell your boss you've quit. I don't want you anywhere near Max again."

The next morning, I did precisely as I was told. I stopped in at my boss's office at my usual start time. He was ready to load up the crates.

"I can't go today," I said.

He furrowed his brow. It wasn't like me to refuse to work.

"I came in to tell you I have to quit."

"Why? Did something happen at the slaughterhouse?"

"No. My parents want me to work as a maid at Wulfshagen Manor."

"But you do well at your job here, and we pay you."

Doubtless he knew how the government's farm assignments typically paid in room and board only. "I have to go," I said. "My parents say I have to."

Sitting at home later that day, I thought of Max looking for me to buy his bottle of milk, looking for me at the end of the day for our walk to the station. It was disappointing, but I truly hadn't grown all that attached. Mostly I felt sad for him, how he'd look and wonder what happened, why I disappeared.

Forty-Four

Tüttendorf

Wulfshagen Manor was nothing like the Wilkens Farm. The estate buildings included a Baroque stone-and-stucco manor house that the count lived in, a property manager's house, two milking barns that held two dozen cows each, a bunkhouse for the dairy workers, and an assortment of sheds and outbuildings scattered about the farmyard and expansive grounds. I never spoke at length with the count. I worked solely for Herr and Frau Lange, the property managers, and shared a bedroom with another maid in the managers' quarters.

That bedroom was on the ground floor, and the other maid let me know this was highly advantageous. "Sometimes I slip out the window at night," she said. "You cover for me; I'll cover for you anytime." I had little idea what I would do once I was outside in the middle of the night, but I wanted to ensure friendship with my roommate and agreed to her request.

Her name was Herta, and she showed me the ropes. No stall mucking or turf cutting. All farm work was the responsibility of the dairy workers, a grimy tough crew that, thankfully, rarely crossed paths with the domestic staff. As the youngest workers on the estate, Herta and I were entrusted solely with the upkeep of the managers' quarters. Our tasks were almost entirely indoors. We woke at five and had breakfast ready for the Langes by six. We washed dishes and cleaned the kitchen daily, cleaned all other rooms weekly, and peeled potatoes endlessly. We cooked the large midday meal and the smaller evening meal. In between, we washed more dishes, peeled more potatoes, beat rugs, and washed laundry. Still, every afternoon we were allowed a one-hour break. Unlike the Wilkens Farm, this assignment was paid—a whole ten Marks per month.

The pay disappeared quickly. Despite, or maybe because of, our confrontation, my father had purchased me a bicycle for twenty-five Marks. He asked me to pay him back for the purchase at a rate of five Marks per month. That was half my paltry salary, but the bicycle would mean a measure of freedom when, every three or four weeks, I received a full day off. After my bicycle payment, I would have enough money to purchase toiletries and soap for the month.

I fast settled into a fairly comfortable routine. Frau Lange was stern, but she was not one to hover; she had her own tasks to attend to at the manor house. For the most part, Herta and I completed our work without any supervisory meddling. The workdays were predictable, uneventful.

Barely two weeks into my term, on a warm summer Saturday afternoon, I heard an incredible racket out on the main driveway. It sounded like a motorcycle had blasted onto the property. The engine continued to rumble in the front courtyard. I peeked out the front door, wondering if the count had taken up a new pastime. It wasn't the count. It was Max. He'd found me. My boss from the grocery must have told him. I ran out the door and down the drive to greet him, but Frau Lange immediately materialized and scowled at me. "You're not to receive guests during your work hours," she said. "And you are never, at any time, permitted to leave the property unless it is your day off."

She let me speak briefly with my guest to inform him of my limitations. Max was still perched on the motorcycle. I stood to the side of the front wheel and explained the situation.

"That's fine," he said. "I'll come back late tonight. Can you get away after dark?"

"I think so…" I now realized why Herta disappeared from our room so often and wondered how she hitched a ride of her own into town.

"Watch for me about ten o'clock. I'll park the bike down at the crossing, then walk to the woods across the road here. I'll wait for you." The bike engine started to sputter and he revved it a little. Then he added, "Brigitte, it's so good to see you."

I smiled. This sounded like a real adventure.

As promised, there he was—I heard the motorcycle and saw its headlight filter through the woods just after dark. I'd told Herta about my plans with Max. She was happy to cover for me. She'd feign snoring if Frau Lange knocked on our door after hours. She never opened the door if she thought we were sound asleep. "Time for me to go," I said when I heard the motorcycle engine stop about a quarter mile away.

I slipped out the window, tiptoed across the front courtyard, and dashed toward the woods. There he was in the shadows. We walked to the bike, and on the way, he asked if I'd ridden on a motorcycle before. I hadn't. He explained how to hold on to him and lean with the turns. "Just follow how I move," he said. "You'll get the hang of it."

That I did. The night air was cool but not cold, and it felt good to wrap my arms around his waist, to lean with each turn and not fight it. I wasn't afraid. I was with Max. He rode all the way back to Kiel and parked the bike by the waterfront. We walked there, looking at the boats moored and docked in the harbor. We didn't talk much and I yawned a lot, as I'd been up and working since five, but I was happy. We strolled for only a few minutes, and then he said he'd better get me back to the manor. Off we went on the motorcycle—back through downtown, past the silent buildings and empty streets, through sleeping neighborhoods, and through the cool mists settling in the farmland.

He parked the motorcycle, again about a quarter mile away, and walked me to the manor drive. There, like old times, we shook hands and wished each other well. "Watch for me again next Saturday night," he said. Then he hurried off into the shadows.

It was a romance, but I did not comprehend that at the time. Or perhaps I simply didn't feel it, not with any significance. I did thrill at doing this secret thing every weekend. My heart pounded at the thought of escaping the manor property. But I did not long for Max, for his presence. Our rather innocent trysts meant much more to him.

Max met me weekly that whole summer, taking me for motorcycle rides back to Kiel, usually to the harbor. Eventually, he asked to take me to his apartment. There was nothing untoward in the request. He shared a luxurious flat with his sister, Elisabeth, and he wanted me to meet her. So then we added visits with Elisabeth to our Saturday-night jaunts. We rarely stayed at the flat more than half an hour or so. Max loved our runaway visits, but he was genuinely concerned about my getting caught or simply not sleeping enough.

Max and Elisabeth's apartment was grand. It was downtown, a second-story flat full of antique trunks and hutches and ornate cabinets and Persian rugs. We sat in overstuffed chairs in the living room, and Elisabeth and I talked about clothes. She owned several elegant dresses, but I never saw her wearing anything other than a casual skirt and blouse. She lived in an opulent home, but she didn't feel the need to flaunt it. Max and his sister never left me feeling like the maid.

They invited me into their world and treated me with the same gentle regard that they had for each other. I did not adore Max, simply because I had no practice at such emotions. But, little by little, my heart opened some. I looked forward to our Saturday visits the whole week.

It wasn't so bad, my life at Wulfshagen Manor. There was, of course, absolutely no opportunity to improve my lot. But I didn't mind for the moment. I grew adept at my tasks, often receiving the highest compliment possible for a maid: not a word of commentary from my supervisor for an entire day. On Saturdays, I had my motorcycle rides with Max, and once a month I got an entire Sunday off. For these holidays, Frau Lange packed my bicycle basket with hard sausage and bread, and off I went to Kiel. It was a fifteen-minute ride on the motorcycle, but it took me closer to two hours using pedal-power. No matter; I cycled all the way to Kiel to say hello to Vati.

My summer took a shape and rhythm so utterly different from my life with Martha and my time with the Wilkens. Being a maid was hard work, but I had these lovely little pleasures each week. I was enjoying myself. Herta ensured that I was never caught for my nighttime escapes, and I returned the favor for her several times.

By autumn, I was decently lulled into the relative pleasantness of my second farm assignment. I grew a little lax about concealing my visits with Max. He wanted to take me to the circus, but it would entail leaving earlier and possibly staying out later than we ever had before. I decided to risk it. I met Max immediately after my evening chores were done. Herta had no idea what she would do if Frau Lange stopped by our room after dinner. She rarely did this though. Everything would be fine.

Off we cruised to the circus at *Exerzierplatz* in the middle of Kiel, and afterward we visited with Elisabeth till after midnight. By the time Max returned me to the manor and I crawled back through my bedroom window, it was one in the morning.

"Please don't do that ever again," Herta whispered to me.

"What's wrong?"

"Frau Lange knocked on our door and called your name," she said. "I was so scared."

"What did you do?"

"What we planned. I acted like I was deep asleep; I breathed heavy and hoped she would go away! Thank God she did."

This might have encouraged me to use more caution in all matters pertaining to Max. It didn't. I kept staying out late with him on Saturday nights. We took long walks by the harbor, and on one of these walks we leaned against a railing and looked out at the water. He had never even kissed me; I think he'd caught on that I was skittish around men. That night, he let his hand perch on the railing next to mine, just barely touching. "Oh, Brigitte," he said. "I'm going to marry you someday. You know that, don't you?"

I only smiled at him, not knowing what to say or what to feel. I should have felt like the young woman in the *Elke* books as she looked forward to starting her own family. I had a vague sense that there ought to be a feeling like that. All that time together, and I still didn't feel what Max felt. I was sure of that. But I never told him. He took my silence as coy, as he always did, and it seemed to make him grow all the more fond of me.

We stopped at his apartment that night to say a quick hello to Elisabeth. We didn't have much time to chat, but she was so excited to show me a dress. "It's lovely, but it doesn't fit me well anymore," she said. "It would fit you though; I'm sure of it." The dress was black with bright colorful flowers embroidered along the neck. I tried it on and it fit perfectly. Elisabeth was delighted. We wrapped the dress in brown paper, and I wedged it between Max and me on the motorcycle.

The next day, Sunday, I wore that extravagant rag. I donned it in the afternoon after my morning chores. I didn't care that I was a maid. I had a gorgeous dress, and I wanted to wear it. Perhaps I would take it off before it was time to peel potatoes again. I was in the farmyard pumping water from the outdoor well when I heard a sharp and familiar voice calling from the drive. It wasn't Frau Lange or Herta. It was Martha. She'd come to check up on me.

"Brigitte, where did you get that dress?"

I was so out of practice with lying that I told her the truth: "Elisabeth gave it to me. I visit her and Max sometimes."

"Oh? Really?"

Then, as if that piece of intelligence were the only reason she'd taken the bus all the way out to the manor, she headed back down the drive. She had nothing further to discuss with me. The following Saturday, I waited for Max, watching the woods across the road, but I never saw the motorcycle's headlight. He didn't appear the next Saturday either. He never showed up again.

I wasn't broken up about this. Really. I did not pine for him, because I hadn't loved him. I only felt disappointed that I no longer had those Saturday-night motorcycle rides. Yes, in my times with Max and his sister, I'd caught a glimpse of how loving people cared for each other. I caught glimpses of it in Anna's family and in Frau Grotjan too, and even Vati gave me his own work-weary love. But I'd always fumbled, in my own hands, the love that they entrusted to me. At sixteen, my mind and heart were honed for survival. I hadn't had enough opportunity to practice love, to know a thing about its natural reciprocation. Not really. So I had never longed for Max—not during our time together or after he disappeared from my life.

Forty-Five

Max was gone. I was well trained to feel nothing when a pleasant thing disappeared, and I settled back into a muted acceptance of my life, my work. Though my father was likely the one who found Max at his workplace and threatened him, I did not feel profoundly bitter about the matter.

I still visited Vati. Heading into that winter, I continued to use my day off to ride my bicycle back to Elmschenhagen, even when the roads got icy. Once, when the snow got deep, I saved up my *Pfennige* to take the bus. But, generally, Frau Lange and I watched the weather, and she gave me a day off when the weather was just mild enough to bundle up and ride the bicycle. I kept visiting, and I never asked Vati about Max. The topic hung in the air between us like the Big Anything back in Seidel, like never mentioning Elke and Rainer.

It was winter. Everything grew quiet under the snow. My daily chores now included the maintenance of heating fires, the cleaning of hearths, and keeping myself just warm enough at night. Winter had always been the coping season. I knew how to do that.

The snows thawed, and mud season arrived. The manor grounds may have been manicured during the summer, but no farmyard was immune to springtime's gloppy stench. Herta and I had a few tasks that took us outside into the muddy yard. We fed the chickens and ducks each day, and once or twice a day one of us refilled the two water vats for the kitchen from the hand pump in the farmyard. Mud made every chore a bit grimier. Still, the sun was warm, and I was grateful our work never took us near the dairy barns and their sickly sweet aroma.

One of those dairy workers often left the barns and loafed around in the yard. He watched us anytime we fetched water or fed the chickens. Sometimes he said *Guten Tag* and we said hello back, but there wasn't any extensive conversation. We never introduced ourselves. In private, Herta and I referred to that man as the lazy one. Regardless, we weren't permitted to mingle with the dairy hands, and though he seemed a nice enough fellow, I had no interest in someone who tromped about in boots caked with mud and manure.

One Tuesday afternoon, Frau Lange surprised me with a task that would send me straight to the dairy barns—even though we maids had always been told to stay away from that side of the farmyard. She called for me after I'd finished washing the midday dishes and asked me to fetch a pair of roof scissors. I had never heard of this term, but Frau Lange was well into spring-cleaning at the manor house. All the roofs on the property were thatch, and I assumed this tool was used for some sort of annual thatch maintenance.

"Find my husband down at the dairy," she said. "He'll get the scissors for you."

She had an odd smirk on her face. I wasn't sure what that was about and I wasn't excited about slogging out to the dairy barns, but she was my boss, so I obeyed. I donned my coat and boots and headed out the door. The first milking barn I entered seemed empty. It was late in the day, milking long done. The cows stood in their stalls munching hay. Frau Lange said her husband would be here, somewhere. I figured I could walk through that barn and then pass through the next one. If I didn't find Herr Lange right away, I'd get out of there and risk returning to my boss empty-handed. The barns were dark, dingy, and reeked. I didn't want to spend any more time in there than absolutely necessary.

As I passed through the barn, I saw someone walking toward me from the other end. My eyes had adjusted to the dark; I could tell it wasn't Herr Lange. It was the loafer that Herta and I saw in the farmyard so often.

"Guten Tag. I'm looking for Herr Lange," I said. "Frau Lange sent me for roof scissors."

"Roof scissors?" he said, then laughed. "There's no such thing as roof scissors."

I considered this new information. Why would my boss send me for a tool that didn't exist? As I pondered the matter, the dairy hand sat down in the straw pile at the end of the stalls.

"Come sit a while," he said, and patted the straw next to him. "Herr Lange isn't here. We can talk a while."

I didn't consider the implications of his gesture, as I had no idea there were any. I thought, momentarily, that he must be truly lazy to avoid his work and persuade me to do so as well. But I figured there was no real harm in talking with the man for a few minutes. Then I could head back to Frau Lange and get to the bottom of her odd request. I walked to the straw pile and sat an arm's length away from the farmhand.

I was looking down, straightening my skirt when he attacked me. One arm wrapped around my midsection, immobilizing my arms; the other reached up my torso, a callused hand clamped over my mouth. I screamed for Herr Lange, but the man edged his grimy hand into my mouth. He knew that would be enough to keep me quiet.

I couldn't breathe to scream anyway; his weight crushed the air out of my lungs as he shoved me onto the manure-packed floor. He was enormous. I fought. I froze. I fought. I collapsed under the weight and stench of him, unable to breathe or scream or fight anymore. Grungy hay stabbed into my back, and I heard the sound of cloth tearing. Arms pinned, body paralyzed, I did the only thing I could do—I disappeared. If the war taught me anything useful, it taught me that. I kept my eyes shut and disappeared.

He pushed himself off when he was done. I heard him cinch his belt and walk a few paces away, then stop. "Don't tell anyone," he said. "No one would believe you anyway."

Then he left the barn. I was alone, my eyes still shut. A cow bawled down the row of stanchions. I lay there, very still. I cried but made no sound, made no tears. I shook. My breath was panicked, shallow, and shaky—but it was breath. I could breathe. I was alive. I needed to get out of the dirt. I needed to find Frau Lange. Needed to get out of the barn. What if that hired hand returned? What if other workers found me there? I needed to get out of there as fast as possible. My arms could move. My fingers. I pulled my torn dress down over my knees and pushed myself up to standing. My legs could move. Somehow.

I staggered out into the farmyard—empty, thank God—and skirted along the edge of the outbuildings to Frau Lange's quarters. I found her in her office and stood in front of her in my filthy, torn dress.

"Brigitte, what have you done?"

"I was in the barn," I said, and told her the truth. "One of your workers attacked me. He beat me and threw me on the ground and forced himself on me."

She scowled. "What on earth were you doing in the barn?"

"You told me to fetch the roof scissors," I said. "I was looking for them, like you asked."

"Tcheh," she said, just the way Martha always did. "That was a joke. It's April Fool's Day. Don't you know that? Don't you know there's no such thing as roof scissors? Shame on you for going into that barn! What did you think would happen?" She told me to get cleaned up, told me she doubted my dress could be mended. I should throw it away and not tell anyone about what happened.

I tried, at first, to wear her scorn—to regard the rape as somehow my fault, a horrible error on my part, a personal embarrassment that I should push out of my mind. I couldn't. After several days of struggling to sleep at night and shaking anytime I stepped outside, anytime my eyes drifted toward the barns, I hit my limit for hating my life.

I told Herta what happened. Our beds were on opposite sides of the room, and we often sat on our beds facing each other, gabbing at the end of the day. I told her what happened in the barn.

"Who was it?"

"The lazy one, the man who always watches us."

"I'm not surprised," she said. Then she began to cry. We both sat there on our opposite beds and cried. It was fine that Herta did not cross the room and hug me or touch my shoulder. We were not especially close, and I don't think I wanted anyone to touch me right then.

The next day, I met with Frau Lange once more.

"I need to go home," I said.

"Your term doesn't end till July."

"That doesn't matter," I said. How thick was she? I bit each word, sturdy anger strangling my tears. "One of your workers raped me in your milking barn. I...can't...stay...here."

Frau Lange begrudged me my early termination, complete with an extra five Marks. I wrote home and told Martha and Vati what had happened; I told them I was raped. Vati came and got me. He didn't hug me, but he looked at me and held my right hand and said how sorry he was that such a bad thing had happened to me. He picked up my suitcase with his free hand and guided me down the drive, still holding my hand, all the way out to the bus stop a half mile away. We were quiet the whole ride home, but at least I was leaving. At least Vati was there—wordless and still, but safe.

Forty-Six

Kiel

They let me go home two months early. That was the reach of
Frau Lange's compassion toward me. I went home. To Martha.
I told her everything, just as I had told her about the man who at-
tacked me in the cemetery. For the second time ever, she believed me.
Just as she'd believed me when I told her about the incident with her
father.

Martha did not slap me or accuse me of lying. She looked at me
and said, "I hope you're not pregnant."

In another month, I knew that I wasn't, but I found this hardly
consoling. My work at the farms was supposed to give me skills to be
a good wife and mother, a decent maid if no man wanted to marry
me. All of that good farm food was supposed to put meat on my
bones. I still weighed ninety-two pounds, and I wanted nothing to do
with men ever again. I wanted nothing to do with anything.

Regina still lived with her sister down the street. She stopped by,
tried to reconnect with me, but I barely spoke to her. We loaned each
other a couple books, took a few walks in the cemetery, but I didn't
say much. I did not tell Regina about the rape. Both Frau Lange and
Martha said I shouldn't talk about it, so I didn't.

Our apartment building had been completely repaired and rebuilt
while I was at Wulfshagen. Everywhere in Kiel there was the sound of

hammers and saws and construction trucks. New shops, new houses, new walls and roofs and stairs and fresh paint. It was an exciting time, and I didn't care about any of it.

It wasn't any one thing that sent me flying. It was a thousand little things over the next two months—and then one measly altercation with Martha. Regina stopped by late one evening, about nine. I greeted her at the entry door, and she dropped off a book she'd borrowed from me. We didn't talk long; Regina knew it was late, and I needed to hurry back upstairs. I took the book, wished my friend goodnight, and returned to the apartment.

Martha shook her head at me and said, "You know you can't have friends over late!"

Ever, I thought. I can't have friends over *ever*.

I let her rail a while, and she ended with her magic words: "You're just like your mother!"

It occurred to me that my mother was beautiful. It occurred to me that it was possible to take Martha's words as one demented and jealous compliment. Martha slapped me—only once—and I went to my back bedroom. Perched on the edge of my bed, I thought of my old suitcase, where I'd hid my real mother's photos and the blouses that I had saved. Then I began to pack. That part was easy; I didn't own much. I packed my clothing on top of Mother's things. I slept well that night. Both Vati and Martha had to work in the morning, and as soon as they left, I would too.

The next morning, after the apartment was empty, I ate one Brötchen, tucked another in my coat pocket, took up my suitcase and left. I didn't leave a note. I didn't care. Frau Müller saw me in the stairwell. She looked at me, at the suitcase.

"Oh, child, you can't do this," she said. "What will become of you?"

I was seventeen. She thought the worst, I'm sure. She thought coping with Martha for another year or two was safer than living on the streets. What did Frau Müller know of the worst? Still her eyes were kind; she'd always been gentle toward me.

"I have to leave," I said.

"Do you have any money?"

"Not enough. I have three Marks." I figured I needed at least ten to take a regional train far enough to reach another city, somewhere I might find work.

"Wait here," she said. "Please."

She ducked back into her apartment, came back a moment later, and pressed three more Marks into my hand. "It's still not enough, I know," she said. "But I hope it helps."

We hugged, and I left. I had no plan. I knew only to leave. Now that I'd done that, I felt capable of considering the where. My mind wandered toward Bremen. My time with the Wilkens outside that city wasn't exactly pleasant. But it wasn't a complete horror either. I knew the area, more or less. It was a sizable town where I might find work as a hotel maid—far enough away that no one would know me, close enough that I could get there in a half day of travel. As far as destinations went, it was as good as any.

Frau Müller was scared someone would hurt me, use me. The worst had already happened to me. The worst had been happening for years. All I knew were my glimpses of something else. I'd seen it in Max and Elisabeth, and in Frau Grotjan and Gisella, and in Anna and her parents. I wanted—I didn't know what I wanted, but I wanted it bad. Martha was not what I wanted. Father was a riddle I could not disentangle, kind to me but so quick to turn a blind eye. I wanted.

I stood on the walk facing the early morning sun. Without enough money to take a train, and a touch too proud to beg, I set off walking toward the industrial fuel station near Kiel's *Hauptbahnhof*.

Other teens like me were there, asking truck drivers where they were headed. The first driver I spoke with was going to Hamburg; that seemed a good enough start for me. So I hitched a ride to Hamburg, and that first driver helped me find another who could get me to Bremen. I arrived in Bremen that evening. I thought nothing of my safety; hitchhiking simply meant that I got to my destination with six Marks still in my pocket. At that time, I hadn't heard of truck drivers treating hitchhikers with anything but compassion. For years after the war, there were plenty of displaced people who relied on that kindness.

In Bremen, the trucker dropped me off at the *Hauptbahnhof.* Every train station still had a Red Cross office for people like me—those still displaced, poor, hungry, or otherwise struggling in the erratic reconstruction economy. I looked for the emblem and marched straight into the office. The woman at the desk wore a crisp Red Cross uniform and cap. I told her my story—mostly true; I couldn't risk being sent home or sent away with no help.

"My name is Brigitte. I've lost my money and I don't have anywhere to go. I don't know what to do."

"Do you have any connections in the area for work?"

"I used to work at a farm in Sagehorn. I could try there."

"Oh, that's far away. And what would you do if they had no work for you?" she said. "There are plenty of jobs here. Let me see what I can do."

The kind woman gave me a form to fill out. My name: Brigitte Zobel; my resources: none; my job skills: two years as a domestic servant; my family connections in the area: none. Then she set about finding me lodging for that night. This part was easier than expected. Within an hour, I had temporary lodging at a shelter for young women, and a lead on a cleaning job at Hotel Columbus in downtown Bremen.

I got that job and moved immediately from the crowded boarding house to the servants' quarters at the hotel. For the next two years, I worked as a maid, receiving room and board as well as a decent paycheck. Initially, I bought only things I needed: two white blouses and a black skirt for my job. Then, that autumn, I bought myself a new coat. It was a blue and white tweed, a wraparound with a tie in back. It felt like wrapping myself in a blanket every time I wore it. I wrapped myself in that coat when I went outside to the cafés in the evening. It warmed me twice: both my body and my heart. It was my coat.

I could afford the new clothes and eating at cafés because the hotel business was booming. Every few weeks, Hotel Columbus hosted major events and diplomatic gatherings. My supervisors notified the cleaning staff of additional tasks we could volunteer for. I always volunteered for coat check. I stood in a booth, and the guests could hand their coats to me across the counter. However, if I left the booth and made a point of taking the coat off the visiting dignitary or businessperson, they tipped me better. I began to practice my English too. I'd learned a little English in school, but now I had opportunities every day to learn another phrase or two. Foreign guests were happy to teach the staff a few new words. A cordial welcome to the British and Americans in both German and English, and my tip jar brimmed over. I learned the key: make guests feel good, make them laugh, and they reward you.

Every day I looked for a way to earn a few extra Marks. If guests were present when I entered a room to clean, I smiled warmly and complimented their attire. I asked where they were from, they told me, and I replied that I'd always wanted to visit that city or country— whether I knew a thing about the place or not. Gleaning good tips felt almost like scavenging for food in Swinemunde. I used the same cleverness, the same improvisations to make money appear. I learned how to spend that money too—mostly on food and shoes and dresses I wore after hours. I'd never learned a thing about saving, had no concept of it, so I spent the money as fast as it came in.

At Christmas, I finally got the courage to contact my father. I sent him a Christmas card: *I am in Bremen working at Hotel Columbus. Merry Christmas.* I used the hotel as my return address. I was sure that I would never go back, but Hans Zobel was still Vati to me. I had to let him know I was alive. I did that much. Vati sent me a reply, thankful that I was safe. We began to correspond occasionally, but I had no intention of returning home for a long time, not even for a visit.

About a year into my work at Hotel Columbus, Father wrote me, asking me to return home. But I already had plans to move; I'd been offered a new position working in a diplomat's home. The diplomat was from Canada. He had been a guest at Hotel Columbus while in Bremen for meetings, and a few days into his stay, he entered his room while I was cleaning. True to my usual method, I got him talking, hoping he would leave a good tip. I asked him about his work and where he was from. He shared those details gladly; people loved to talk about themselves. I figured they tipped you well simply for being a good listening ear.

"You live in Bonn?" I spoke to him in halting English. "I always want to visit there."

"Oh? Are you interested in any other work?" he asked. "We would have to discuss the matter further, but my wife and I are looking for an au pair."

"Really? Yes, I am interested."

"We have two children. You would take care of them. You would need to learn more English too."

That was no hardship to me. I had been working on my English; here was a chance to become fluent. If I knew another language well enough to translate, I could have any hotel job I wanted, not just cleaning. A few days after the diplomat left, he sent me a letter. Having discussed the matter with his wife, he offered me the job.

I spent the next year in this fashion—jumping from job to job as a maid or au pair. Whenever a diplomat moved on, I found another position easily with another family or at a hotel. I gave my employers every reason to adore me, and they did. The only challenge was that the jobs were inherently short term or seasonal. I moved every few months, and sent single-sentence postcards to Vati: *I am in Bonn now. I am in Heidelberg.* Everywhere I went, there were newly renovated hotels and travelers who needed their rooms cleaned, or diplomats who needed their homes and children cared for. My pay was steady, but I continued to spend money as fast as I made it. I concluded the solution was to make more money.

In Heidelberg, I enrolled in a technical college that offered hotel management classes; at the time, such programs didn't require a high school diploma. With a certificate, I could make the big money and would never run out of cash again. I worked at Hotel Heidelberg as a maid, lived in their workers' quarters, attended classes in the evening, and still found time to get to know the other hotel workers. And these friends taught me that it was always possible to find time to party.

Two young women from Holland worked at the front desk, answering the phones and registering guests. They were cousins, Gretje and Carin, and one was blond and charming, the other dark haired and canny. These two befriended me and introduced me to *Zum Roten Ochsen—To the Red Ox.* Heidelberg was a university town, and this was the best student bar in the restaurant district. I joined my Dutch friends there a few nights a week, before or after my classes. If we worked too hard and never played a little, we might turn dull— that was Gretje and Carin's philosophy. So we drank and we danced with our workmates from the hotel and young men from the university. After Wulfshagen Manor, I had no interest in finding a boyfriend, but dancing was all right. It was okay to touch a man's hand and foxtrot for a number or two. That felt good. There were about a dozen of us, a little gang, and we took our party from bar to bar, ate spaghetti for the first time at an Italian restaurant, treated ourselves to ice cream, and always ended our nights at Zum Roten Ochsen. In that bar, there was a wall where everyone carved their initials. My girlfriends and I borrowed a pocketknife from one of the university boys and added our marks on that wall.

A beer or glass of wine every night helped me laugh at the day's frustrations, spaghetti was my new favorite food, Italian shoes were my remedy for any glum day, and dancing was the best way to forget everything from the past. I purchased a second suitcase to accommodate my growing collection of shoes and dresses. I spent about a year in Heidelberg, and by April 1955, I had perhaps spent too much time and money fulfilling Gretje and Carin's philosophy of life.

I couldn't afford my next tuition payment and had to drop out of school. Worse, I learned that Hotel Heidelberg was making cuts; the winter had not been lucrative, and cleaning staff were the first to go. We were all encouraged to return in the summer months. Surely things would pick up again. That was little comfort to me in the moment. I had no money and, for the first time, had no lead on another job. No families in need of an au pair, no other hotels looking for maids—we were still in the off-season, after all. I had two suitcases full of Italian shoes, wool skirts, fine hosiery, and a Viennese dress—and only one hundred Marks left in my wallet after my final paycheck. It was enough to buy a train ticket to Kiel, with a little left for food. Dismayed, disheartened, I said farewell to my Dutch girlfriends and lugged my suitcases to the *Hauptbahnhof*. Two years after running away, I was heading home broke.

Nothing, thank God, was entirely the same. For starters, I had grown a backbone during my time away. Vati and Martha still lived in the apartment on Landskroner Weg, but the units had been entirely repaired and remodeled while I was gone. More significant, my father and stepmother now had a baby. His name was Wolfgang, and he was just over a year old. Vati invited me to stay and help take care of Wolfgang because Martha had a heart problem that had grown worse. I said no. I'd had enough of my stepmother, even if she no longer seemed interested in hitting me. She still had plenty of energy to scoff at the contents of my suitcase. Such opulent clothing and barely a Pfennig to my name. It was true; I didn't talk back to her on that matter.

I also did not wait for Martha to find me a job. I made it clear that this was a temporary stay till I found work elsewhere. My humble return home should last days, not weeks. I skipped the local classifieds and spent the next few days reading the postings in regional hotel and tourist magazines instead—I wanted out of Kiel as soon as possible. There were openings posted at a bed and breakfast in Timmendorfer Strand, about fifty miles west on the Baltic coast. Perfect. Vati gave me the bus fare to visit the venue, and I interviewed during that first visit. The owner liked me, liked that I had plenty of cleaning experience, and liked that I knew English. Hired immediately, I returned to Kiel to collect my suitcases and wish Vati well, then moved to Timmendorfer Strand the next day.

Part 5

Flight
1955

Brigitte at about age 17—first portrait after
leaving home and living on her own

Forty-Seven

Timmendorfer Strand

I'd learned one significant lesson about money: if you spent it as fast as you made it, there was soon nothing left. There would be a crisis at some point, and it was easier to survive that crisis if you had a little something socked away. So on my first day at the Haus Waldschmidt Bed and Breakfast, I had a frank conversation with the owner, Elizabeth.

"You pay me both in room and board and in cash as well?"

"Yes, just as we discussed. One hundred Marks per month for four months."

"Instead of paying me each month, could you set my money aside and give it to me at the end of the season?"

Elizabeth looked at me funny. "I've never had such a request. But I see no reason why not."

"I need to be more careful about my spending."

"Ah," she said. She nodded in approval, and from then on, she was quite fond of me, impressed with my dedication to work and frugal living.

So I swung the pendulum. I worked at Haus Waldschmidt for two summer seasons, letting my boss hold my pay for the off-season. That winter, between my resort summers, I returned to Kiel for a few months and worked in the kitchen at a retirement home. The job kept me out of Martha and Vati's house from dawn to dusk, but even the hour or two I spent with them each day was intolerable.

It was a relief to return to Elizabeth's bed and breakfast, even though my life there hardly resembled my party days in Heidelberg. Sometimes my tips alone exceeded my monthly wage, so I was never hurting. But I exchanged partying for walking along the Baltic shore alone in the evening. Instead of eating out, I sat at a café table in the garden behind Elizabeth's bed and breakfast and ate perfectly fine meals for free. I bought no new clothing, instead enjoying the lovely rags I already had. And I quit running to bars to find friendship, instead initiating more meaningful conversations with the inn's guests.

That was how I met Miriam. She and her father were on holiday for a month. As usual, I introduced myself while cleaning their room. They invited me to coffee in the garden when I was on break that afternoon. With my newly simplified lifestyle, I never refused such invitations. Miriam was the most beautiful girl I'd ever met. She had long brown hair and sparkling dark eyes. She was about my age, well educated, and intelligent; I marveled at how she and her father debated politics and world happenings when we met in the garden. I had no idea what they were talking about, but did my best to pretend I was following along with the conversation. Miriam must have known I could not keep up with her. She befriended me anyway. We met often for afternoon coffee, and soon the father-daughter duo invited me to lunches at cafés in town, once to an extravagant dinner at a restaurant on the pier. Please, they said, I shouldn't be concerned; Miriam's father would pay. They enjoyed my company.

They owned a Volkswagen, and I sat in back while they drove around town. I didn't always pay close attention to their conversations, but I realized on one particular drive that their words had turned dark and hushed. They spoke about places I hadn't heard of—Auschwitz, Dachau, Ohrdruf—and people who had died there.

They talked about the merits of moving to America or staying on in Germany, as they had been. They would stay on. Germany was home; they had survived and they would stay there. I caught on that Miriam and her father were Jews, but I still didn't know precisely what a Jew was. None of my family, biological or foster, had spoken a word about Judaism to me. I had a vague awareness from confirmation classes that Jews might be members of another denomination of the church, like Catholics and Lutherans. Just not as common. I'd never met a Jewish person before.

I couldn't listen in silence any longer and spoke up from the back seat. "Excuse me, what are you talking about?"

"The war," Miriam said. "What happened to our people."

"What...happened?"

She turned in her seat to look back at me. "Brigitte, you don't know about the camps?"

"The camps?" I thought of my life in Seidel, of Otto's brief internment in the labor camp.

"The Nazis tried to kill us all. You know about this, yes?"

I held very still. I thought of my time as a refugee, my tunnel-vision devotion to finding food, and I thought of my schooling in Melsungen and Kiel, where the history books ended before the war years. I thought of my life with Martha, where all my thought and focus were channeled into appeasing or avoiding my stepmother. My work on the farms and at the grocery store kept me similarly small. Then I traveled Germany as a runaway; I should have learned something about my nation then. But I didn't. Not really. My friends were drinking companions; we spoke of nothing serious, certainly not the war. Interacting with hotel visitors, I learned to say *Welcome* in several languages, to offer fresh linens, and scrub a toilet till it shined. I learned to spend all my money on new fashions. I learned nothing of any consequence at all.

I couldn't meet Miriam's gaze and looked down at my lap. "I don't know," I said.

The next day, Miriam met me once more for coffee during my break. We sat at a table apart from the other guests in the garden. Miriam told me everything then, everything about the war. She explained to me what it meant to be Jewish, correcting my naïve assumption that Judaism was simply a rare denomination of Christianity. She told me about what happened to her people before and during the war: about forced evacuations and deportations at gunpoint, about families watching their sons and fathers shot in the street, about people hiding in attics and people found in cellars, and about how the people found in hiding were sent to the camps and that the compassionate souls who hid them were shipped off to the camps as well. She told me about empty houses and stolen possessions and stolen art and lost culture and lost livelihoods and stolen lives and hearts and families ripped to tatters. She spoke plainly about the death camps.

"You mean the work camps?" I asked, still thinking of Onkel Otto's experience.

"No," she said. "These were very different." Miriam told me about the concentration camps, how her people were starved and mass murdered—thousands upon thousands, probably millions. They were still counting. No one knew yet how many. And other people were killed too—Christians who opposed the Nazis, people deemed mentally ill or poor-witted, anyone who was not Aryan. "They killed anyone who did not obey, anyone who was not like them, anyone who did not keep quiet."

It couldn't be. But my heart knew every word she said was true. The why and the how of all my own wartime memories collapsed over the course of an afternoon conversation. Her stories dismantled mine. Dismantled them and rebuilt them in an unfamiliar form— more horrifying, more confusing. We did not compare sufferings;

nothing could ever compare. I never told Miriam my own story. In a way, Miriam never told me hers, not the story of her own personal survival, and I knew not to ask.

A few days later, their holiday over, Miriam and her father left. I never asked her why she traveled alone with her father, never asked her where her mother was or if she had any siblings. I never found out how she and her father had survived the war, whether they lived in hiding or were liberated from a camp. These were the things about which we did not speak. It was the most frightening mystery, the Biggest Anything.

At the end of the summer, Elizabeth reminded me of my upcoming paycheck. It was time to decide where I might go next. My boss urged me to head to a winter paradise, to Bad Tölz in Bavaria; there might be year-round jobs there at the ski resorts. I had never seen the mountains. It would have been wise to return to Kiel, to correspond with a few Bavarian hotels and confirm that they had several open positions before I moved across country. Perhaps that would have been wise.

There were plenty of jobs in Kiel too. Everything was new: clothing stores and bakeries, cafés and hotels, offices and houses. Everything was new, bright brick and metal and glass. Yet none of the new buildings and fresh concrete and repaired roads and young trees planted in boulevards and parks—none of it—could completely cover the shattered things. The ground would weep rubble for years to come. Gardeners would find shards of broken dishes, concrete fragments, coins, arms of dolls, and wheels from toy trucks every time they turned the dirt each spring.

I could not go home. Elke was almost fourteen years old and Rainer twelve. I barely knew my siblings, and there was no assurance that I ever would. Vati and Martha had Wolfgang now. There was no changing any of it. I had no family to hold me.

I saw them all, while not perfectly, a little more clearly: Mother, my real mother, stunning in her cocktail dress, heading out to meet a girlfriend; Mother promising me ice cream and never showing up; Father, the mild and silent citizen, the soldier fighting for a nation not worth fighting for; Father lifting me from the stream in Seidel; Father yelling at Martha and yet leaving me with her the next morning; Martha stitching me a dress out of an old blue-checked curtain; Martha running after me with the rug beater. I remembered Martha standing in the stairwell chatting with Herr Steiner after he tried to attack me. I heard them both laughing softly. They knew the truth. Knew it all along.

I saw them all, and knew no other way to live. But I trusted a way might make itself known. The surety came in flashes, like the flutter of a person ducking into a room on the periphery of my awareness. If I turned to look, the shadowy form was gone. But someone had been there. I knew it.

I saw Miriam and her father and their incomprehensible grief and unstoppable gentleness with each other. I saw Max and Elisabeth and how they lived with each other with respect and harmony, how Elisabeth gave me her dress, and how Father and Martha forbade me to spend time with them. I saw Anna standing under the light in the train station crying for me. I saw.

I saw hundreds and thousands of other young women and men like me working in the hotels and the restaurants. We were all learning English and meeting Americans and other Europeans—and learning what really happened. We all felt angry and ashamed, and angry about feeling ashamed, and no one knew what to do with the shame. We all stayed up late dancing and drinking and dancing some more, drinking to forget and dancing the shame away.

At the end of that summer, I stood on the platform waiting for a train to take me away from Timmendorfer Strand. I wasn't going back to Kiel to piece together another off-season. Instead, I held a ticket to München to meet a girlfriend at Oktoberfest. We would dance and drink to another season survived. Then off to Bad Tölz to find work at the ski resort hotels. I was bound for Bavaria, to the mountains I'd never seen.

Epilogue

An Interview with Brigitte

When the book ends, you are a young adult. You'd survived a lot at that point. What kind of a life did you make for yourself after all you'd been through?

As a young woman, I eventually settled in Bavaria, in Bad Tölz, a beautiful mountain town. There was an American military base there and tourism was growing, so there were lots of jobs. I got a job with Deutsche Bundesbahn, the passenger rail line. They managed hotels designed for their employees, and I worked in one of those hotels cleaning and waitressing. I got to know people quickly, and I had a rail pass to travel anywhere I wanted to.

The husband of one of my girlfriends was the local hockey coach. He coached the Americans in a team they started on the military base nearby. My girlfriends and I often watched the games and chatted with the players afterward. Everyone was having fun learning English and getting to know the Americans.

A few years later, I got a job working at the NCO club on the base. The exchange rate was four Deutsche Mark to the American dollar, so financially things began to stabilize for me. While working at the NCO, I got to know the man I would eventually marry. His name was Don, and he began to spend more and more time with me.

I told him I wasn't interested in romance. But Don was patient. It took him a year to convince me that he loved me, and we dated for another year before we married in January 1964.

About a year later, we moved to the U.S. and settled in Hope Mills, North Carolina. We raised four daughters together. Don and I had been married for forty-two years when he passed away in 2006. A few years after that, I moved to Montana to be closer to one of my adult daughters.

In Montana, I met a man named Frank. His spouse had passed away too, and we began spending time with each other. I now consider him my best friend and soul mate. He still gives me butterflies! I am so thankful to live in the mountains once again and enjoy this landscape with Frank and my family.

Did you ever get to see your Aunt Anna again?
Yes, I did! But not until 1982, almost forty years since I'd last seen her. I was almost fifty and was back in Germany visiting my sister. I brought my daughter Mary Ann. My sister and I were talking about the war, and I mentioned Anna and how much her family had cared for me. I told Elke I wanted to try to find Anna.

My sister helped me. We got a phone book for Melsungen and found a listing with the same last name. We called, and one of Anna's cousins picked up! She put me in touch with Anna.

On our first visit, my daughter and I got to spend an afternoon with Anna. When Mary Ann got out of the car, Anna said, "Oh my God, it's Brigitte!" Mary Ann was twelve at the time and looked so much like me at that age. Anna could not stop looking at her.

From then on, I visited Anna every two years or so until she passed. We'd stay up late at night talking. We didn't talk about the war much. Mostly we talked about Seidel, about the good memories. At some point, she told me she had restored the amber necklace that I had carried during the war, and she gave it to me. I still have it and wear it often.

You said that your sister helped you find Anna. So you reconnected with Elke as well?
Yes, my sister Elke and I became close friends as adults. We are still very close. After I moved to America, I visited her a lot in Germany; she has visited me here too. Anika has seen us together and says we act like girls having a sleepover. I also reconnected with Rainer. He still lives near Kiel, and I have visited him many times there. He surprised me by showing up unannounced at my eightieth birthday party in the U.S. You can imagine the look on my face when I looked out and there was Rainer on my doorstep! I am so thankful I have been able to rebuild my relationships with my siblings as adults.

As an adult, did you ever talk to your father about the war? What did he say?
He didn't want to talk about it. A lot of people were like that. Everyone stayed a little alert; even after the war, they were afraid to talk about the Nazis. They still wondered what would happen to them if they said anything against the Nazis. They also wondered what might

happen to them if they admitted they'd been in the German military or had held a government job.

After the war, because my father had been drafted into the German army, he had to go through a denazification interview overseen by the Allies. I still have the papers that say he completed this. Did it help him? Did he actually believe Nazi ideas before and during the war? Honestly, I will never know now.

As a young woman, I found a photo of my father, the only portrait of him as a young man. I noticed a tiny portion of the photo was scratched off and filled in with black ink. The scratch was on my father's lapel. I knew it was where a Nazi pin had been. When he got the job in the submarine shipyard, everyone there was required to be a party member, and so he was.

Did he agree with their ideas? Was he "only complicit," like so many others? Did he know what was happening to Jews and other minorities? Was he totally ignorant? No one was. So why didn't they do anything? How frightened was he of questioning the government? Or did he even think to? Of course I wanted to know. As a grown woman, I visited him and asked him more than once. Every time, he held up his hand and brushed the questions away.

"That is the past," he said. "I don't want to talk about it."

The last time I asked him, I showed him the portrait with the lapel pin scratched off.

"Did you do this?" I asked.

"Yes," he said. "It needed to be done."

Then he looked away and wouldn't say anything more to me. It was the most I ever got out of him. Finally, I quit trying.

Sometimes I wish I had started writing my book while he was still alive. I would have sat him down and said, "I'm writing this book, and now you need to tell me some things!"

It bothers me that I have no way of knowing now. It bothers me because I want to think only good things about him. Compared to Martha, my father was the kind and gentle parent to me, but there will always be these questions.

What inspired you to write your story?

During the years that I had young children at home, I was so busy caring for them, I didn't think much about my past. There wasn't time to. My twin girls and a third daughter were born in Germany, and my fourth daughter was born in North Carolina after my husband Don and I moved there.

Eventually, my daughters asked me about my childhood. When they were learning about World War II in their history classes, they'd come home and ask me questions. They were old enough to hear a few of my stories, so I told them some. They were shocked and said, "Mom, you should write a book!" I wound up going to their history classes to share about my experience. That got me thinking about writing it all down, but life was busy with four teenagers at home. So I put the idea on the back burner.

Then, long after my girls had moved out and were raising their own families, the topic came up again. There was a group of German women in my North Carolina community who got together regularly near the base. We met at a bakery every Thursday for coffee and to chat with each other *auf Deutsch*. A reporter had heard about us and stopped by one week to interview everyone. That is, everyone but me. I hadn't made it to coffee that week.

My girlfriends told this reporter to contact me. "Brigitte has the story you really need to hear," they said.

So the reporter wrote his story about our little *Kaffeeklatsch* group and sent another reporter to interview me privately. She wrote an article just about my survival story. That feature appeared in the Saturday Extra of the *Fayetteville Observer*. There was my story and my picture in the paper. Of course, it got me thinking about the book again.

That was in 2000. My children were all grown; I certainly had time to write. But shortly after that, I wound up caring for one of my grandchildren, and then Don grew ill. Once again, I was too busy caring for others to make time for writing a book.

Still, my daughters reminded me that I ought to. "I will, I will," I would say. "Someday."

That someday didn't happen for several more years. Occasionally I would write a few pages, then set it aside. It wasn't until I was widowed and moved to Montana in 2009 that I realized, *I certainly have the time now.*

I had written a draft that was about twenty pages long. It was just a summary of what I had lived through—being part of the child transports, being a refugee, losing a friend to an explosion, and escaping to West Germany. I explained all those things really quickly; it wasn't as long as a book. But it was something.

A couple of my friends were writers and editors, and they helped me at first, but no one had the time to help me grow it into a full-length memoir. My pastor's wife, Mary Wagner, knew about the situation. In 2011, she met Anika at an interfaith event at Congregation Beth Shalom. Mary connected us. And the rest is history!

You survived so much. How do you approach the concept of forgiveness today? Has your understanding of forgiveness changed over the years?

As a child, I didn't understand anything. I didn't know a thing about why the war was happening. I hated and feared the Russians who raped my girlfriend. I hated the Polish people who stole from us. After the war, at first we German kids played with the Polish kids in the street. Then they turned on us and began stealing our clothing. I didn't know why any of this was happening. Of course I was angry and scared and hated the people who had hurt me and my family.

It was years before I learned about the Holocaust. I was a teenager before I learned what Germany had done to the Polish people. Then I began to understand. Understanding like that definitely makes it easier to forgive. Of course, in the long run, you forgive for your own good. Forgiveness is important, whether you really understand the person who hurt you or not.

It's been much harder to forgive the abuse that happened at home. As for Martha, my stepmother, I don't know that I can honestly say I've forgiven her. The intensity of the hurt has faded over time, and I think about it less. Yet even today, I sometimes still feel it, how confusing and frightening it all was. And I still don't understand why she was as cruel as she was and why she never changed.

The fact is, forgiveness isn't a one-time thing. It's something you have to keep doing, something you practice. Saying you practice something means you're probably bad at it. So you keep practicing!

Have you done a lot of healing work over the years?
Do you mean therapy? No. That wasn't a common thing to do in my generation. Not in Germany; not in the U.S. either at that time. For the most part, I was so busy raising my family, I didn't think about the war or my childhood experiences much. I was raising my girls, and then I helped care for a grandson, and then I was caring for Don toward the end of his life. When you're taking care of other people, you're not really thinking of anything but the problem you need to solve right then.

So for all those years, I didn't think much about my past. To honor my daughters' requests, I finally sat down to write the book. I had to remember all those past memories, over and over, as Anika worked with me to write and rewrite the scenes. It wasn't exactly a fun thing. But it was good to do it. Frank, my partner, was really my rock during that time.

Writing down my memories—all of them—that was my healing work. It was not easy, but I think it was good for me. These days, it's not that I'm too busy to think about it; it's that I *have* thought about it, and now I can put it all aside. It feels like it's done.

The Authors

As a German child, **Brigitte Yearman** survived World War II, Russian military occupation, the refugee experience, and harsh reconstruction years. Her memoir recounts her journey of survival and how she came to learn about the Holocaust and the frightening realities in her country's recent history.

Later as a young woman, Brigitte met and married an American soldier. They moved to the United States where they raised four daughters. After her husband passed away in 2006, Brigitte moved to Montana to be closer to one of her adult daughters. She still lives in Montana with her partner, Frank, who encouraged her throughout the memoir-writing process.

Anika Hanisch has worked as a freelance writer, ghostwriter, editor, and author coach for over fifteen years. She co-writes both instructional and narrative non-fiction and also coaches fiction authors. Her own writing has appeared in several national and regional magazines including *Guideposts* and *Montana Quarterly*.

68655304R00171

Made in the USA
San Bernardino, CA
06 February 2018